DUMBARTON OAKS STUDIES

XVIII

THE NATURE OF THE *BIBLIOTHECA* OF PHOTIUS

Lavra cod. 449, folio 0^{v}, detail. Photius (seated) and his friend Amphilochius

The Nature of the *Bibliotheca* of Photius

Warren T. Treadgold

Dumbarton Oaks
Trustees for Harvard University
Washington, DC

Manufactured in the United States of America by
Sheridan Books, Inc., 450 Fame Avenue, Hanover, PA 17331 | (717) 632-3535

Photius, approximately 820–approximately 891.
Treadgold, Warren T., 1949–
The Nature of the *Bibliotheca* of Photius
(Dumbarton Oaks studies; 18)

ISBN 978-0-88402-090-5 (first clothbound)
ISBN 978-0-88402-474-3 (first paperbound)

LCCN permalink: https://lccn.loc.gov/80067452

1. Photius I, Saint, Patriarch of Constantinople,
approximately 820–approximately 891. Bibliotheca.
2. Greek literature—History and criticism.
3. Christian literature, Early—History and criticism.

EU GPSR Authorised Representative
LOGOS EUROPE, 9 rue Nicolas Poussin, 17000, La Rochelle, France
E-mail: Contact@logoseurope.eu

TO MY PARENTS

Preface

The nature of the so-called *Bibliotheca* of Photius cannot be accurately explained in a word or a phrase. To say that it is a collection of descriptions by Photius of ancient and medieval books which he had read is true as far as it goes. But the *Bibliotheca* belongs to no recognized category of writing. In certain places and in certain respects it resembles a history of literature, a literary autobiography, a work of literary criticism, an anthology, an annotated bibliography, a library catalogue, or a research notebook; but it is none of these consistently. It is rather an untidy compilation of various elements composed in different ways, so that an adequate explanation of its nature must depend on a series of explanations describing how each element was composed and how the whole was compiled. Until now, the only work to offer a complete explanation of the nature of the *Bibliotheca* was the *Photiana* of Emil Orth, much of which has long been refuted. Though other books and articles have made substantial contributions, they have not attempted to solve the problem fully, and their partial solutions often contradict one another.

To try to arrive at a comprehensive explanation in this book, I have studied the entire *Bibliotheca* thoroughly, the relevant secondary literature somewhat less completely, and the surviving books read by Photius only for limited purposes. My principal aim has been to show how Photius' own statements about the composition of the *Bibliotheca* can be reconciled with the text as we have it. To be sure, my judgment that Photius' statements are candid is a conjecture. But the opposite judgment—that Photius does not mean what he says—is also a conjecture and leads to more and more conjectures as we try to determine the truth that he is supposedly withholding from us. If it can be demonstrated that the *Bibliotheca* could have been composed as Photius says it was, as I think it can, we ought to believe him. A demonstration that the *Bibliotheca* could also have been composed in some different way can no doubt be provided as well, but this is not enough to justify our rejecting what Photius says.

As for Photius' individual descriptions of texts, anyone who studies one of them will of course soon know much more about it than this book can tell him. For such research, the main use of this book and its tables will be to indicate what sort of document the description comes from, and how the description compares to and fits in with the others. Neither my text nor my tables pretend to independent research on the books read by Photius, which are necessarily treated briefly and imperfectly.

For purposes of reference, it should be noted that I use the traditional forms for Greek names: Anglicized when there is an accepted English form, and otherwise Latinized. The forms based on ancient or medieval Greek pronunciation, which are seldom used consistently anyway, seem particularly inappropriate when applied to names that cover fourteen centuries during which the pronunciation of Greek changed drastically.

This book was written during the course of two junior fellowships at the Dumbarton Oaks Center for Byzantine Studies, which I thank for two happy years, the use of a splendid library that includes microfilms of the manuscripts of the *Bibliotheca,* and the means of publishing this study. I am particularly thankful to have worked at the Center when there were faculty members in full-time residence. This book has profited from advice and information given by practically every one of its faculty, visiting scholars, and fellows between 1975 and 1977. My very best thanks go to the Dumbarton Oaks editorial staff, especially Miss Julia Warner and Dr. Timothy Miller (since 1979 at the University of Washington), who have produced this book at the highest editorial standard.

Among others who have helped me, Professor Kurt Weitzmann gave his kind permission to publish the illumination of Photius and his friend Amphilochius as a frontispiece, and Professor L. G. Westerink read and commented on earlier versions of Chapters II and III, also sharing some of his findings on Photius' *Amphilochia.* Much credit goes to Mr. Frank Trombley, a doctoral candidate in history at U.C.L.A., who conscientiously checked and corrected my footnotes on a grant from the U.C.L.A. Department of Classics. I am especially grateful to Professor Tomas Hägg, who has corresponded with me for over four years, sent me proofs of his own book, read my typescript, and contributed so much invaluable advice that I can fairly call myself a student of his. My greatest debt is to Professors Ihor Ševčenko and Herbert Bloch, who jointly supervised the writing of this book in the somewhat different form of a Harvard doctoral dissertation in Byzantine Greek. Professor Bloch first suggested that I write on this topic, gave me my start on it, and continued his sound advice throughout. Professor Ševčenko, though he does not subscribe to all my conclusions, has contributed more to my work than anyone else by his Photius-like learning, ingenuity, and scholarly example.

Seattle
July 1978

Table of Contents

List of Abbreviations

AnalBoll	*Analecta Bollandiana*
Bardenhewer	O. Bardenhewer, *Geschichte der altkirchlichen Literatur,* 5 vols. (Freiburg, 1913–32)
Beck	H.-G. Beck, *Kirche und theologische Literatur im byzantinischen Reich* (Munich, 1959)
Becker	P. Becker, *De Photio et Aretha lexicorum scriptoribus* (diss. Bonn, 1909)
BHG	F. Halkin, *Bibliotheca Hagiographica Graeca,* 3rd ed., 3 vols. (Brussels, 1957) (ref. to entry no.)
Bibliotheca	Photius: *Bibliothèque,* ed. R. Henry, 8 vols. (Paris, 1959–77); *Bibliotheca,* ed. I. Bekker, 2 vols. (Berlin, 1824–25)
Bonn ed.	Corpus scriptorum historiae byzantinae, ed. B. G. Niebuhr et al. (Bonn, 1828–97) (with date of individual volumes in parentheses)
Bury, *Eastern Roman Empire*	J. B. Bury, *A History of the Eastern Roman Empire from the Fall of Irene to the Accession of Basil I* (London, 1912)
BZ	*Byzantinische Zeitschrift*
CahCM	*Cahiers de Civilisation Médiévale, Xe–XIIe siècles*
cod. (codd.)	Photius: *Bibliothèque,* ed. R. Henry, 8 vols. (Paris, 1959–77); *Bibliotheca,* ed. I. Bekker, 2 vols. (Berlin, 1824–25) (reference to codex number, then page, column, and line of Bekker edition, retained by Henry edition)
DOP	*Dumbarton Oaks Papers*
FGrHist	*Die Fragmente der griechischen Historiker,* ed. F. Jacoby, 3 vols. in 16 parts (1923–58) (ref. to entry no.)
CPG	M. Geerard, *Clavis Patrum Graecorum,* vols. II, III (Tournot, 1974–79) (ref. to entry no.)
GCS	Die griechischen christlichen Schriftsteller der ersten [drei] Jahrhunderte (1897–)
GRBS	*Greek, Roman and Byzantine Studies*
Hägg, *Photios*	T. Hägg, *Photios als Vermittler antiker Literatur: Untersuchungen zur Technik des Referierens und Exzerpierens in der Bibliotheke* (Upsala, 1975)
Henry	*Photius: Bibliothèque,* ed. R. Henry, 8 vols. (Paris, 1959–77)
Homilies	*The Homilies of Photius, Patriarch of Constantinople: English Translation, Introduction, and Commentary,* ed. C. Mango (Cambridge, Mass., 1958)
Klinkenberg	J. Klinkenberg, *De Photi Bibliothecae codicibus historicis* (diss. Bonn, 1913)
KP	*Der Kleine Pauly,* ed. K. Ziegler and W. Sontheimer, 5 vols. (Stuttgart, 1964–75)

Krumbacher	K. Krumbacher, *Geschichte der byzantinischen Litteratur*, 2nd ed. (Munich, 1897)
Lemerle, *Humanisme*	P. Lemerle, *Le Premier humanisme byzantin: Notes et remarques sur enseignement et culture à Byzance des origines au Xe siècle* (Paris, 1971)
Letters	*Photiou Epistolai*, ed. I. Valettas (London, 1864)
Lexicon	*Photii patriarchae Lexicon*, ed. S. A. Naber (Leiden, 1864–65)
Mango, "Books"	C. Mango, "The Availability of Books in the Byzantine Empire, A.D. 750–850," *Byzantine Books and Bookmen* (Washington, D. C., 1975), 29–45
Mango, "Liquidation"	C. Mango, "The Liquidation of Iconoclasm and the Patriarch Photios," *Iconoclasm*, ed. A. Bryer and J. Herrin (Birmingham, 1977), 133–40
Mansi	G. Mansi, *Sacrorum Conciliorum nova et amplissima collectio*, 31 vols. (repr. Paris-Leipzig, 1901–)
Martini, *Textgeschichte*	E. Martini, *Textgeschichte der Bibliotheke des Patriarchen Photios von Konstantinopel.* I, *Die Handschriften, Ausgaben, und Überträgungen* (Leipzig, 1911)
OCD	*The Oxford Classical Dictionary*, 2nd ed. (Oxford, 1970)
ODCC	*The Oxford Dictionary of the Christian Church*, 2nd ed. (Oxford, 1974)
Orth, *Photiana*	E. Orth, *Photiana*, Rhetorische Forschungen, I (Leipzig, 1928)
PG	Patrologiae cursus completus, Series Graeca, ed. J.-P. Migne
Pinax	E. Martini, "Studien zur Textgeschichte der *Bibliotheke* des Patriarchen Photios von Konstantinopel. I, Der Alte *Pinax*," Ὁ ἐν Κωνσταντινουπόλει νέος Ἑλληνικὸς Φιλολογικὸς Σύλλογος, Πεντηκονταετηρὶς 1861–1911, suppl. to 34 (1921), 297–318
Quasten	J. Quasten, *Patrology*, 3 vols. (Westminster, Md.-Utrecht, 1950–60)
RE	*Paulys Realencyclopädie der classischen Altertumswissenschaft*, new rev. ed. by G. Wissowa and W. Kroll (Stuttgart, 1893–1979)
REG	*Revue des Etudes Grecques*
Ševčenko, "Hagiography"	I. Ševčenko, "Hagiography of the Iconoclast Period," *Iconoclasm*, ed. A. Bryer and J. Herrin (Birmingham, 1977), 113–31
Severyns, *Chrestomathie*	A. Severyns, *Recherches sur la Chrestomathie de Proclos*, 4 vols. (Liège-Paris, 1938–63)
"Sophronius"	*Hieronymi de viris inlustribus*, ed. O. von Gebhardt, *TU*, 14.1B (1896)
Suda	*Suidae Lexicon*, ed. A. Adler, 5 vols. (Leipzig, 1928–38)
TM	*Travaux et Mémoires*, Centre de Recherche d'Histoire et Civilisation byzantines (Paris, 1965–)
Treadgold, "Photius"	W. Treadgold, "Photius on the Transmission of Texts (*Bibliotheca*, Codex 187)," *GRBS*, 19 (1978), 171–75

Treadgold, "Preface"	W. Treadgold, "The Preface of the *Bibliotheca* of Photius: Text, Translation, and Commentary," *DOP*, 31 (1977), 343–49
TU	*Texte und Untersuchungen zur Geschichte der altchristlichen Literatur*
Wentzel, "Übersetzung"	G. Wentzel, "Die griechische Übersetzung der *Viri inlustres* des Hieronymus," *TU*, 13.3 (1895)

CHAPTER ONE

Introduction

From the end of the eighth century, Byzantine scholars began to copy, read, and write literature on a scale that had not been equaled for some two hundred years. Particularly during the first period of iconoclasm, hardly anyone inside the Empire had copied or written books. Soon after 787, however, when the Seventh Ecumenical Council restored the icons, a generation of notable scholars appeared. Abbot Plato of Saccudium and others were developing the minuscule hand, an invention that made copying quicker and cheaper and reading easier. The Patriarchs of Constantinople were first Tarasius, an expert in classical metrics, and then Nicephorus, a theologian and historian. Abbot Theodore of Studium wrote theology, poetry, and letters, and George Syncellus and Theophanes Confessor composed an important world chronicle. Though these scholars were and remained iconophiles, several distinguished scholars were ready to accept iconoclasm when it was reintroduced in 815. Among them were John the Grammarian and Leo the Mathematician, both of whom concentrated on mathematics and the natural sciences, and Ignatius the Deacon, an epistolographer, poet, and biographer. When the icons were again restored in 843, Leo and Ignatius again conformed, and some new scholars appeared. The most important of these was Photius, the author of the *Bibliotheca.*[1]

Photius was born about the year 810 into a family that was well-connected, well-educated, rich, and iconophile.[2] He was related on

[1] On the whole subject of the revival of learning, see J. Irigoin, "Survie et renouveau de la littérature antique à Constantinople (IXe siècle)," *CahCM,* 5 (1962), 287–302; Lemerle, *Humanisme,* 109–76; Mango, "Books"; and W. Treadgold, "The Revival of Byzantine Learning and the Revival of the Byzantine State," *American Historical Review,* 84 (1979), 1245-66.

[2] Lemerle, *Humanisme,* 180–82. The traditional date of *ca.* 820 has nothing in its favor and much against it. On Photius' family, see Nicetas Paphlago, PG, 105, cols. 509A-B.

his father's side to the scholar-patriarch Tarasius.[3] His father, Sergius, held the rank of *spatharius* and was probably the "Sergius Confessor" who came to be venerated as a saint and wrote an ecclesiastical history that Photius describes in the *Bibliotheca*.[4] The brother of Photius' mother Irene married a sister of Theodora, consort from 830 of the iconoclast Emperor Theophilus.[5] Among Photius' collected correspondence are letters addressed to his four brothers: Tarasius, Sergius, Constantine, and Theodore.

A source who shows a rabid hostility to Photius declares that he had received his classical education from a Jewish magician in return for denying the sign of the Cross.[6] From this we should probably conclude only that, even at an early date, nothing was known of Photius' teachers, whom he never mentions himself. No doubt Photius, like his older contemporary, Leo the Mathematician, acquired a primary and secondary education in grammar and poetry at a school in Constantinople. Leo pursued his studies further with an unnamed man of learning but had to complete his education himself by private reading.[7] Presumably Photius had some instruction after he left school from his father and from others, among whom Leo may conceivably have been included; but no teacher seems to have had a very great influence upon him.[8] His private reading of the books reviewed in the *Bibliotheca* must have been the most important part of his education.

During the persecution of iconophiles that began in 832 or 833, Photius' whole family was condemned as iconophile and sent into exile, in the course of which both Photius' parents died.[9] When the

[3] Photius calls Tarasius his πατρόθειος, which I take to mean "father's uncle" (*Letters*, no. 3, p. 159; no. 4, p. 180; and no. 5, p. 198). On Tarasius' learning, see Lemerle, *Humanisme*, 129.

[4] Pseudo-Symeon, Bonn ed. (1838), 668–70. On the rank of *spatharius*, see N. Oikonomidès, *Les Listes de préséance byzantines des IXe et Xe siècles* (Paris, 1972), 297–98. On Photius' father, see Mango, "Liquidation," 135–39.

[5] Theophanes Continuatus, Bonn ed. (1838), 175 (cf. Bury, *Eastern Roman Empire*, 156 note 1). On the date of Theodora's marriage to Theophilus, see W. Treadgold, "The Problem of the Marriage of the Emperor Theophilus," *GRBS*, 16 (1975), 325–41. If the "Arsaber the patrician" of Theophanes Continuatus, p. 175, is the same as that of p. 156, and if Bury has interpreted Theophanes Continuatus, p. 175, correctly, Irene was also the sister of the learned iconoclast John the Grammarian, who would therefore be Photius' uncle; but this is far from certain.

[6] Pseudo-Symeon, 670.

[7] Theophanes Continuatus, 191–92.

[8] Lemerle, *Humanisme*, 182, thinks that Leo contributed substantially to Photius' education, but no source links these two well-known scholars as teacher and pupil.

[9] On the family's exile, see *Letters*, no. 164, p. 501. For the date, see Lemerle, *Humanisme*, 181 and note 19. See also Mango, "Liquidation," 136–39, who interprets the letter slightly differently. On Photius' parents' death, see *Letters*, no. 2, p. 145 and no. 142, p. 459.

Emperor Theophilus died in 842, however, the crown passed to his infant son, Michael III, and power passed to his iconophile widow Theodora and her family. In that year, Photius seems to have returned to Constantinople and begun teaching.[10] His students included St. Constantine-Cyril, future missionary to the Slavs, and Thomas, later a high-ranking Imperial official.[11] With their connections with the Empress' family, Photius and his brothers rose to high offices in the imperial government. Sergius and Constantine attained the high rank of *protospatharius,* Tarasius the still higher rank of patrician, while Photius himself became not only a *protospatharius* but *protoasecretis,* the head of the imperial chancery.[12] Photius continued teaching informally while he held this office.[13]

Photius' career did not suffer in 855 and 856, when Theodora's brother, Bardas, took over her power on behalf of Michael III. In 858, Bardas decided to depose the Patriarch Ignatius, a partisan of Theodora and a critic of Bardas' liaison with his daughter-in-law. To replace Ignatius, Bardas chose Photius, an unmarried layman. The appointment was a mixed success. Photius' patriarchate of nine years was disturbed by increasing challenges from the partisans of Ignatius and from the Papacy and ended in 867, when Basil I, who had already had Bardas murdered, killed Michael III and became emperor. Basil deposed Photius and restored Ignatius.

Photius was exiled, imprisoned, and in 870 condemned by the Council of Constantinople, considered the Eighth Ecumenical Council by the Western Church. Nevertheless, he soon managed to gain favor with the Emperor Basil, who made him tutor to the future Emperor Leo VI. When Ignatius died in 877, Basil returned Photius to the patriarchate for another nine years. In 886, however, Leo succeeded Basil and deposed and exiled his controversial former teacher. This time the septuagenarian Photius was unable to return to imperial favor. He died in exile, no earlier than 893, but probably not much later.[14]

During this varied and stormy career, Photius produced a sub-

[10] F. Dvornik, *Les Légendes de Constantin et de Méthode vues de Byzance* (Paris, 1933), 352 (cf. *ibid.,* 34). See also *infra,* p. 28 and note 33.

[11] See note 10 *supra* and the heading to Photius' *Lexicon,* ed. S. A. Naber (Leiden, 1864–65).

[12] *Letters,* nos. 15, 12, and 7 (titles), and Nicetas Paphlago, PG, 105, col. 509A. For the importance of these titles, see Oikonomidès, *op. cit.* (*supra,* note 4), 297 (*protospatharius*), 294–95 (patrician), and 310 (*protoasecretis*).

[13] *Letters,* no. 3, pp. 149–50. Lemerle, *Humanisme,* 197–99, notes that this is not a description of a school in a strict sense, but he seems to me to press his point too far.

[14] Cf. Mansi, XVI, col. 452A, a summary of the Eighth Ecumenical Council, which indicates that Photius was still alive in 892. Because his feast day is February 6, that day in 893 would seem to be the first possible date for his death.

stantial body of philological and theological literature. When he was very young he compiled a lexicon, of which his surviving *Lexicon* may be a later, expanded version.[15] Probably in 843 he wrote a work against the Paulician heretics, entitled *Against the Manichaeans*, which he expanded in 871 or 872 into the version that is preserved.[16] All his collected homilies date from his first patriarchate.[17] The main collection of his letters dates from before 868–72; at that time he used many of them in his *Amphilochia*, a set of answers to mostly theological questions addressed to his friend Amphilochius of Cyzicus.[18] Probably Photius' latest work is his *Mystagogia*, a treatise on the procession of the Holy Spirit, written after his second deposition in 886.[19] He also composed a few minor works, of which some are lost and others unpublished.[20] When the *Bibliotheca* itself was completed is highly controversial. Suggested dates have ranged from 838, still under Theophilus, to a date of completion after 875 and even to a posthumous publication.

Photius himself gave the *Bibliotheca* the unwieldy title *Inventory and Enumeration of the Books That We Have Read, Of Which Our Beloved Brother Tarasius Requested a General Analysis*. The preface, postface, and contents all corroborate that it was meant to be a collection of descriptions of practically all the books which Photius had read and that it was addressed to Photius' brother Tarasius. The earliest specific Byzantine reference calls it a letter from Photius to Tarasius, which in form it is.[21] While the title *Myriobiblon* is of late Byzantine origin, the title *Bibliotheca* was coined in the sixteenth century; I use it here only for the sake of convenience.[22] The name originally implied only that the work could be used as a sort of library, not that

[15] P. Becker (*De Photio et Aretha lexicorum scriptoribus* [diss. Bonn, 1909], 7–62) and Lemerle (*Humanisme*, 185–87) have argued that Photius composed the *Lexicon* as a young man and before the *Bibliotheca*; K. Tsantsanoglou (Τὸ Λεξικὸ τοῦ Φωτίου, Χρονολόγηση-Χειρόγραφη Παράδοση, *Hellenika*, suppl. 17 [1967], 11–35) has argued that Photius composed it as an old man and after the *Bibliotheca*; and K. Ziegler (in *RE*, XX, 733–34) throws up his hands at the contradictory indications of the *Lexicon*'s date. Without having studied the problem extensively, I am inclined to think that Photius wrote an earlier version of the *Lexicon* when he was very young (*Amphilochia*, PG, 101, no. 21, col. 153C), before he had composed the *Bibliotheca*, and then, after he had composed the *Bibliotheca*, expanded it into the version we now possess. On the text of the *Lexicon*, still not completely edited, see Tsantsanoglou, *op. cit.*

[16] See pp. 28–29 *infra*.

[17] *Homilies*, 18–24.

[18] Lemerle, *Humanisme*, 199–201.

[19] Beck, 521.

[20] *Ibid.*, 520–28.

[21] See A. Diller, "Photius' *Bibliotheca* in Byzantine Literature," *DOP*, 16 (1962), 391.

[22] *Ibid.*, 392 and 395–96.

it was an inventory of Photius' own books, as some have mistakenly assumed.

Photius gives the number 279 for the "books" that he had read. In fact, the *Bibliotheca* contains 280 numbered descriptions, including one (number 268) of a book that Photius says he had not read. Aside from that, almost all the descriptions begin with the word Ἀνεγνώσθη (There was read), followed by the title of the book.[23] Continuing the comparison of Photius' compilation to a library, scholars have named these numbered descriptions "codices," though some of them describe more or less than one manuscript volume. For example, "codex" 145 describes a lexicon that Photius found in seven volumes, and "codices" 151 through 157 describe eight lexica that Photius found bound together in a single volume.[24] Many "codices" include several different works, such as "codex" 189 on three works by three different paradoxographers. Further, apparently by accident, sixteen "codices" describe a second time books that have already been treated in earlier "codices."[25] In short, Photius was not consistent in dividing up his work, a process that sometimes had to be arbitrary. By leaving out the repeated reviews and by dividing "codices" into different works—i.e., by counting collections of similar works as one "book" but collections of dissimilar works as different "books"—I have arrived at a figure of 386 "books."[26] I use the term "codex," hereafter without quotation marks, only for convenience, as I do the title *Bibliotheca*.

The codices are of different kinds. There are those which give only the author and title of the book, sometimes vaguely or inaccurately, sometimes accurately, including the exact number of parts or chapters of the book. Others give short summaries, which are in some cases vague and general, in others accurate and specific, down to a table of contents of the book. Many codices give long and detailed epitomes in the order of the original, either in a conversational manner which addresses Tarasius in the second person or in the remote and disconnected form of notes. To these references, summaries, and epitomes Photius usually adds an appraisal of the book's style and content, often including a short biographical sketch

[23] There are 16 exceptions: codd. 110, 111, 113, 133, 134, 135, 157, 173, 174, 217, 218, and 219 refer back to previous codd. that begin with Ἀνεγνώσθη; that Photius read 89, 92, 152, and 155 can be inferred from what he says about them.

[24] Cf. the beginnings of these codd.; cod. 155 implies, but does not state, that it continues the same volume.

[25] See p. 41 note 13 *infra*.

[26] My divisions are indicated in Table I. The figure 386 includes cod. 268 on a book that Photius did not read. Ziegler, *op. cit.* (*supra*, note 15), 691–713, does not divide up the codices, with the result that his numbers differ from mine.

of the author and occasionally some information about the form of the manuscript. From codex 234, however, these additional elements practically disappear, and the codices consist not of summaries but of nearly literal excerpts, some of which are as brief as a few words quoted out of context. Apparently in reference to this excerpting, most of the codices from 234 to 280 begin with the words 'Ανεγνώσθη ἐκ (There was read *from*), not with the simple 'Ανεγνώσθη that begins the earlier codices.

In his preface, Photius says that he has made no systematic attempt to organize his material, and this is borne out by his text. Nonetheless, a number of codices of the same kind are often grouped together, e.g., codices 27 through 31 on ecclesiastical histories or codices 252 through 258 on saints' lives, though other ecclesiastical histories and saints' lives appear outside these groups. Several works by the same author are sometimes grouped together, as in codices 172–74 dealing with writings of John Chrysostom, though other works by the Saint are described elsewhere. Photius also tends to group secular and religious codices in different places. All but three of codices 1 through 56 are on religious subjects, all but four of codices 57 through 84 are on secular subjects, and this approximate alternation of religious and secular works recurs throughout the *Bibliotheca.*[27]

Photius explains in his postface that he deliberately excluded from the *Bibliotheca* those books "whose study and perusal commonly constitute the arts and sciences," by which he must mean school texts.[28] Accordingly, he leaves out all the poetry that a well-educated Byzantine would have read at school: Homer, Hesiod's *Works and Days,* the selected plays of Aeschylus, Sophocles, Euripides, and Aristophanes, Pindar's *Olympian Odes,* Theocritus, Theognis, and Pseudo-Menander's *Gnomic Sayings.*[29] Of the standard prose texts, he omits Thucydides, even the best-known works of Plato and Aristotle, some common orations of Aristides, and Gregory of Nazianzus' *Eulogy of St. Basil;* he seems to have included Demosthenes only to avoid spoiling a complete set of biographies of the ten Attic orators.[30] Neither does he review standard textbooks, such as Nicoma-

[27] For a possible explanation of this, see pp. 24–25 *infra.*

[28] Postface, *Bibliotheca*: 545 lines 13–14: χωρὶς ὧν ἡ σπουδὴ καὶ μελέτη τέχνας φιλεῖ καὶ ἐπιστήμας ἐργάζεσθαι. . . . Cf. Plato, *Republic* VII.522C: τοῦτο τὸ κοινόν (arithmetic), ᾧ πᾶσαι προσχρῶνται *τέχναι* τε καὶ διάνοιαι καὶ *ἐπιστῆμαι,* ὃ καὶ παντὶ ἐν πρώτοις ἀνάγκη μανθάνειν.

[29] See A. Dain, "A propos de l'étude des poètes anciens à Byzance," *Studi in onore di Ugo Enrico Paoli* (Florence, 1956), 195–201, especially 198–99.

[30] Lemerle (*Humanisme,* 210–13) notes that both Plato and Aristotle were fairly well known in Byzantium. I. Ševčenko, "Theodore Metochites, the Chora, and the

chus of Gerasa's *Introduction to Arithmetic,* Euclid's *Elements,* Aphthonius' *Progymnasmata,* and Hermogenes' *De Ideis.*[31] Naturally he omits the Bible as well.

That Photius had read all of these books, or virtually all, goes without saying. We learn from incidental remarks in the *Bibliotheca* that he had read Thucydides, some Plato, Nicomachus, and also some Xenophon, whom he apparently counted as a standard author.[32] We can also tell that he did not consider Herodotus, Aeschines, and Isocrates as standard authors, because he reviews them in codices in the usual way. In most cases, it is not difficult to determine whether Photius omitted a book because every educated man had read it or because not even he had read it; those who conclude from the absence of school texts that Photius neither knew nor cared about classical poetry and philosophy are certainly mistaken. Therefore, in reckoning Photius' reading, we must add to the books reviewed in codices a list such as the one suggested here, comprising perhaps twenty to thirty standard works. Aside from these, however, Photius says in his postface that the books in the *Bibliotheca* represent the sum total of his private reading.[33]

Although Photius describes 239 Christian and Jewish works and only 147 secular and pagan works, the bulk of his reading seems to have been slightly on the secular side. Not only were some secular

---

Intellectual Trends of His Time," in *The Kariye Djami,* ed. P. Underwood, IV (Princeton, 1975), 37–38 and note 148, lists as standard prose works Gregory's *Eulogy,* Demosthenes, and some Aristides. Photius does include two works of Aristides in the *Bibliotheca* (codd. 246–48), but I doubt that they were all he had read.

[31] On textbooks, see particularly Lemerle, *Humanisme,* 252–55. G. Kustas, *Studies in Byzantine Rhetoric,* Analekta Vlatadon, 17 (Thessalonica, 1973), 22, notes that Aphthonius and Hermogenes were standard textbooks in Byzantium and observes that the *Bibliotheca* in particular shows familiarity with Hermogenes (pp. 20–21). Three Byzantine scholars list some authors whom they read at school; unfortunately they all studied in the thirteenth century. Nicephorus Blemmydes read Homer, other unspecified poets, Aphthonius, Hermogenes, Nicomachus, and part but not all of Diophantus (*Curriculum Vitae,* ed. A. Heisenberg [Leipzig, 1896], 2 and 5). Gregory of Cyprus studied the poets and dramatists, including the *Iliad* and Aeschylus' *Seven Against Thebes,* Aristotle, Euclid, and Nicomachus (*Autobiography,* ed. W. Lameere, in *La Tradition manuscrite de la correspondance de Grégoire de Chypre* [Brussels-Rome, 1937], 183–85). Theodore Metochites studied Aristotle, Nicomachus, and Euclid (K. N. Sathas, *Μεσαιωνικὴ Βιβλιοθήκη,* I [Venice, 1872], πζ').

[32] Photius' comparisons at cod. 71: 35b lines 30–32, cod. 82: 64a lines 17–20, and cod. 213: 171b lines 9–12 show that he had read Thucydides, and his remarks at cod. 37: 8a line 7, cod. 155: 100a lines 21–24, and cod. 209: 165b lines 20–23 show that he had read some works of Plato, including the *Republic.* His comparisons at cod. 187: 142b lines 19–21 show that he knew Nicomachus' *Introduction,* and his remark at cod. 58: 17b lines 20–21 indicates that he had read some Xenophon.

[33] This does not include books that his brother had read aloud in his presence (see pp. 21–22 *infra*), books Photius forgot (see p. 23 *infra*), and, of course, books Photius read after compiling the *Bibliotheca* (see pp. 32–34 *infra*).

authors excluded as school texts, but many of the secular works were or are massive, e.g., the complete histories of Diodorus Siculus and Dio Cassius, while the average length of the religious works was definitely less. Of the text of the *Bibliotheca* itself, about 57 percent describes secular and pagan works, 43 percent Jewish and Christian ones.[34]

The secular titles include many histories and collections of orations, which together are the majority, rounded out by prose fiction, medicine, mythology, biography, epistolography, paradoxography, poetry, philosophy, and science. Codex 163 is a manual of agriculture, codex 187 a treatise on arithmology. Most of the religious titles are works of apologetic, dogmatic, or exegetical theology, but along with them appear sermons, religious letters, devotional works, saints' lives, ecclesiastical histories, religious poems, monastic rules, Easter tables, and the acts of thirteen church councils. Photius' neglect of poetry and philosophy have been considerably exaggerated by some modern scholars. Although he must have left out the poets and philosophers who were school authors, Photius describes nine works in verse and two anthologies with many verse selections, as well as three works of pagan philosophy, three biographies of philosophers, several scientific works, and some works by Christian philosophers such as Clement of Alexandria and Methodius of Olympus. The whole selection is in fact remarkably comprehensive, though mathematics and the natural sciences (apart from medicine) are underrepresented.

The chronological distribution of the books reviewed is also wide. The earliest is Herodotus, treated in codex 60; the latest is the ninth-century ecclesiastical history of Sergius Confessor, reviewed in codex 67. Every century beginning with the fifth before Christ is represented, but the representation is naturally very uneven. After he had excluded the principal classics, Photius had only 22 works from the pre-Christian centuries to include, with only 3 from the third and second centuries combined. He describes 27 to 29 works from the first Christian century, 59 to 61 from the second, and 41 or 42 from the third. The fourth century is the best represented of all, with 99 to 103 works, but the fifth and sixth centuries have almost as many. The three centuries closest to Photius' own time, however, the seventh through ninth, have only 28 to 30 works among them. Obviously, these figures reflect both fluctuations in literary production over the centuries and Photius' inability to obtain many early works. He often mentions that he has been unable to find ancient books and

[34] This figure is based on my own classification as it appears in Table III. Hägg (*Photios*, 8 note 2) calculates 58% secular material and 42% Christian.

that even some of those he found, like the histories of Theopompus and Memnon, were in incomplete manuscripts.[35] What is surprising is how much Photius did find and want to read.

Of the books that Photius read, 211 (about 55 percent) do not survive in as complete a form as he had them. 110 are entirely lost, except for the description the *Bibliotheca* preserves of them and sometimes a bare attestation elsewhere. Another 51 survive outside the *Bibliotheca* only in fragments, and still another 27 are missing substantial parts in our texts. A further 13 are fully preserved only in Latin, Coptic, or Slavonic versions. Of the books whose texts are lost, the *Bibliotheca* seems to be the only evidence that 81 ever existed.

Although Photius gives long summaries and excerpts of a number of books that still survive in complete form, as a rule he describes lost books at greater length than preserved ones. This is probably the result of his intention, stated in his preface, to treat rare books more extensively than common ones. For example, though the first-century manual of mythology by Conon is known only from Photius' codex 186, it is hardly to be considered a "lost" book. Since Photius notes that it was short and rebukes himself for practically transcribing it, his epitome, consisting of twenty-four columns in the Bekker edition of the *Bibliotheca* divided into the original fifty chapters with their titles, probably includes most of the wording and all the substance of the original text.[36] Though this seems to be the work that Photius preserved most completely, other codices preserve large parts of other "lost" works: the fifth-century B.C. *Persica* and *Indica* of Ctesias (codex 72), the first-century A.D. *New History* of Ptolemaeus Chennus (codex 190), the *Chrestomathia Grammatica* of Proclus (codex 239), and, among Christian works, the sixth-century *On the Incarnation* of Jobius the Monk (codex 222) and several works by Ephraem of Amida and Eulogius of Alexandria (codices 225–30).[37] Even the summaries and excerpts of surviving works have their value, since they sometimes give better readings than our manuscripts and provide a means of controlling Photius' habits in transmitting lost texts.

In 194 of the first 233 codices, beginning with codex 2 and ending with codex 233, Photius gives formal judgments of different kinds on the books. Generally, he gives a criticism of both style and content, and, for religious works, of orthodoxy. The appraisals of style,

[35] See cod. 176: 120a lines 6-14 and cod. 224: 239b lines 9-11.

[36] See cod. 186: 130b lines 25-28 and 131a lines 19-20 (cf. Henry, III, 229-30). The titles of the chapters, which are preserved in both MSS and are evidently original, are unjustifiably omitted by Bekker and Henry, but are included in *FGrHist*, 26.

[37] The chapter numbers in codd. 72 and 222 are preserved in both MSS (though they do not always quite agree with the indications of chapters in the text) but are omitted by Bekker and Henry.

content, and orthodoxy are remarkably independent of each other. For example, Photius praises the style and argumentation of the Origenist Pierius in codex 119 but condemns his heresy; in codex 192A, he praises the orthodoxy of Maximus Confessor but notes that the style of his book is mediocre, the arguments unfounded and irrelevant.[38] Photius' appreciations of the classics are often refreshing. He praises Arrian enthusiastically for his clarity and criticizes Isocrates sharply for his affectation and verbosity.[39]

In about sixty of the codices, usually at their end, Photius gives short biographical sketches of the authors. The first such sketch closes codex 13; the last begins codex 228. Photius obviously composed some of these sketches from what the authors say about themselves. Many other sketches, however, do not derive from the books under review and are often introduced by the words "they say" or "it is said." In 1895, Georg Wentzel demonstrated that Photius' source for most of this material was a biographical dictionary that largely survives in the biographical articles in the *Suda,* the tenth-century Byzantine encyclopedia. The principal sources of this dictionary, which Wentzel called the "Hesychius epitome," were the lost sixth-century *Onomatologus* of Hesychius of Miletus and the surviving Greek translation of St. Jerome's fourth-century *Famous Men.*[40] Though the parts of the *Bibliotheca* based on the dictionary have no independent authority, they are witnesses to the texts of the "Hesychius epitome" and its sources.

The text of the *Bibliotheca* itself is preserved in twenty-five manuscripts, plus a number of manuscripts with excerpts from it. In his history of the text of the *Bibliotheca,* Edgar Martini determined that only two of the manuscripts of the entire work are independent. These are Marcianus Graecus 450, conventionally called A, which dates from the tenth century, and Marcianus Graecus 451, or M, which dates from the twelfth century.[41] Though the end of A is missing, it can be mostly recovered from its thirteenth-century apograph, Parisinus Graecus 1266 (= B). Among the indirect witnesses are an anonymous ninth-century scholion taken from codex 239 on

[38] Cod. 119: 93a lines 36-40 and 93b lines 5-7 and 10-18; cod. 192A: 156b line 26-157a line 9.

[39] Cod. 92: 72b line 40-73a line 30; cod. 159: 102b lines 4-19. The latter review is evidence against the conjecture of Romilly Jenkins that Photius "reintroduced [Isocrates] as the basis of rhetorical education" in Byzantium ("The Classical Background of the *Scriptores Post Theophanem,*" *DOP,* 8 [1954], 16).

[40] On the "Hesychius Epitome," see Wentzel, "Übersetzung"; see also pp. 31–32 and Chapter IV *infra.*

[41] See Martini, *Textgeschichte*; cf. Diller, *op. cit.* (*supra,* note 21), 389–90, who thinks that A is "somewhat earlier" than the second half of the tenth century, when Martini dated it, and mentions (note 3) a MS overlooked by Martini.

Proclus' *Chrestomathia*, and two scholia taken from four other codices by Arethas of Patras about 913. Arethas was probably also responsible for many, mostly incorrect emendations that appear in M but not in A.[42] Because these manuscripts are early and good, the text of the *Bibliotheca* presents few serious problems.

Until recently, the standard edition was that of Immanuel Bekker (1824–25), reprinted by Migne in volumes 103 and 104 of his *Patrologia Graeca* (1860). Bekker's edition has now been superseded by that of René Henry, with French translation and notes (1959–77). Since Henry has retained the page and line numbers of Bekker, I make my references to them, but I follow Henry's text except where I specify otherwise. A column in Bekker's edition, which I often use as a standard of length, is roughly equal to an ordinary page, though Bekker's own pages have two columns each. For the *pinax* of the *Bibliotheca*, which Bekker and Henry omit from their editions quite unjustifiably, I refer to a separate edition by Martini (1921). An edition and study of the marginalia in the manuscripts is badly needed. By consulting microfilms of manuscripts A and M, I have come to the conclusion that all the present editions of the *Bibliotheca* ought to be used with some caution.[42a]

Though Henry's translation and notes contain a number of errors, they still do a great service to the user of the *Bibliotheca*. In addition, nine secondary works are particularly valuable. First, Cardinal Hergenröther's three-volume study of Photius (1867–69) is largely outdated but not superseded as a whole. As I have noted already, an article by Georg Wentzel on Photius' biographical sketches (1895) and Martini's work on the text (1911) are still fundamental. The dissertation of Johann Klinkenberg on the historical codices (1913) contains the first careful analysis of Photius' method and some reasonable conclusions, occasionally led astray by the limitations of treating only a fraction of the whole *Bibliotheca*. Emil Orth's two pamphlets (1928–29) do cover the whole and are often valuable for their rhetorical analysis and word indices, though not for their conjectures about how Photius composed, which are little better than fantasy. Albert Severyns' monograph on codex 239, the *Chrestomathia* of Proclus (1938), contains detailed research on the text in general, unfortunately marred by a complete acceptance of Orth's conjectures. The best brief discussion of the *Bibliotheca* is in Konrat Ziegler's article on Photius in Pauly-Wissowa (1941), which refutes the ideas of Orth that are unacceptable. The remarks on the *Bibliotheca* in Paul Lem-

[42] Severyns, *Chrestomathie*, I, 339-57; Diller, *op. cit.*, 390-91.

[42a] See W. Treadgold, "The Recently Completed Edition of the *Bibliotheca* of Photius," *Byzantinoslavica*, 41 (1980) (forthcoming).

erle's *Le Premier humanisme byzantin* (1971) are also of interest. Finally, Tomas Hägg's study of Photius' methods of excerpting and summarizing (1975) covers ten codices thoroughly and includes some useful generalizations. Full references to these and other works on the *Bibliotheca* and its various codices will be found in my bibliography.

Despite the contributions made by these studies, there is no scholarly consensus at present about the date, method of composition, or nature of the *Bibliotheca.* Only parts and aspects of the work have been studied in detail, often with results that flatly contradict one another. In particular, most theories about the date and circumstances of composition have been based on only a few passages in the text, especially on Photius' preface, or even on ideas that have no basis in the text at all. On the other hand, most of the detailed studies of various codices have avoided general questions and developed a theory about Photius' method on the basis of only one or a few codices. Consequently, many of these theories can be disproved simply by referring to evidence in the text that they do not take into account.

Much about how and why the *Bibliotheca* was written depends on its date and the circumstances under which it was composed. Before 1963, scholars generally agreed that Photius composed it before he became patriarch in 858. From the preface and postface, Hergenröther concluded that it was written to describe books that Photius had read himself, just before Photius left on the embassy of 855–56 to the Arab-Byzantine border, or possibly on an earlier one, such as that of 845 to the Caliph's capital at Samarra.[43] Orth, followed by Severyns, adopted the date of 855 but somehow concocted the theory from the preface, postface, and some corruptions in the text that the books were read under Photius' direction by an itinerant reading circle of ambassadors on their way to Baghdad and that the *Bibliotheca* was written down and sent to Tarasius before their return.[44] Ziegler noted that this theory is pure "myth," absolutely excluded by the preface and postface; much like Hergenröther, he concluded that Photius compiled the *Bibliotheca* in Constantinople before his departure on the embassy of 855 to the Byzantine frontier (*not* Baghdad),

[43] J. Hergenröther, *Photius, Patriarch von Konstantinopel: Sein Leben, seine Schriften und das griechische Schisma,* I (Regensburg, 1867), 14; III (1869), 341–43.

[44] Orth, *Photiana,* 6–10; Severyns, *Chrestomathie,* I, 1–4. The beginning 'Ανέγνων on which Orth relied so much is a corruption of A's abbreviation ἀνεγνώ (= 'Ανεγνώσθη); see Hägg, Photios, 133. In his subsequent work, *Die Stilkritik des Photios,* Rhetorische Forschungen, II (Leipzig, 1929), 134, Orth corrected his error that the embassy of 855 went to Baghdad, but Severyns seems not to have noticed this.

using notes that he had taken during his private reading of many years.[45] In 1956, B. Hemmerdinger produced the new myth that Photius read all the books and composed the *Bibliotheca* in Baghdad in 855–56 (presumably because he had nothing else to do, being many miles from his embassy at the frontier and from the Arab government at Samarra).[46]

Then, in 1963, François Halkin challenged the widely accepted date of 855 by arguing that the preface and postface are literary fictions and that Photius must have composed the *Bibliotheca* after 875, the earliest date for a book that Halkin identified with one reviewed in codex 252.[47] In 1965, however, Hélène Ahrweiler, unconvinced by Halkin's identification, dated the *Bibliotheca* to 838, when, according to her, Photius dictated it from books and reading notes that he had brought to the Byzantine army camp in Asia Minor, before he left on an embassy to the camp of the invading Caliph.[48] This theory was tentatively accepted by Lemerle.[49] On the other hand, Cyril Mango accepted Halkin's identification of the book in codex 252 and argued that Photius wrote an earlier, much shorter version of the *Bibliotheca* before going on an embassy but continued adding to his work throughout his life.[50] Of all these theories, I believe that the text of the *Bibliotheca* rules out all but the original explanation of Hergenröther, retained by Ziegler. I shall argue that the most likely date for the *Bibliotheca* is 845.

Until now, no scholar seems to have identified all the peculiarities of form and content of the latter part of the *Bibliotheca* or noticed that these begin abruptly with codex 234. Some have at least tried to explain the much greater length of the later codices by supposing that they were composed under different circumstances. J. B. Bury assumed that Photius wrote the earlier part before his embassy and the latter part at leisure after he returned.[51] Severyns argued that Photius dictated the earlier part just after he had found his secretary so as to cover the books that his reading circle had already read, adding the latter part as his reading circle read new books.[52] Not only do these theories presuppose circumstances of composition that

[45] Ziegler, *op. cit.* (*supra*, note 15), 685–91.

[46] Henry (I, li-lii) has unfortunately taken this theory seriously.

[47] F. Halkin, "La Date de composition de la *Bibliothèque* remise en question," *AnalBoll*, 81 (1963), 414–17.

[48] H. Ahrweiler, 356–61.

[49] Lemerle, *Humanisme*, 42; cf. 179-80.

[50] Mango, "Books," 37-43.

[51] Bury, *Eastern Roman Empire*, 446 and note 1.

[52] Severyns, *Chrestomathie*, I, 7.

are at variance with the text of the *Bibliotheca*, but they do not explain why the later codices are written in a peculiar, impersonal manner and consist almost entirely of excerpts from the books. To explain these facts, I shall argue that the later codices were copied into the *Bibliotheca* by the secretary from notes that Photius had taken earlier.

Though Photius is often cited as if he were a primary source for the literary history of authors who lived long before his time, he is obviously nothing of the kind. Aside from the partially lost dictionary identified by Wentzel, Photius seems to have consulted the books that he reviews in the *Bibliotheca* and little or nothing else. Even in using these materials, he makes a number of errors and leaves a number of spaces blank. Although some of these errors have been identified and explained, others have been overlooked or misinterpreted because of a tendency to accept Photius' authority uncritically and because of a lack of familiarity with the *Bibliotheca* as a whole.

All these problems bear on the question of how Photius composed his descriptions of the books. Nigel Wilson has suggested that Photius relied mostly on an extraordinary memory; but Hägg has shown from the text that, while some parts probably were composed from memory, others could not have been.[53] Hägg has distinguished those descriptions which seem to have been composed while Photius was reading from others which seem to have been composed after the readings.[54] The former include all the codices from 234 on and a few earlier ones. I shall argue that the few in the first part, like those in the second, were copied for the *Bibliotheca* from Photius' reading notes. Of the remaining codices, I shall argue that Photius composed some from memory and at least the majority of the others with his own copies of the books before his eyes.

The selection of books in the *Bibliotheca* has often been taken to indicate what Photius' interests were. But because Photius seems to have read and reviewed in the *Bibliotheca* nearly everything he could find, the selection probably reflects the availability of books to Photius rather than his interest in them. The space he devotes to describing books and especially what he has to say about them are better guides to his interests, suggesting that Photius found and read more religious books but was more interested in secular books. I shall not attempt a full discussion of Photius' stylistic criticisms here, because the topic is large, extends beyond the question of the nature of the *Bibliotheca*, and has already been extensively treated by Orth

[53] N. G. Wilson, "The Composition of Photius' *Bibliotheca*," *GRBS*, 9 (1968), 451-55; and T. Hägg, "Photius at Work: Evidence from the Text of the *Bibliotheca*," *GRBS*, 14 (1973), 213-22.

[54] See pp. 81–82 *infra*.

and George Kustas.[55] They have established that Photius' criticisms are essentially his own and are based on his actually having read the books.

In short, the *Bibliotheca* is many things, not all of them of the same nature. Most of the codices before 234 are fairly orderly descriptions addressed to Tarasius; the later codices are rather disconnected excerpts addressed to no one in particular. Some of the descriptions are vague and unreliable, probably done from memory; others are specific but superficial, probably done from the manuscripts; still others are textual but unfocused, probably copied from notes. The biographical sketches are derivative; the stylistic judgments, on the other hand, are original. Thus, the question of what the *Bibliotheca* is must be given not merely an answer but a set of answers.

[55] See Orth, *Photiana*, and *idem*, *Stilkritik* (*supra*, note 44); also G. Kustas, "The Literary Criticism of Photius: A Christian Definition of Style," *Hellenika*, 17 (1962), 132–69; *idem*, "History and Theology in Photius," *Greek Orthodox Theological Review*, 10 (1964), 37–74; and *idem*, *Studies* (*supra*, note 31).

CHAPTER TWO

The Circumstances and Date of Composition

Photius himself speaks several times of the date and circumstances under which he composed the *Bibliotheca,* particularly in his preface and postface. Since these form the beginning and end of a letter to his brother, Tarasius, the whole work has the form of a huge letter. Though the preface and postface are generally admitted to be authentic compositions of Photius, scholars still disagree about how they are to be interpreted and reconciled with the text of the *Bibliotheca* that comes between them. Indeed, certain scholars have maintained that no satisfactory interpretation or reconciliation is possible and declared that the preface and postface are either literary fictions of some sort or parts of a different version of the *Bibliotheca* of which our text is a revision. As always, however, the burden of proof is on those who reject the source material.

The right place to start is with the text of the preface and postface. Although the only primary manuscript of the former is quite worn, with several readings uncertain and a corner missing, these textual problems fortunately do not affect any controversial passage, and can for the most part be cleared up with the help of parallels elsewhere in Photius' work. Without putting any title before his preface, Photius begins as follows.

> Photius to his beloved brother Tarasius, greeting in the Lord.
>
> When we were chosen by the members of the embassy and by imperial appointment to go on an embassy to the Assyrians, you asked us to write down for you summaries of those books that had been read when you were not present, my dearest brother Tarasius, so that you might have some consolation for the separation that you bear unwillingly, and also the knowledge, even if somewhat impressionistic and rather general, of those books that you have not yet read in our hearing. These are the fifteenth part plus one short of three hundred and no more [i.e., 279], for that is the number, I believe, that happened to be read when

you did not happen to be there. Though later, perhaps, than was your burning desire and warm entreaty, nevertheless more quickly than anyone else would have expected, we, finding a secretary, have edited as many of the summaries as our memory preserves, satisfying your desire and claim.

The summaries will be treated in whatever order my memory presents each of them, though it would not be difficult, if someone should choose, [to distribute all] those of them that are of history in one place and those that relate to one subject or another in other places [according to] their kind, with [much(?) learning,] but excessive [and officious pe]dantry. On the other hand, [one] who considers [mixture] an admirable thing, and [chooses(?)] variation as well, in many places at many times harmo[nizes] even [the most dissimilar things,] and cannot produce boredom in his read[er.]

And if it seems to you, whenever you come upon [the] volumes themselves one by one and study them, that some of the summaries have been recorded inadequately and inexactly, do not be surprised. For it is no trouble for a man who reads through one book by itself to compose its summary and to commit it to memory and writing if he wishes, but for a man who reads many books together to come to an exact recollection of them, especially when some time passes in the interval, is not, I think, an easy thing. Besides, for our part, with those books that we have read that are common and probably, because of their availability, have not eluded your studies either, we have not taken as much care as with the others; in the case of these exactitude has been deliberately neglected. But if anything else useful and beyond what you requested finds its way in along with the summaries, you will see it better than I.

These materials that we have edited will no doubt be of use to you for your general memory and remembrance of the [books that(?)] you have encountered in your reading [either with others (?)] or by yourself, and for finding readily what you look for in them, as well as for your easier comprehension of those things that have not yet come to be read by your perceptive self.[1]

[1] Φώτιος ἠγαπημένῳ ἀδελφῷ Ταρασίῳ ἐν Κυρίῳ χαίρειν.

Ἐπειδὴ τῷ τε κοινῷ τῆς πρεσβείας καὶ τῇ βασιλείῳ ψήφῳ πρεσβεύειν ἡμᾶς ἐπ' Ἀσσυρίους αἱρεθέντας ᾔτησας τὰς ὑποθέσεις ἐκείνων τῶν βιβλίων, οἷς μὴ παρέτυχες ἀναγινωσκομένοις, γραφῆναί σοι, ἀδελφῶν φίλτατέ μοι, Ταράσιε, ἵν' ἔχοις ἅμα μὲν τῆς διαζεύξεως ἥν βαρέως φέρεις παραμύθιον, ἅμα δὲ καὶ ὧν οὔπω εἰς ἀκοὰς ἡμῶν ἀνέγνως εἰ καὶ διατυπωτικήν τινα καὶ κοινοτέραν τὴν ἐπίγνωσιν (ταῦτα δέ ἐστι πεντεκαιδεκάτῳ μέρει τῶν τριακοσίων ἐφ' ἑνὶ καὶ οὐ πλέον ἀπολείποντα, τοσαῦτα γάρ, οἶμαι, τῆς σῆς οὐ τυχόντα παρουσίας ἀναγνωσθῆναι συνέπεσεν), ὀψὲ μὲν ἴσως τοῦ σοῦ διαπύρου πόθου καὶ τῆς θερμῆς αἰτήσεως, θᾶττον δὲ ἢ ὅσọṿ ἄν τις ἄλλος ἐλπίσειε, τυχόντες ὑπογραφέως, ὅσας αὐτῶν ἡ μνήμη διέσωζε, τὸν σὸν ὥσπερ ἀφοσιούμενοι πόθον καὶ τὴν ἀξίωσιν ἐκδεδώκαμεν.

Οὕτω δὲ τάξεως αἱ ὑποθέσεις ἐπιλήψονται, ὡς ἂν ἑκάστην αὐτῶν ἡ μνήμη προβάλοι, οὐ χαλεπὸν ὂν καὶ εἴ τις ἕλοιτο ἰδίᾳ μὲν τούτων ὅσα τῆς ἱστορίας ἐστίν, ἰδίᾳ δὲ ὅσα πρὸς ἄλλον καὶ ἄλλον σκοπὸν ἀναφέρẹṭ[αι πάντα διελεῖν κατ'] εἶδος, μẹṭạ̀ [πολλῆς (?) φιλοπονίας] ἀλλὰ περιττῆς [καὶ περιέργου φιλο]τιμίας. Μᾶλλον [δ' ὁ τὸ ἀναμιγμένον] νομίζων ἀξι[ό]λ̣ọγọṿ, [αἱρούμενος(?)] δὲ καὶ τὸ ποικίλον, κ̣ạ̀ị̀ [ἀνομοιότατα] ἐν πολλοῖς πολλάκις ạ̔ρμό[ζεται,] καὶ κόρον οὐκ οἶδε τίκτειν εἰς ἀκρọạ[τήν.]

After this comes the *pinax*, which is in both manuscripts, though not in the editions of Bekker and Henry.[2] Then the body of the work is introduced by a title that is evidently the author's own: "Inventory and Enumeration of the Books That We Have Read, of Which Our Beloved Brother Tarasius Requested a General Analysis (They Are Three Hundred, Lacking Twenty Plus One [i.e., 279])."[3] After the last codex, numbered 280, Photius completes the letter to his brother as follows.

> Those books, therefore (except for those whose study and perusal commonly constitute the arts and sciences), that it happened to come to our memory that we have studied by ourself during our life, from the time that any kind of perception and judgment of literature came to us up to the time of the present composite edition in outline of what we have read, amount, I believe, to a number that is short of three hundred by the three-hundredth part of it plus the fifteenth [i.e., 279].
>
> But, most beloved of those who had a share in my mother's labor pains, if, as we are accomplishing this embassy, the common end of mankind should befall, you would still have a favor that does not entirely miss what you had hoped for, a summary and memory of my love and of consolation, and so both a first and a last offering to satisfy the whole of your requests concerning literary study. But if, bringing us back safely from there, the benevolent will of God restores us to seeing each other and to enjoying each other's company as before, then perhaps this will be the beginning of other edited materials no shorter than these, which will give you benefit in a similar outline.[4]

Εἰ δέ σοί ποτε κατ᾽αὐτὰ γενομένῳ [τὰ] τεύχη καὶ φιλοπονουμένῳ τινὲς τῶν ὑποθέσεων ἐλλιπῶς ἢ οὐκ εἰς τὸ ἀκριβὲς δόξουσιν ἀπομνημονεῦσθαι, μηδὲν θαυμάσῃς. Μίαν μὲν γὰρ ἑκάστην βίβλον ἀναλεγομένῳ τὴν ὑπόθεσιν συλλαβεῖν καὶ μνήμῃ καὶ γραφῇ παραδοῦναι οὐκ ἔργον ἐστὶ τῷ βουλομένῳ· ὁμοῦ δὲ πλειόνων, καὶ τότε χρόνου μεταξὺ διαρρυέντος, εἰς ἀνάμνησιν μετὰ τοῦ ἀκριβοῦς ἐφικέσθαι οὐκ οἶμαι ῥᾴδιον εἶναι. Ἡμῖν δὲ καὶ ὅσον ἐπιπολάζει τῶν ἀνεγνωσμένων καὶ οὐδὲ τὰς σὰς διὰ τὸ πρόχειρον ἴσως διαπέφευγε μελέτας, οὐδὲ τούτοις τὴν ἐπὶ τοῖς ἄλλοις ὁμοίαν ἐθέμεθα φροντίδα, ἀλλὰ κατὰ τὸ ἑκούσιον τὸ ἀκριβὲς αὐτῶν ὑπερώφθη. Εἰ δέ τι καὶ ἄλλο χρειῶδες καὶ τῆς σῆς αἰτήσεως ἐπὶ πλέον ταῖς ὑποθέσεσι συνεισπίπτει, αὐτὸς μᾶλλον συνήσεις.

Χρησιμεύσει δέ σοι δηλονότι τὰ ἐκδεδομένα εἴς τε κεφαλαιώδη μνήμην καὶ ἀνάμνησιν τῶν⟨βιβλίων ἃ εἴτε μετ᾽ ἄλλων (?)⟩ εἴτε κατὰ σεαυτὸν ἀναλεξάμενος ἐπῆλθες, καὶ εἰς ἕτοιμον εὕρεσιν τῶν ἐν αὐτοῖς ἐπιζητουμένων, οὐ μὴν ἀλλὰ καὶ εἰς εὐχερεστέραν ἀνάληψιν τῶν οὔπω τὴν ἀνάγνωσιν τῆς σῆς συνέσεως ὑπελθόντων. For this text, which differs significantly from that of Bekker and Henry, see W. Treadgold, "The Preface of the *Bibliotheca* of Photius: Text, Translation, and Commentary," *DOP*, 31 (1977), 343–49.

[2] Edited in *Pinax*.

[3] Ἀπογραφὴ καὶ συναρίθμησις τῶν ἀνεγνωσμένων ἡμῖν βιβλίων ὧν εἰς κεφαλαιώδη διάγνωσιν ὁ ἠγαπημένος ἡμῶν ἀδελφὸς Ταράσιος ἐξῃτήσατο· ἔστι δὲ ταῦτα εἴκοσι δεόντων ἐφ᾽ ἑνὶ τριακόσια. Bekker and Henry place this title before the preface without any justification in the MSS.

[4] Ἃ μὲν οὖν ἐν βίῳ φιλολογουμένοις ἡμῖν καθ᾽ ἑαυτοὺς εἰς ἀνάμνησιν ἐλθεῖν συνηνέχθη, χωρὶς ὧν ἡ σπουδὴ καὶ μελέτη τέχνας φιλεῖ καὶ ἐπιστήμας ἐργάζεσθαι, ἀφ᾽ οὗπέρ τις αἴσθησις ἡμῖν ἀμηγέπη καὶ κρίσις λόγων ἀνεφύη μέχρι τῆς παρούσης τῶν

The only reason for classing this preface and postface as literary fictions seems to be dissatisfaction with what they imply about the composition of the *Bibliotheca*. They belong to no known family of literary fictions, and even as some sort of deliberate deception they have no apparent point. Nor do they say anything that is in itself fantastic or even unlikely. The Byzantines sent out many real embassies and often appointed well-informed and able men like Photius to go on them. Photius had a real brother named Tarasius, who would naturally have known that Photius had read a great deal and who also seems to have read aloud, on occasion, in Photius' presence. Without making any extraordinary imposition, Tarasius could have taken the opportunity before his brother left on the embassy to request some "impressionistic" and "general" summaries of the books that Photius had read but he had not. Further, since Photius addressed thirteen other extant letters to Tarasius, all of which appear to be real letters, it seems likely that he addressed and sent this preface and postface to him as well.[5]

Of course, the principal point in dispute is whether Photius composed not just the preface and postface in the manner he describes, but the whole thousand-page text of the *Bibliotheca*. Yet the preface and postface do not stand alone. Twenty-nine times in nine of the codices Photius addresses his brother in the second person. In codex 165 he refers to Tarasius as "your studious self," in codex 187 as "dearest brother," and in codex 191 as "your perceptive self," all of which correspond to words used of Tarasius in the preface; the last reference in the second person occurs in codex 230.[6] The proof that

---

ἀνεγνωσμένων ὡς ἐν τύπῳ συνεκδόσεως, εἰς τοσοῦτον, οἶμαι, συνάγεται πλῆθος, τριακοσιοστῷ καὶ πεντεκαιδεκάτῳ μέρει προελθεῖν ἄχρι τῶν τριακοσίων κωλυόμενον.

Σὺ δ' ὦ τῶν ἐμοὶ κεκοινωνηκότων μητρικῶν ὠδίνων ἐρασμιώτατε, εἰ μὲν ⟨ἡμῶν⟩ ταύτην τὴν πρεσβείαν διαν[νό]ντων τὸ κοινὸν καὶ ἀνθρώπινον καταλάβοι τέλος, ἔχοις τὴν αἴτησιν τῆς ἐλπίδος οὐ διαμαρτοῦσαν, φιλίας τε ἅμα καὶ παραμυθίας ὑπόθεσιν καὶ ἀνάμνησιν, καὶ δὴ καὶ ἀπαρχὴν καὶ τελευτήν, ἀφοσιουμένην τῶν σῶν κατὰ λογικὴν θεωρίαν αἰτήσεων τὴν ἐκπλήρωσιν. Εἰ δ' ἐκεῖθεν ἡμᾶς ἀνασωσάμενον τὸ θεῖον τε καὶ φιλάνθρωπον νεῦμα εἰς τὴν ἀλλήλων θέαν καὶ προτέραν ἀπόλαυσιν ἀποκαταστήσει, τάχα ἂν ἑτέρων ἐκδόσεων οὐκ ἐλαττόνων ἀρχὴ ταῦτα εἴη, παραπλησίῳ τύπῳ παρεχομένων σοι τὴν ὠφέλειαν (postface: 545 lines 13–22). I have added ἐν βίῳ from M after οὖν in line 13, supplied ἡμῶν in line 17 (no lacuna in M), and completed M's διαν..ντων in line 17, where Henry prints διανοοῦντα. I have also replaced Henry's ἔχεις in line 18 with M's ἔχοις and deleted Henry's line 23, which is not in M.

[5] *Letters*, nos. 12, 13, 14, 142, 143, 220, 223, and 224; *Amphilochia*, PG, 101, nos. 133 and 135 (Professor L. G. Westerink has informed me that these questions in the *Amphilochia* appear as letters to Tarasius in one MS); *Sancti Patriarchae Photii archiepiscopi Constantinopoleos epistolae XIV*, ed. A. Papadopoulos-Kerameus (St. Petersburg, 1896), nos. 4, 6, and 8 (nos. 3, 5, and 7 are letters from Tarasius to Photius).

[6] The words are τὴν σὴν φιλοπονίαν (cod. 165: 108b lines 29–30; cf. preface, *Bibliotheca*: 1 lines 12–13, σοὶ...φιλοπονουμένῳ), φίλτατε ἀδελφῶν (cod. 187: 145a line 30; cf. preface, *Bibliotheca*: 1 lines 1–2, ἀδελφῶν φίλτατέ μοι), and σοῦ τὸ συνετόν (cod.

all the other codices were also meant for Tarasius is the number 279 given so elaborately in the preface, title, and postface, and a note in the *pinax* under the last codex: ". . . with which things note, dearest brother, that the things you earnestly requested come to an end also."[7] In an inconspicuous place where literary fiction would have been particularly pointless, this last note completes the case for taking Photius' account of the composition of his work at face value. If the *pinax* had been printed in the editions where it belongs, much scholarly controversy might have been avoided.

Though Photius probably expected Tarasius to show the *Bibliotheca* to other people, the preface and postface do not speak of any formal publication. The word ἐκδεδώκαμεν at the end of the first paragraph of the preface cannot mean "we have published" in the sense of producing several manuscripts for distribution, because it merely describes what Photius and his secretary have already done by producing one manuscript for Tarasius. I have therefore used the more neutral word "edited" in my translation. Like the *Bibliotheca,* most of Photius' letters, including the majority of those to Tarasius, answer requests for information or opinions, sometimes at great length. And three of Photius' other works are introduced by prefaces that show that Photius composed them for particular people. He addressed his *Lexicon* to his student, Thomas the *Protospatharius,* his *Amphilochia* to his friend, Amphilochius of Cyzicus, and his *Against the Manichaeans* in its first edition to the "Manichaean" Berzelis and in its second to his friend, Arsenius of Hiera.[8]

The whole *Bibliotheca,* then, as most modern scholars have assumed, seems really to have been sent by Photius to Tarasius in the manner he describes. Since it is a primary document, whatever information it gives ought to be believed in the absence of a good reason to the contrary. Still, as is natural in a letter between two brothers, it takes a good deal of knowledge for granted. And, as is natural in any letter not intended as a positive affidavit, it is not totally self-consistent. It therefore needs some interpretation, but this must have an adequate basis in the text.

According to both the preface and the postface, Photius composed the *Bibliotheca* shortly before he was to leave on his embassy. Some scholars have believed that Photius composed it during the course

191: 154a line 19; cf. preface, *Bibliotheca*: 1 line 21, τῆς σῆς συνέσεως). For the other passages, see p. 40 *infra* and notes 8–11.

[7] *Pinax,* 318 lines 25–27: ...οἷς συναπαρτίζεσθαί σοι, φίλτατε ἀδελφῶν, ἴσθι καὶ τὴν ποθουμένην ἐξαίτησιν. Henry has interpolated this clause into the beginning of the *text* of cod. 280 without justification.

[8] For the references, see my bibliography. (For the *Contra Manichaeos,* consult the edition of Astruc et al., in *TM,* 4 [1970], 181.)

of the embassy, but in the postface he calls the destination of the embassy "there" and refers to it as a future event. Therefore, he was still in the place from which the embassy was to set out, which, unless it was a very exceptional embassy, was Constantinople. Many scholars have applied the preface's words "more quickly than anyone else would have expected" not to Photius' completing the *Bibliotheca* but to his finding the secretary, and they concluded that Photius was in some remote or foreign place where Greek secretaries were difficult to find. But, as the earlier translators of the *Bibliotheca* saw, the sense and syntax lead the other way. The temporal clause applies more naturally to the main verb ("we have edited") than to the participle ("finding"), and naturally Tarasius had to wait some time for Photius to finish compiling this immense work, however hurriedly.[9]

Tarasius may well have been in Constantinople himself, but he wanted to have the summaries of the books in writing, both as a work of reference and as a memento of his brother during their separation. His presence in the capital seems to be implied by the fact that he learned at once of his brother's appointment as ambassador and made his request in enough time to permit the *Bibliotheca* to be written before the embassy left. The "separation" that distressed Tarasius was plainly the imminent one occasioned by the embassy, not some hypothetical separation before it. That Tarasius was not present to read every book in the *Bibliotheca* does not mean that he was out of town but only that he had something to do besides read books. Likewise, many of Photius' other correspondents were presumably in Constantinople but wanted his answers in writing for purposes of reference. Besides, Photius was obviously a man who liked to show off his learning in writing. Thus it is not a problem that Photius had the *Bibliotheca* written down instead of going to his brother's house for a week-long conversation about literature.

Photius says that the books which he included in the *Bibliotheca* were those he had read by himself when Tarasius was not present. In fact, there are two exceptions to this. At codex 268, Photius says that he has not yet had time to read the works of the orator Lycurgus but that he is giving information about Lycurgus from a "history," evidently the same lost history from which he took information about the other nine Attic orators.[10] Bury has given this as the simplest and most reasonable explanation for Photius' repeatedly and elaborately saying that he had read 279 books when, as the last codex number

[9] Cf. Schott (PG, 103, col. 43A); and J. H. Freese, *The Library of Photius*, I (New York, 1920), 15. I thus disagree with Henry (I, 1).

[10] Cod. 268: 496b lines 38–41. On the history, see pp. 48–50 *infra*.

and the *pinax* prove, there are 280 codices in the *Bibliotheca.*[11] Thus Photius seems to have remembered this exception and indirectly acknowledged it.

The second exception is codex 165, where, after a summary of the contents of the orations of Himerius, Photius adds, "I think it was only these orations of the sophist Himerius, about seventy of them, that your studious self read in our presence."[12] This is in flat contradiction to the preface and to the statement in the postface that Photius had studied the books he reviewed by himself. But in a work of a thousand pages, composed in haste, a man is entitled to a few inconsistencies. Since this codex occurs in the first quarter of the *Bibliotheca* and that concerning Lycurgus in the last quarter, by the time the preface and postface were completed Photius had probably forgotten about codex 165 but still remembered 268. All the other books in the *Bibliotheca* were evidently read by Photius alone, as he says. The persistent and unfounded theory that a "reading circle" read the books may perhaps have arisen because Photius habitually refers to himself in the plural.[13]

Though some incidental references in the *Bibliotheca* show that Photius had read a few books which he does not review in codices, he gives three possible reasons for this himself. First, besides Himerius, Tarasius may have read other books aloud in Photius' presence that Photius did leave out. But the word "only" in codex 165 may well mean that the only such books were the orations of Himerius; in any case, these books seem to have been few enough that Photius could forget in the course of his work whether he was including them or not. Second, there is the exception mentioned in the postface of books "whose study and perusal commonly constitute the arts and sciences." This corresponds to the preface's "books that are common and probably, because of their availability, have not eluded your studies either," with which Photius was not careful; probably he described some summarily and omitted the most common altogether. I have already argued that among such standard texts were

[11] Bury, *Eastern Roman Empire,* 446 note 2. Other suggestions seem not to have taken into account the *pinax,* which proves that the original number of codices was 280.

[12] Τούτους οἶμαι τοὺς λόγους μόνους τοῦ σοφιστοῦ Ἱμερίου, περί που ο´ ὄντας, κατὰ πρόσωπον ἡμῶν τὴν σὴν φιλοπονίαν ἀνεγνωκέναι (cod. 165: 108b lines 28–30).

[13] "We" can mean a reading circle only if the whole circle were made ambassadors (preface, *Bibliotheca*: 1 line 1), composed the *Bibliotheca* (preface: 1 lines 7–9), had read together since childhood (postface: 545 lines 1–8), and were Tarasius' brothers (title); 545 lines 8–9 is proof that Tarasius was Photius' physical brother. Cod. 165, and the reference in the preface to Tarasius' reading books "in our hearing," implies no wider "circle" than the two brothers.

four of those that Photius mentions but does not review.[14] Finally, as Photius acknowledges when he says that he included as much material as he remembered, no doubt he simply forgot a few books he had read, or he did not recall whether he had already included them. This probably accounts for the remaining four or five books that he had evidently read but did not review.[15] Otherwise, he says that he has included every book he had read since he had attained the age of reason. In nine-tenths of the cases in which Photius mentions a book that he is not reviewing, the book he mentions is reviewed in another codex.[16] The proportion of the total of his reading which is reviewed in the *Bibliotheca* was probably not much different.

When he notes that he found a secretary and put in writing "as many of the summaries as our memory preserves," Photius implies that he dictated at least part of the *Bibliotheca.* The secretary must have done the writing, while the source for what Photius merely remembered must have been his own mouth. But, when Photius says that he summarized as many books as he could remember, this means simply that he may have forgotten some books, not, as some have supposed, that he worked entirely from memory without recourse to notes or texts. In fact, in the middle of codex 186 he stops and asks rhetorically, "But why should I almost transcribe (μεταγράφειν) these things, when I should proceed much more summarily?"[17] Here Photius must have been working with either notes or the text before his eyes, as Hägg has proved he did in ten other codices. In fact, what Photius says about his secretary is vague enough to allow the possibility that the secretary copied part of the *Bibliotheca* from texts or notes.

But could Photius' secretary have copied the *Bibliotheca,* from

[14] See pp. 6–7 *supra.*

[15] Photius' comments imply that he had read John Chrysostom's *On Priesthood* (cod. 168: 116a lines 26–29), the medical works of Alexander of Tralles and Paul of Aegina (cod. 178: 123b lines 31–37), and the *Against Severus* of Jobius the Monk (cod. 222: 181b lines 5–6), though none of these is reviewed in a codex. Photius also implies (cod. 164: 107b lines 5–12 and cod. 178: 123b line 42–124a line 12) that he had read other works of Galen besides the one reviewed in cod. 164, but here he may be referring to Oribasius' voluminous abridgments of Galen (codd. 216–19). Photius need not actually have read the agricultural manuals he mentions in cod. 163: 107a lines 11–15 (note his ὅσα ἐμὲ εἰδέναι). His history of the ten orators and "Hesychius Epitome" are not formally reviewed but are special cases; see pp. 50 and 58 *infra.*

[16] I have counted 168 incidental references to books reviewed in other codices, against the four references to standard texts (note 14) and four others to unreviewed texts, with one case (Galen) doubtful (note 15).

[17] Ἀλλὰ τί μοι δεῖ μικροῦ μεταγράφειν ταῦτας, δέον πολλῷ κεφαλαιωδέστερον ἐπελθεῖν (cod. 186: 131b lines 19–20).

dictation or notes or texts, in the time between Photius' appointment to the embassy and his departure? A good Byzantine, Western, or Armenian scribe could copy fifteen to eighteen folios a day.[18] Manuscript A of the *Bibliotheca* originally had 537 folios, and M 441 folios.[19] If Photius employed his secretary full time, seven days a week, the *Bibliotheca* could have been copied in a month. In practice, the task probably took longer, but Photius emphasizes that it was done extraordinarily quickly. The Patriarch Methodius was able to copy seven complete psalters, about the equivalent of the *Bibliotheca*, in the seven weeks of Lent.[20] Of course, whatever part of the text was copied from written materials could have been written after Photius had left.[21] For the text to be copied under the circumstances described in the preface is certainly possible.

The beginning of the *Bibliotheca* actually seems to show changes in subject and method at intervals of about fifteen folios. Since Bekker's edition, which omits the *pinax*, has 545 pages, one Bekker page is a little less than one folio. The first fifty-six codices of the *Bibliotheca*, all very short and all but three on Christian or Jewish subjects, take up about fifteen Bekker pages. The next eleven codices are all historical, with the last eight arranged in chronological order from the oldest book in the *Bibliotheca* to the newest; this section consists of approximately eighteen Bekker pages. The next five codices, all on chronicles, take up about sixteen Bekker pages.[22] Though the next codex, describing a novel, marks the end of these neat divisions,

[18] The figure of 15 folios (30 pp.) a day is given on the basis of several examples by E. Lesne, *Histoire de la propriété ecclésiastique en France:* IV, *Les livres: "scriptoria" et bibliothèques* (Lille, 1938), 376–77. The western scribe Wandalgarius recorded that he copied 55 folios between 30 October and 1 November 794, a rate of at least 18 folios a day (G. Scherrer, *Verzeichniss der Handschriften der Stiftsbibliothek von S. Gallen* [Halle, 1875], 240, on MS 731). An Armenian scribe, who complained of very bad working conditions, says in a colophon, "Every night I copied eight folios, but during the day only two or three folios" (A. Sanjan, *Colophons of Armenian Manuscripts, 1301–1480* [Cambridge, Mass., 1969], 22); this points to a normal rate of about 15 folios a day. St. Methodius, Patriarch of Constantinople from 843 to 847, once copied one complete psalter (the equivalent of 70 to 80 ordinary folios) during each of the seven weeks of Lent, presumably not working Saturdays or Sundays (*Vita Methodii*, PG, 100, col. 1253B); again, this was about 15 folios a day. On dictation, see T. C. Skeat, "The Use of Dictation in Ancient Book-Production," *Proceedings of the British Academy*, 42 (1956), 179–208. Photius would presumably have mentioned it if his secretary had used tachygraphy, which Tarasius would have had trouble reading and of which there is no evidence in corruptions in the MSS.

[19] See Martini, *Textgeschichte*, 6, 7, and 12. (Note that a few folios are lost today.)

[20] See note 18 *supra*.

[21] In Chapters III and VI I argue that this was slightly more than half the text.

[22] The groups are codd. 1–56, 57–67, and 68–72. I count cod. 61 (Aeschines) as historical because it is almost totally a summary of a biography of Aeschines, placed in chronological order after Herodotus and before Praxagoras.

sometimes a similar pattern can be detected in the alternation of religious and secular sections after this point. To begin a new day's work with a new subject would have been a natural thing. In any event, the idea of several scholars that Photius reviewed the books in the order in which he had read them is excluded not only by the preface but by many references in the text to books that are only described later on.[23]

If the impression given by the preface and postface is trustworthy, the *Bibliotheca* was thrown together hurriedly in response to a request from its author's brother, done partly from memory, and arranged without organization or proportion. The codices are longer or more detailed not according to the importance or quality of the book, but according to its rarity, or to how much Photius remembered of it or had in notes or texts. The arrangement is not by subjects nor deliberately random for variety, but it is simply the order in which the books occurred to Photius. The sixteen cases in which books were reviewed a second time without even a cross-reference were apparently unintentional; otherwise, the preface, title, and postface would at least give a lower number for the books, if they did not mention the repeated reviews specifically.[24] The text of the *Bibliotheca* in fact displays so many careless errors, blank spaces, and inadvertent repetitions that it could hardly even have been proofread. But in a work composed in the manner that the preface and postface describe these things are not surprising.

This still leaves the problem of the identification of the "embassy to the Assyrians." The embassy must have been real: as the preface shows, Tarasius had already heard about it and actually requested a report on Photius' reading because of it. With the identification of this embassy goes the date of the *Bibliotheca,* which was written just before the embassy was to leave and can hardly contain later additions. That no codices were added at a later date is proved by the number 279 in the preface, title, and postface, and by the note at the end of the *pinax.* In view of the unfilled blanks and lack of proofreading, it is improbable that Photius added anything at all to his

[23] Cf. cod. 29: 6a line 28 (referring to cod. 31), cod. 33: 6b line 28–7a line 2 (to cod. 76), cod. 38: 8a lines 22–25 (to cod. 43=240), cod. 41: 9a lines 12–15 (to cod. 55), cod. 58: 17a lines 24–27 (to codd. 91 and 93), cod. 60: 19b lines 36–38 (to cod. 70=244), cod. 61: 20b lines 12–17 (to codd. 159=260, 262, and 265), and 61: 20b lines 23–28 (to cod. 158), etc. This misconception evidently arose from the myth that Photius both read his books and composed the *Bibliotheca* during his embassy, but it is shared even by some scholars who do not believe the myth; e.g., J. Irigoin, "Survie et renouveau de la littérature antique à Constantinople (IXe siècle)," *CahCM,* 5 (1962), 296.

[24] On these repeated reviews, see p. 45 *infra*.

work after it was sent to Tarasius. Indeed, he could not even have kept a copy for himself, because he had no time to have one made and mentions only one secretary.

But who these "Assyrians" were, or what place is meant by the reference to them, is not clear. Though the usual modern assumption is that "Assyrians" here means "Arabs," this particular classical affectation does not seem to be paralleled in other authors of Photius' time, and there were several embassies to various places in the Caliphate and elsewhere during Photius' career. Before searching for this embassy, which after all may have passed unrecorded in the sources, or even have been called off before it left or arrived, we should try to determine on other grounds as many probabilities as we can about both the embassy's date and the date of the *Bibliotheca*.

First, the period before the death of the Emperor Theophilus (20 January 842) can definitely be excluded. Theophilus was an active persecutor of iconophiles in general and of Photius and his family in particular; he would not have allowed Photius to be his ambassador. Under Theophilus, as we have seen, Photius and his parents were condemned and exiled.[25] Furthermore, the *Bibliotheca* is openly the work of an iconophile. It includes observations that certain authors can be used to defend the icons, condemns a source which Photius says the iconoclasts cited in their favor, and praises Sergius Confessor's anti-iconoclast history, repeating its condemnation of Constantine Copronymus.[26] On the other hand, the total absence of iconoclast writers from the *Bibliotheca* probably reflects the ban on them imposed by the iconophile council of 843.

Second, it is highly unlikely that Photius would have been appointed to an embassy while he was patriarch of Constantinople. It is not only that documented cases of sitting patriarchs who went on embassies are not to be found; unique and unexpected events do happen. But if the Patriarch Photius, about whose two patriarchates the sources say so much, had been made an ambassador, someone would have mentioned it; it would have been a major event. Moreover, a patriarch would surely have been chosen by the emperor to head the embassy, not chosen by the other ambassadors as a subordinate member, as the preface implies Photius was. This eliminates the periods between November or December 858 and 23 September 867, and between 26 October 877 and 29 or 30 September 886.[27]

[25] See p. 2 *supra*.

[26] References to the icons are at cod. 29: 6a line 33; cod. 52: 13a lines 36–37; cod. 110: 89b line 8; cod. 119: 93b lines 7–10; cod. 160: 103a lines 13–15; to the iconoclasts, at cod. 114: 91a lines 4–5; and to Sergius Confessor, cod. 67.

[27] V. Grumel, *La Chronologie*, Traité d'études byzantines, I (Paris, 1958), 436.

The period after Photius' second patriarchate can also be ruled out. Photius was disgraced and exiled during this period and was, moreover, very old. Finally, the years between Photius' two patriarchates are at least very improbable. In the first part of this period Photius was in disgrace, condemned by the Council of Constantinople (869–870) and obviously not about to go on an embassy. Photius returned to favor, but the sources record that Basil then made him tutor to Leo VI, not that he sent him on an embassy.[28] That the ambassadorship of such a famous man would have passed unrecorded is almost as unlikely in this period as during one of his two patriarchates. Furthermore, Photius never once refers in the *Bibliotheca* to his troubles, fall, or exile, as he does in his letters, *Against the Manichaeans*, and *Amphilochia*.[29] Finally, the fact that the preface does not address Tarasius as "patrician," as Photius' other letters do, suggests a date before his other letters, most of which seem to date from his first patriarchate. This leaves the years between 843 and 858 as the only probable time for the embassy to the "Assyrians."

We may now examine what Photius' incidental remarks in the *Bibliotheca* reveal about the time of its composition. First, he was particularly interested in the icons, indicating that iconoclasm was still an issue. In codex 114, he says of Pseudo-Leucius Charinus, "In his *Acts of St. John* he seems, in the opinion of the iconoclasts, to teach a doctrine against the icons."[30] This sounds as if iconoclasts were still to be found who had not abjured their heresy or disappeared from sight. On the other hand, it is remarkable that the *Bibliotheca*, among its many theological works, does not include a single work of iconophile theology, unless we count the acts of the Seventh Council: nothing by John of Damascus or Theodore of Studium and only a historical work of the Patriarch Nicephorus. One possible explanation is that the iconoclasts had suppressed such books so successfully that they were still very difficult to find. These arguments, which are by no means conclusive, point to a date soon after the restoration of the icons in 843.

Second, the *Bibliotheca* shows a Photius whose main occupation was scholarship—scholarship that was very much still in progress. In a dozen or more places in his compilation, he says that he has "not yet" found a book, resolved a bibliographical problem, or, in the case

[28] See F. Dvornik, *The Photian Schism, History and Legend* (Cambridge, 1948), 161–73.

[29] *Contra Manichaeos* (*supra*, note 8), preface; *Letters*, nos. 50 (pp. 348–52), 146 (pp. 471–85), 164 (p. 501), 211 (pp. 525–26), 218 (pp. 530–33); *Amphilochia*, PG, 101, title and preface (cols. 46A–48B) and no. 78 (col. 489C).

[30] Δοκεῖ δὲ καὶ κατ' εἰκόνων τοῖς εἰκονομάχοις ἐν ταῖς 'Ιωάννου πράξεσι δογματίζειν (cod. 114: 91a lines 4–5).

of the orator Lycurgus, had time to read the book.[31] In the postface he tells Tarasius that he hopes to read and report on as many books again when he returns, a plain indication that Photius was not very old. Nowhere in his work does he mention any ecclesiastical or administrative duties apart from the embassy. He must have been spending a large part of his time reading, which would have been difficult for a man with the extensive secretarial and judicial duties of a *protoasecretis,* a post Photius held for some time before 858. Rather, what the *Bibliotheca* seems to show is Photius' continuing process of self-education before the busier part of his career.

In codex 187, on a work of arithmology by Nicomachus of Gerasa, Photius says to Tarasius, "in our day, in geometry, arithmetic, and the other sciences, as you know as well as I do, there are many among our acquaintances who have no less exact knowledge, I dare say, than the son of Hermias (for you, of course, know the skill of Ammonius in those fields), and none of the propositions that Nicomachus piles up together in his work on numbers would be obscure to them."[32] Such comprehensive knowledge of mathematics, to which Photius himself does not pretend, was the particular pride of the iconoclast scholars of the generation before Photius: John the Grammarian, his cousin Leo the Mathematician, and their circle. John is not heard of after 847, and, according to the Slavonic *Life of St. Constantine,* Leo and Photius both taught the young Constantine in the early 840's.[33]

Photius' great but far from exclusive interest in theology in the *Bibliotheca* is only what one would expect from any well-educated Byzantine layman, especially one who, like Photius, had planned in his youth to become a monk.[34] But one theological passage demands close scrutiny. In codex 52, on a collection of conciliar acts combating the Messalian heresy, Photius adds, "And there were charges of

[31] Codd. 14: 4a lines 19–21; 35: 7a lines 31–33; 48: 11b lines 40–42; 58: 17b lines 21–22; 88: 66b line 35-67a line 1; 166: 111b line 43-112a line 3; 170: 117b lines 27–30; 172–74: 119a lines 41–42; 213: 171a lines 19–21; 228: 245a lines 28–33; 261: 488a lines 15–16; 268: 496b lines 38–41; and 273: 507b lines 15–20.

[32] . . . νῦν τά τε γεωμετρικὰ καὶ ἀριθμητικὰ καὶ τἄλλα τῶν μαθημάτων, ὡς καὶ σὺ συνεπίστασαι, πολλοὶ τῶν ἡμᾶς ἐγνωκότων οὐκ ἔλαττον, οἶμαι, τοῦ παιδὸς Ἑρμείου (οἶδας γὰρ πάντως τὴν περὶ ταῦτα δεξιότητα τοῦ Ἀμμωνίου) διακριβοῦσι, καὶ οὐδὲν αὐτοὺς λάθοι ἂν τῶν θεωρημάτων, ἃ συνεπεισκυκλεῖ Νικόμαχος τῷ περὶ ἀριθμῶν πόνῳ (cod. 187: 145a.35–40). For corrections to and further commentary on this text, see Treadgold, "Photius."

[33] On John, see Lemerle, *Humanisme,* 144, and on Leo and Photius, see F. Dvornik, *Les Légendes de Constantin et de Méthode vues de Byzance* (Prague, 1933), 34 and 352. I do not share the skepticism of Lemerle (*Humanisme,* 163–65) about the latter passage. A letter from Photius to Leo, of uncertain date, appears among Photius' correspondence (*Letters,* no. 77, pp. 403–4).

[34] *Letters,* no. 2, p. 145.

many other impieties done and said by the Messalians; in the same way, in leading away from a similar heresy, as far as we were able, certain men who have newly begun to propagate it from that source, we have found a great corruption of passions and malice feeding upon their souls."[35]

This heresy "similar" to Messalianism can only be Paulicianism, which was closely related to it and sometimes identified with it.[36] Against Paulicianism, Photius wrote his *Against the Manichaeans*. Its full title is *Against the Newly-Sprung Heresy of the Manichaeans*, for Paulicianism was also regarded as a recrudescence of Manichaeanism.[37] The title's word "newly-sprung" (ἀρτιφυοῦς) neatly parallels codex 52's "newly begun to propagate" (ἄρτι βλαστάνειν . . . ἀρξαμένους). The best explanation of this passage seems to be that Photius is referring to his own book.

In its original edition, *Against the Manichaeans* was addressed to a "Manichaean" named Berzelis, who had converted by the time of the second edition. Hélène Ahrweiler has identified "Berzelis" with a "Manichaean" named Zelix (a Syrian Bar Zelis?), who was condemned with his followers at the council of 843 but was soon afterward converted by the Patriarch Methodius (843–47).[38] Paul Lemerle has doubted this identification because it would mean that Photius kept his *Against the Manichaeans* for almost thirty years before preparing its second edition in 871 or 872; but why should he not have done so?[39] If Berzelis and Zelix were not two different "Manichaeans," Photius wrote his original treatise about 843. If codex 52 refers to it, the event was still recent. Although all these interpretations of Photius' incidental remarks are guesswork, they seem to point to a date not very long after 843. No remark of Photius' seems to require a later date.

On the other hand, some have used arguments based on specific books which Photius included in the *Bibliotheca* to argue for a very

[35] Καὶ ἄλλα ἄττα ἀθέμιτα διεβέβλητο, ἃ τοῖς Μεσσαλιανοῖς καὶ ποιεῖται καὶ λέγεται, καθὼς καὶ ἡμεῖς, ὡς οἷον τε ἡμῖν, τινὰς τῆς τοιαύτης πλάνης ἀπάγοντες, ἄρτι βλαστάνειν ἐκεῖθεν ἀρξαμένους, πολλὴν σηπεδόνα παθῶν καὶ κακίας τὰς ἐκείνων ψυχὰς ἐπιβοσκομένην ἑωράκαμεν (cod. 52: 13b lines 11–16).

[36] P. Lemerle, "L'Histoire des Pauliciens d'Asie Mineure d'après les sources grecques," *TM*, 5 (1973), 55 and 133.

[37] Κατὰ τῆς τῶν Μανιχαίων ἀρτιφυοῦς πλάνης (*Contra Manichaeos* [*supra*, note 8], 181).

[38] H. Ahrweiler, "Sur la carrière de Photius avant son patriarcat," *BZ*, 58 (1965), 361–62. On Zelix, see also J. Gouillard, in *Byzantion*, 31 (1961), 371–87.

[39] Lemerle, "Pauliciens," 42–43. Lemerle's further objection, that Methodius and not Photius converted Zelix, does not apply because it is plain from the preface to the second edition that the *Contra Manichaeos* did not immediately succeed in converting Berzelis.

late date for its composition. In particular, considering the preface and postface to be literary fictions, François Halkin dated the *Bibliotheca* no earlier than 875, and probably a good deal later. Halkin's argument concerns only codex 252, on a *Life* of St. Gregory the Great. Halkin conjectured that this was a short Greek *Life* that has been preserved. Hippolyte Delehaye had earlier asserted that this Greek *Life* was derived from the Latin *Life* composed by John the Deacon between 873 and 875 or 876. Halkin's Greek *Life* includes only two related incidents, both of which appear in Photius' codex. But since codex 252 has no verbal parallels with Halkin's text and includes information that is not in Halkin's text at all, under Halkin's theory Photius would have had both to revise and to expand his source.[40]

At the beginning of codex 252, however, Photius announces "*The Life of St. Gregory Dialogus,* of which [my] edition records a certain selection."[41] Therefore codex 252, like all the other codices after 233 that can be checked, seems to be merely a selection of excerpts from its original.[42] It follows that the *Life* read by Photius differed in wording from Halkin's text and included material that is not in it. The date of the *Life* read by Photius may be indicated by a passage in codex 252 (not paralleled in Halkin's text) that describes the translation of Gregory's works into Greek by Pope Zacharias (741–52) and shows parallels of wording and content with the anonymous preface that was appended to Zacharias' translation of Gregory's *Dialogues* at least by the late eighth century.[43] The most natural interpretation of the evidence is that, like this preface, the Greek *Life* of Gregory read by Photius was produced under Zacharias or very soon after his death.[44] In any event, Photius' *Life* could not have been identical

[40] F. Halkin, "La Date de composition de la *Bibliothèque* remise en question," *AnalBoll,* 81 (1963), 414–17. Cod. 252: 467a line 40–467b line 14 has no parallels in Halkin's text (ed. *Archiv für slavische Philologie,* 18 [1896], 152–55).

[41] Γρηγορίου τοῦ διαλόγου ὁ βίος, οὗ ἡ ἔκδοσις ἐκλογήν τινα ἀναγράφει. Instead of this, Henry prints a text that he himself realizes to be "visiblement un remaniement" of the right one, for the incredible reason that he wants to preserve the line numbers of Bekker! See Henry, VII, 207 note 1, and his apparatus. Bekker's erroneous text apparently led Halkin to think that Photius' *Life* consisted of excerpts (ἐκλογαί), as did the *Life* that he identified with it. The word ἔκδοσις refers to Photius' own "editing" (cf. his preface and postface). On the word ἐκλογή, see pp. 45–46 *infra.*

[42] See Chapter III.

[43] Cf. cod. 252: 467a line 40–467b line 12 with PL, 77, cols. 147B–150A. On the date of the preface, cf. B. Hemmerdinger, "Le 'Codex' 252 de la *Bibliothèque* de Photius," *BZ,* 58 (1965), 1.

[44] This lost Greek *Life* seems to have derived from a lost Latin *Life* that was the source of Halkin's Greek text and one of the sources of John the Deacon. A student in my seminar at U.C.L.A., Miss Ruth Anne Lawn, has argued with probability in a paper that Halkin's text is not derived from John the Deacon, since it groups together two incidents that John separates widely but were obviously grouped together in their source (cf. John's Book I, chap. 10 and Book II, chap. 23 in PG, 75, cols. 66A–C and

with Halkin's text, which itself was probably not even derived from John the Deacon's work, and Halkin's date for the *Bibliotheca* is not justified.

This means that the latest book formally reviewed in the *Bibliotheca* is Sergius Confessor's ecclesiastical history, which ended with the year 828 and was presumably compiled shortly thereafter.[45] Besides this, there is the biographical dictionary which Wentzel identified as Photius' source for passages that begin with "they say" or "it is said." This "Hesychius Epitome" largely survives in the biographical articles of the *Suda,* the latest of which is on Ignatius the Deacon and mentions his *Lives* of the Patriarchs Tarasius and Nicephorus, written a little earlier than Ignatius' death soon after 845.[46]

There are several reasons for believing that the compiler of the "Hesychius Epitome" was Ignatius himself or at least a close associate of his. First, just as the compilers of its two main sources, Hesychius of Miletus and St. Jerome, added biographies of themselves as their latest entries, one might expect the latest compiler to follow their example.[47] This seems particularly likely because Ignatius' biography

96A–D). Halkin's text was translated from the Latin independently from Photius' and more literally, because it includes Latinisms that are paralleled in John the Deacon but not in Photius (e.g., βεστιάριος, *vestiarius* in John, διακονησάμενος in Photius; σκουτέλιον, *scutella* in John, πινακίσκος in Photius). My stemma is therefore as follows:

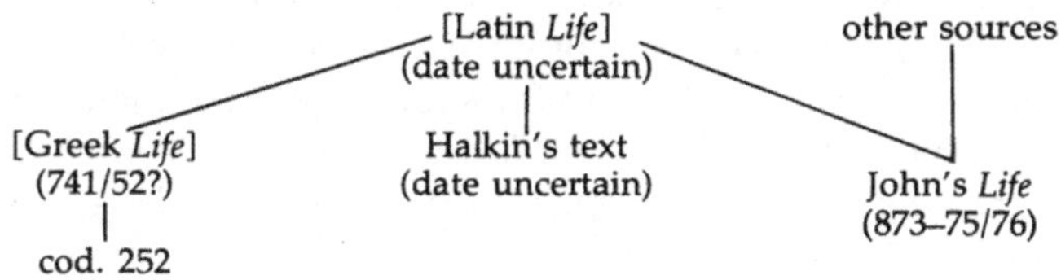

Note that this stemma differs from that of Hemmerdinger, *op. cit.* (*supra,* note 43), 2, who also assumes a lost Greek *Life* but supposes that it was translated for John by Anastasius Bibliothecarius and thus became one of John's sources.

[45] Cod. 67: 33b lines 33–34. Cf. Mango, "Liquidation," 135–39.

[46] Wentzel "Übersetzung," 57; *Suda,* II, 607–8. On the date of Ignatius' death and of the *Lives* of Tarasius and Nicephorus, see Ševčenko, "Hagiography," 122–25. The *Suda* also mentions Ignatius' letters, which are of different dates both before and after 843 according to C. Mango, "Observations on the Correspondence of Ignatius, Metropolitan of Nicaea (First Half of the Ninth Century)," *Festschrift Marcel Richard* (forthcoming). Professor Mango, who is reediting the letters, kindly supplied me with a copy of his article. (Because the letters mentioned in the *Suda* need not have included all those that we possess, the mention of letters is not a reliable indication of the date of the prototype of the *Suda*'s entry.)

[47] For Jerome's autobiography, see "Sophronius," chap. 135, 62. For Hesychius' autobiography, see *Suda,* II, 594 (the words οὐ ἐπιτομή ἐστι τοῦτο τὸ βιβλίον and the last sentence are additions by the compiler of the "Hesychius Epitome"; see Wentzel "Übersetzung," 2–4). It may be that the biography of Ignatius originally mentioned his making the epitome, but the editor of the *Suda* abbreviated it; as it is, the list of Ignatius' works ends with the words καὶ ἄλλα (*Suda,* II, 608).

is one of only three post-Hesychian biographies in the collection, along with those of the much more famous George of Pisidia and John of Damascus.[48] Further, Ignatius' biography does not mention that he had been an iconoclast before 842; perhaps significantly, the biography of John of Damascus does not mention John's iconophile theology but dwells instead on the beauty of his hymns. Finally, Ignatius is known to have been both a classical scholar and a biographer.[49]

Unless the reference to the works written after 842 is a later addition, the "Hesychius Epitome" could not have been compiled before 843; but it need not have been compiled later and indeed could not have been compiled much later if Ignatius was the compiler. As for the *Bibliotheca,* Photius kept up to date on literary affairs, sometimes read manuscripts at their authors' request even before they were published, and in 871 or 872 plagiarized the history of Peter the Sicilian a year or less after it had been written.[50] Thus the *Bibliotheca,* once again, cannot be earlier than 843, but need not be later.

Mango argued that correspondence between the books used in Photius' other works and those in the *Bibliotheca* indicates that its date was late.[51] Correspondence alone, however, would seem to be compatible with any possible date for the *Bibliotheca.* Photius could have read and referred to a book at an early date and included it in the *Bibliotheca* much later; he could also have referred at a late date to a book that he had read and included in the *Bibliotheca* much earlier. Especially if Photius owned the book, had taken notes on it, or reread it, he could have displayed detailed knowledge of it many years after his original reading.

Of course, since the *Bibliotheca* purports to include, with some limited exceptions, every book that Photius had ever read, nearly complete correspondence between it and Photius' other works would suggest a late date. But the correspondence is very far from being

[48] On Ignatius' iconoclasm, see Ševčenko, "Hagiography," 125. The biographies of George of Pisidia and John of Damascus are in the *Suda* (I, 517 and II, 649).

[49] See Ševčenko, "Hagiography," 121–25 and 129; W. Wolska-Conus, "De quibusdam Ignatiis," *TM,* 4 (1970), 329–60; and R. Browning, "Ignace le diacre et la tragédie classique à Byzance," *REG,* 81 (1968), 401–10. With Browning and Ševčenko and against Wolska-Conus, I believe that there was only one Ignatius.

[50] On the "advance copies," see *Letters,* no. 114, p. 435, and no. 244, p. 550. On Photius' plagiarism of Peter and its date, see Lemerle, "Pauliciens" (*supra,* note 36), 31–47.

[51] See Mango, "Books," 41. As evidence, Mango cites only two of Photius' homilies that were delivered in 861 or 867. In the *Homilies,* 237–38, Mango, the editor, shows that most of the sources of these orations appear in the *Bibliotheca.* But since these seem to be the only references to books in the *Homilies,* they are too few to give a reliable picture of Photius' reading by themselves. For a discussion of them, see p. 95 *infra.*

complete. For example, in a letter to his friend, Amphilochius of Cyzicus, who had asked him for models of epistolary style, Photius mentions twelve titles, all of which he seems to have read: Plato's dialogues, Plato's letters, Aristotle's letters, Aristotle's other works, and the letters of Pseudo-Demosthenes, Pseudo-Phalaris, Pseudo-Marcus Junius Brutus, Marcus Aurelius, Libanius, St. Basil, Gregory of Nazianzus, and Isidore of Pelusium.[52] Of these, only St. Basil's letters appear in the *Bibliotheca,* in codex 143. Like all of the letters from Photius' main collection, this one must date before 868–72. Yet its date seems to have been considerably later than the *Bibliotheca*'s, leaving Photius time to read many more books which relegated to the back of his mind the many collections of letters in the *Bibliotheca.*[53]

In the *Amphilochia,* which dates from 868–72, Photius gives another list, this one of books concerning the incomprehensibility of God.[54] He cites five, which again he apparently had read: Pseudo-Dionysius, "Athanasius," St. Basil's *Against Eunomius,* Gregory of Nazianzus' *Theological Orations,* and John Chrysostom's *On the Incomprehensible Nature of God.*[55] There is no way to be sure whether Photius means the works of Athanasius that he describes in the *Bibliotheca* (codices 32, 139, and 140) or others, but the other four works are not in the *Bibliotheca.*

In the whole body of his letters, Photius refers to thirty-three titles as if he had read them. Of these, seven are in the *Bibliotheca,* and one more may be. Another five titles could plausibly be considered school texts. This leaves twenty that are neither school texts nor reviewed in the *Bibliotheca.* The pattern is similar in the *Amphilochia,* where Photius refers to forty-two titles that he had apparently read: six titles are definitely in the *Bibliotheca,* seven more may be, and seven could be considered school texts, leaving twenty-two which are neither school texts nor in the *Bibliotheca.*[56] If the ambiguously described books and the possible school texts are excluded, the titles that are not in the *Bibliotheca* outnumber those that are by nearly three to one in the letters, and by more than three and a half to one in the *Amphilochia.* These books vary widely in length, but, if anything, the books that are not in the *Bibliotheca* tend to be longer than those that are.

[52] *Letters*, no. 208, p. 545. That Photius means Marcus by ὁ ἐν βασιλεῦσι φιλόσοφος, see B. Laourdas, Τὰ εἰς τὰς ἐπιστολὰς τοῦ Φωτίου σχόλια τοῦ κωδίκου Baroccianus Graecus 217, in Ἀθηνᾶ, 55 (1951), 135 note 2.

[53] On the date of the letters, see p. 4 *supra.* 15 codices review letters (see under "letters" in both parts of Table III).

[54] On the date of the *Amphilochia,* see Lemerle, *Humanisme,* 200.

[55] *Amphilochia,* PG, 101, no. 119, cols. 697D–700B.

[56] For all the references, see Table VI, in which possible school texts not in the *Bibliotheca* are marked with an asterisk.

To be sure, a few of these could be books that Photius forgot to put into the *Bibliotheca* or read with Tarasius, but such books could hardly have amounted to more than three times those that were reviewed. The assumption that Photius pretended to have read many books that he had not is not only unsupported by the evidence but applies equally to the *Bibliotheca* and the other works; so it does not help to explain the discrepancy. The only satisfactory explanation seems to be that, by the time he wrote most of his letters, Photius had read many books which he had not read when he composed the *Bibliotheca* and had read still more by the time he composed the *Amphilochia*. Again, this is evidence for an early date for the *Bibliotheca*, certainly a good number of years before 868–72.

Therefore, according to several different lines of argument, Photius was chosen for the embassy to the "Assyrians" and composed the *Bibliotheca* sometime between 843 and 858. Two embassies are recorded for this period, both to the Arabs.

One of these embassies, that of 855, was considered to be Photius' by almost all scholars until recently; it still is by many. According to a somewhat vague account in the Arabic chronicle of Al-Ṭabarī, which is much the fullest source for this embassy, the Byzantine ambassadors never left Imperial territory. The chief ambassador, a certain George, conducted negotiations with the Caliph through an Arab intermediary which resulted in an exchange of prisoners at the Lamus River, the Arab-Byzantine border in Cilicia.[57] But western Cilicia is not "Assyria," and "Assyrians" is not one of the many names used elsewhere for the Arabs. Nevertheless, "Assyrians" could somehow mean the Arabs, and 855 could possibly have been the date of Photius' embassy, though it seems somewhat too late.

The other embassy went in 845 to Samarra, to give the Assyrian name by which that city is generally known. It was refounded in 836 to be the capital of the Abbasid Caliphate under the name of Surra Man Ra'a, retaining its status until 892. It is located on the east bank of the Tigris in ancient Assyria.[58] This location agrees with the only reference in the body of the *Bibliotheca* to "Assyrians" (besides three references to the ancient Assyrians), in codex 63 on Procopius' *Wars*. In it, Belisarius sends his general Arethas "among the Assyrians" (ἐν Ἀσσυρίοις) from the Byzantine camp in the area of Nisibis.[59] Photius has quoted the phrase from Procopius, who makes it clear that this was the land east of the Tigris.[60] I would guess that Photius,

[57] A. A. Vasiliev, *Byzance et les Arabes,* I (Brussels, 1935), 224–26 (passage translated 317–18).

[58] P. K. Hitti, *A History of the Arabs,* 9th ed. (London, 1968), 466.

[59] Cod. 63: 26a line 2: Photius' references to the ancient Assyrians are at codd. 69: 34b line 1, 72: 35b line 37, and 189: 146a line 12.

[60] Procopius, *De Bellis* II.19, 17.

who had read Procopius carefully and knew where his embassy was going, decided to use this classicism for his destination. The only other recorded Byzantine embassy to Samarra occurred in 859, the very beginning of Photius' patriarchate, about which the sources give quite full information. Since there was no government in Baghdad at any time during the probable period of Photius' career, the common opinion that his embassy went to Baghdad is indefensible.

The chronology of the embassy of 845 can be reconstructed approximately as follows. On 6 March 845, the Caliph Al-Wāthiq executed forty-two Byzantine prisoners who had been captured during the sack of Amorium seven years before and now chose death rather than conversion to Islam.[61] The news of their martyrdom probably reached Constantinople quickly, because an optical telegraph was then in operation between the frontier and the capital.[62] The impression—reflected in contemporary hagiography—made on the Byzantines by these executions presumably influenced the government's decision to send an embassy to request an exchange of the Greek prisoners still held by the Arabs. The ambassadors' activities when they arrived at Samarra are described by Al-Ṭabarī, who quotes a friend of the Arab who managed the embassy, the eunuch Khāqān:

> Then the ambassadors of the Emperor of the Romans (he was Michael [III], the son of Theophilus, the son of Michael [II], the son of Leo, the son of George) came before [the Caliph] Al-Wāthiq, asking him to make an exchange for whoever of the Muslim captives was in the Emperor's hands. Then Al-Wāthiq sent Khāqān for that purpose. Then Khāqān and whoever was with him set out for the exchange of the Muslim captives at the end of the year 230 A.H. [ended 6 September 845], on the date specified between Khāqān and the ambassadors of the Emperor of the Romans. The meeting for the exchange was on the day of Ashūra (that was the tenth of Muḥarram of the year 231 A.H. [16 September 845]).[63]

[61] Bury, *Eastern Roman Empire*, 271–72.

[62] *Ibid.*, 246–48; and Lemerle, *Humanisme*, 154–55.

[63] فقدم على الواثق رسل صاحب الروم وهو ميخائيل
ابن توفيل بن ميخائيل بن اليون بن جورجس يسئله ان
يفادى بمن فى يده من اسارى المسلمين فوجه الواثق خاقان
فى ذلك فخرج خاقان ومن معه فى فداء اسارى المسلمين فى آخر
سنة ٢٣٠ على موعد بين خاقان ورسل صاحب الروم الالتقاء
للفداء فى يوم عاشوراء وذلك العاشر من المحرم سنة ٢٣١
Al-Ṭabarī, *Annales*, ed. M. J. De Goeje, ser. 3, II (Leiden, 1883–84), 1352. See Vasiliev, *op. cit.*, I, 198–204 (passage translated 311).

Ṭabarī's account goes on to say that, before the exchange, Khāqān had sent an envoy to Constantinople to complete the arrangements. This would mean that the Byzantine ambassadors had probably left Constantinople sometime in June or a little earlier.[64]

If this was the embassy to which Photius was appointed, the *Bibliotheca* was composed in the spring of 845, before its author left Constantinople. Thus the "Hesychius Epitome," which Photius used, was apparently completed between 843 and 845, and codex 52 could refer to Photius' *Against the Manichaeans,* written about two years earlier. In this period, as far as is known, Photius was still only a teacher and scholar and had not attained any high office or gained any great fame. The Greek sources had no reason to mention his ambassadorship at this time, and by the time he became patriarch this embassy was thirteen years in the past and fading from memory. Though Photius at the time was about thirty-five, he was a voracious reader; it is perfectly possible that he had read 386 books plus some school texts by that age.

The *Bibliotheca* could have been composed in 855; it could also have been composed on the occasion of an embassy between 843 and 858 of which our sources say nothing. But the available evidence seems to indicate that it was composed in 845, informally and hastily, by a young man with an enthusiasm for learning that he wanted to share with his favorite brother.

[64] Between the departure of the ambassadors from Constantinople and the departure of Khāqān for the actual exchange about September 6, we must allow time for the ambassadors to travel to Samarra and for Khāqān's emissary Abū Qaḥṭaba to travel from Samarra to Constantinople and back. We may safely assume that the Byzantine ambassadors, Abū Qaḥṭaba, and Khāqān all followed the main post-road between the two capitals, with Khāqān leaving the road at Adana to follow the spur road to the Lamus. Khāqān took about ten days to travel from Samarra to the Lamus (*ca.* 700 miles), which would mean some nine days to travel from Samarra to Adana (*ca.* 650 miles). The stretch from Adana to Chrysopolis (Scutari), across the Bosporus from Constantinople, took a courier seven days in the seventeenth century (*ca.* 500 miles). (This was part of Evlija Tshelebi's twelve-day trip from Damascus to Scutari; see F. Taeschner, *Das Anatolische Wegenetz nach Osmanischen Quellen,* I [Leipzig, 1924], 103.) Allowing a rest day, the journey from Samarra to Constantinople would have taken about seventeen days. Thus the three journeys alone would have taken nearly two months, while even the straightforward negotiations described by Ṭabarī must have taken a week or two; nine or ten weeks before September 6 puts the Byzantine embassy's departure in June.

CHAPTER THREE

The Second Part (Codices 234–280)

Photius gives us no details about the part that his secretary took in the composition of the *Bibliotheca*. His only reference to the secretary is the one he addresses to Tarasius in the preface: "Though later, perhaps, than was your burning desire and warm entreaty, nevertheless more quickly than anyone else would have expected, we, finding a secretary, have edited as many of the summaries as our memory preserves, satisfying your desire and claim." This could mean that Photius personally dictated the whole *Bibliotheca* to his secretary between the time of Tarasius' request and the time of the embassy's departure.

This passage, however, is imprecise enough to cover just as easily a more complex and varied process of composition. For example, Photius might have used the secretary for only part of the work and written the rest with his own hand. Alternatively, Photius could have dictated or written only part of the work and left the secretary, with more or less full instructions, to copy the rest from the original books or from notes which Photius had previously taken on the books. The methods of copying, dictation, writing, or having the secretary copy could have been used alternatively from one codex to another, or even combined within a single codex.

Without a more explicit statement than the one Photius gives us about the composition of his work, we have no practical way to distinguish material which he wrote with his own hand, if there was any, from material that he dictated. Because, however, Photius' letters indicate that he habitually dictated when he composed at any length, my analysis here will disregard the unverifiable and unnecessary hypothesis that he wrote some part of the *Bibliotheca* by himself.[1] Having the secretary copy from the original manuscripts would

[1] In a letter that Photius wrote during his first exile, he complains that he cannot write at length because he has been deprived of a secretary (*Letters*, no. 146, pp.

have saved Photius still more time and trouble than dictating would. But in cases in which the original survives, a comparison with even the most detailed excerpts reveals pervasive, though often minor, paraphrasing, condensing, and glossing of the original text which cannot be plausibly explained by any instructions which Photius might have given his secretary, even in the form of marginal notes in the texts.[2] Thus the possibility that the secretary sometimes copied directly from the original books can be safely ruled out.

This leaves the possibility that Photius had his secretary copy part of the *Bibliotheca* from notes which Photius had taken previously. In this case, the text would not have been composed for Tarasius at all but only copied for him. In fact, Photius used a procedure of this kind when he prepared his *Amphilochia,* a collection of about three hundred answers to questions, for his friend Amphilochius of Cyzicus. Beginning with question 81 in Migne's edition, the *Amphilochia* is made up of a variety of materials, most of which were certainly not composed for Amphilochius. At least eighty questions are verbatim copies of letters which Photius had already written to answer questions addressed to him by various people and which are separately preserved among his correspondence.[3] At least sixty-one more "questions" are summaries or plagiarizations of the work of other authors, including thirty-three "questions" taken from Theodoret's *Commentary on the Octateuch,* eleven "questions" summarizing Aristotle's *Categories,* and thirteen "questions" which repeat excerpts from sermons of Pseudo-Modestus of Jerusalem and John Chrysostom that are found in codices 275 and 277 of the *Bibliotheca.*[4] This mechanical copying, which includes no references to Amphilochius, was plainly done by a secretary on Photius' orders, not by Photius himself. Evidently Photius chose from his papers those that he wanted to send to Amphilochius and had them copied as part of the manuscript of the *Amphilochia.*

If Photius had the thirteen "questions" which correspond with

---

480-81). He notes at the end of another, very short letter that he had written it with his own hand, thus implying that this was unusual for him (no. 225, p. 540).

[2] This was already recognized by Severyns, *Chrestomathie,* I, 5-6.

[3] Cf. *Amphilochia,* PG, 101, cols. 1173-76, Index III. Professor L. G. Westerink has given me a more complete list of the questions that were originally letters, which includes nos. 81-121, 131-36, 171-73, and 193-222 (*Amphilochia,* PG, 101).

[4] Nos. 137-47 (*Amphilochia,* PG, 101) are summaries of the *Categories;* no. 149 is plagiarized from St. Germanus, and 152 from Polychronius; nos. 158-70 correspond with the *Bibliotheca*'s codd. 275 and 277; nos. 188 and 191 are plagiarized from Jobius the Monk, and 249-81 from Theodoret. Cf. the notes to the relevant questions, *Amphilochia,* PG, 101; for the correspondences with the *Bibliotheca,* which are not quite exact, see *Amphilochia,* ed. S. Oikonomos (Athens, 1858), 244-53 notes. This list of "foreign elements" in the *Amphilochia* is probably not complete.

material in the *Bibliotheca* copied from the *Bibliotheca* itself, this would be the only indication that Photius ever returned to the *Bibliotheca* after sending it to Tarasius. On the contrary, at the end of the "question" that immediately precedes these thirteen "questions" in Migne's edition, Photius refers to the confiscation of his books during his exile, telling Amphilochius, "We have transcribed these things from rough versions (ἀπὸ σχεδαρίων) as best we could, but the books, as your archpriestly perfection knows as well as we, captivity took for plunder, along with the other things that make life worth living."[5] To judge from the context, these σχεδάρια were notes, including considerable parts of books, that Photius had made earlier. Probably Photius' excerpts from Pseudo-Modestus and Chrysostom were originally such notes, which were successively transcribed for both the *Bibliotheca* and *Amphilochia,* with appropriate headings for each.

Another set of Photius' notes on a book, this one on Philostorgius' *Ecclesiastical History,* is preserved entirely independently.[6] It is about the length of one of the longer codices of the *Bibliotheca* and, like the codices that parallel the *Amphilochia* and many other codices as well, it consists only of excerpts without any commentary. Though Photius reviews Philostorgius briefly in codex 40, he mentions nothing that is in these excerpts, which do not appear in either of his compilations.

Thus Photius seems to have had the habit of taking extensive notes, primarily in the form of excerpts, when he read certain books. This is not a strange habit for a scholar and teacher, especially in a society in which books were expensive and scarce. Probably Photius used these notes for his own reference and in his teaching, and apparently he passed them on to colleagues like Tarasius and Amphilochius. At least codices 275 and 277 seem to have come from this collection of notes and not to have been composed originally for the *Bibliotheca* as such. A number of other codices are of a type that is very similar to these two. Can the parts of the *Bibliotheca* which were copied from such notes be distinguished from parts that Photius composed particularly for Tarasius?

[5] Ταῦτα μὲν ἀπὸ σχεδαρίων, ὡς ἠδυνήθημεν, μετεγράψαμεν, τὰ δὲ βιβλία, ὡς καὶ ἡ σὴ ἀρχιερατικὴ τελειότης συνεπίσταται, μετὰ τῶν ἄλλων, ἐξ ὧν ἦν δυνατὸν ζῆν, ἡ αἰχμαλωσία λάφυρον ἔθετο (*Amphilochia,* ed. Oikonomos, no. 148, p. 225 [not edited in PG, 101; see no. 148, cols. 811–12]). Our present knowledge of the *Amphilochia* is insufficient to determine whether Photius compiled the work itself without books or only some elements of it, including no. 148. The latter seems more probable to me.

[6] See *Philostorgios Kirchengeschichte,* ed. J. Bidez and F. Winkelmann, 2nd ed. (Berlin, 1972), 4–150. The title is Ἐκ τῶν ἐκκλησιαστικῶν ἱστορίων Φιλοστοργίου ἐπιτομὴ ἀπὸ φωνῆς Φωτίου πατριάρχου. See M. Richard, Ἀπὸ Φωνῆς, *Byzantion,* 19 (1949), 191–222 for a demonstration that here this phrase simply means "by" (cf. the beginning of cod. 241).

Some material composed for Tarasius can be identified easily, because it includes remarks addressed to him in the second person. Besides those in the preface, *pinax,* title, and postface, we have already seen three such passages in codices 165, 187, and 191, which, to judge from parallels in the preface, must have been addressed to Tarasius.[7] Another remark that is evidently addressed to him occurs in codex 161.[8] Eight times in codex 222, the longest codex in the *Bibliotheca,* Photius apparently addresses comments on Jobius the Monk's *On the Incarnation* to his brother in the second person, thus differentiating his own observations from Jobius'. "Now you consider this point too with me" is the first of these remarks.[9] Seventeen more such comments appear in four other long codices: 223 on Diodorus of Tarsus, 225 on Eulogius of Alexandria, 229 on Ephraem of Amida, and 230 again on Eulogius.[10] But Photius does not seem to address Tarasius directly in any codex after 230.[11]

Although these passages do not prove that all the material as far as codex 230 was composed for Tarasius, their distribution indicates that the bulk of it was. Besides, most of the codices in the first half of the *Bibliotheca* are worded more formally than one would expect rough notes to be. As late as codex 233, Photius reviews St. Germanus' *Retribuens aut Legitimus* in a manner closely comparable to that of the earliest codices: in roughly a page of Bekker's edition, he gives the title, the subject, a stylistic criticism, and a general summary of the contents. But with codex 234, a little more than half way through the *Bibliotheca,* the nature of the codices changes abruptly, with a corresponding change in their form.

Codices 234 through 280 are distinguished from the codices that precede them in a number of ways. Not only do they include no second-person references to Tarasius; they include only four first-person references to Photius himself, though these are common in the codices before 234. The codices from 234 on contain only four

[7] See p. 19 note 6 *supra.*

[8] Ταῦτα δὴ πάντα, καὶ εἴ τι ὅμοιον, ὁ πέμπτος ἀναγινώσκοντί σοι παραστήσει λόγος (cod. 161: 103b lines 30–32).

[9] Σὺ δέ μοι κἀκεῖνο σκόπει. . . . (cod. 222: 186a lines 5 and 11, 188a lines 28–29 and 40, 189a line 34, 196a line 41, 196b line 9, 202a lines 17–18, and 202b line 6. This is Photian language; cf. *Letters,* no. 16, p. 273 to his brother Constantine (Καὶ σκόπει μοι συνετῶς); no. 19, p. 278 to Amphilochius of Cyzicus (Σὺ δέ μοι σκόπει); no. 25, p. 296; no. 40, p. 334; no. 71, p. 394; etc.

[10] Cod. 223: 214b line 1; cod. 225: 241b line 29; cod. 229: 253b line 41, 258a line 33, 262a line 20, 263b line 16; cod. 230: 269b line 3, 271a line 33, 272a line 6, 272b line 25, 273a lines 41–42, 276a line 9, 276a line 40, 276b line 16, 277a line 36, and 280b lines 19–20.

[11] I do not count two passages in which the second person seems to be used impersonally: cod. 199: 162b lines 7–8 and cod. 237: 313a lines 11–32, which may even be a scholion in Photius' MS (see Hägg, *Photios,* 156–57).

passages that might reasonably be called criticisms of style or content, though these appear in about 200 of the first 233 codices. In fact, the codices after 233 contain almost no general information of any kind about the books. It is only in the loosest possible sense that they could be called "summaries," which is what Photius' preface says he composed for Tarasius. Instead, they are all selections of more or less literal excerpts, including ten codices on the Attic orators that are excerpts from a history of the orators. All these selections differ from the earlier summaries by being much more literal, less coherent, and on the average much longer. Photius has composed them in a strangely impersonal manner, introducing even his own explanatory remarks with the particle ὅτι.[12] Codices 234-80 also include eleven of the sixteen cases in which a book already reviewed is reviewed a second time; all of the long second reviews are among these codices.[13]

The majority of these codices differ in form from the earlier ones; they are introduced by the curious formula Ἀνεγνώσθη ἐκ (There was read *from*). In about half of these codices there is a reference to a "selection" (usually ἐκλογή); scholars have interpreted this expression differently in studying each of the codices in which it appears. Unlike any preceding codex, about a third of the codices after 233 are divided into sections by subordinate headings that tell either the principles on which the extracts were made or the book, chapter, oration, or sermon from which the extracts come: for example, Ἐκ τοῦ β′ λόγου (From Book II). The interpretation of these introductory formulas, of references to selections, and of subordinate headings is often problematical even in their context.

Most of these peculiarities have been noticed before, though no connection seems to have been made between the pecularities of form and those of content. Severyns and Henry noticed the formula Ἀνεγνώσθη ἐκ, which they thought Photius used of books he had read only in part.[14] Hägg, however, concluded from his detailed comparison of the codices to their originals that this is not so; he attached no particular importance to these formulas.[15]

Bury and Severyns, among others, noticed that the codices of the latter part of the *Bibliotheca* are much longer and more literal than those of the earlier part, though neither scholar identified an exact

[12] For this usage of ὅτι in four earlier codices, see pp. 88–90 *infra*.

[13] The "doublets" after cod. 233 are codd. 238 (=76), 240 (=43), 241 (=44), 242 (=181), 243 (=165), 244 (=70), 250 (=213), 251 (=214), 260 (=159), 264 (=61), and 280 (=182=208, a triplet). The other doublets are codd. 88 (=15), 169 (=49), 191 (=144), and 211 (=185, though 185 is not in A).

[14] Severyns, *Chrestomathie*, II, 31 and 65; and Henry, V, 155 note 2.

[15] Hägg, *Photios*, 131–37.

point of division between the parts. Bury conjectured that Photius wrote the earlier part before his embassy and the second part at his leisure after he returned to Constantinople.[16] Severyns, accepting Orth's hypothesis of an itinerant reading circle of ambassadors, conjectured that Photius found his secretary along the way, quickly dictated the first part to cover books which the ambassadors had already read, and then dictated the second part as the readings were going on.[17] As has been seen, both of these theories are based on misinterpretations of the *Bibliotheca*'s preface and postface. Still, some such conjecture is needed to explain not only the differences in the content of the codices after 233 but their peculiarities of form.

I therefore conjecture that all of codices 234 through 280, which I shall now call the "second part," were copied by Photius' secretary from rough notes that Photius had taken before he composed the *Bibliotheca*. These notes could be long and literal because they were taken at Photius' leisure, with manuscripts of the books at hand. They do not address Tarasius because they were not composed for him. In a very few cases they include first-person statements, stylistic criticisms, or general information about the books which Photius wanted to record for himself or for others who might use the notes. But usually Photius did not expect to need a record of such things, wanting only notes on the contents of the book in a form that he, but not necessarily others, could understand. The meaningless initial ὅτι, found also in his independently preserved excerpts from Philostorgius, is evidently a characteristic of Photius' note taking.[18]

At the time of Tarasius' request, Photius first dictated most of codices 1-233. Then, probably because he was running short of time before his embassy was to leave, he gave a collection of his reading notes to his secretary with instructions to copy them and to add a codex number and an initial Ἀνεγνώσθη to each, thus continuing the format of the first part of the *Bibliotheca*. Photius was evidently unaware that these notes included extracts from some books that he had already reviewed; the secretary copied these along with the others, producing the repeated reviews. Most of the sets of excerpts had headings in the form Ἐκ τῆς βίβλου (From the book) at the beginning, with subordinate headings such as Ἐκ τοῦ β' λόγου in the middle. Thus, when the secretary mechanically added a codex number and an Ἀνεγνώσθη to the first heading of each set of excerpts, he produced the meaningless formula Ἀνεγνώσθη ἐκ τῆς βίβλου (There was read from the book). Otherwise, the secretary

[16] Bury, *Eastern Roman Empire*, 446 note 1.
[17] Severyns, *Chrestomathie*, I, 7.
[18] See p. 39 note 6 *supra*.

presumably copied Photius' notes word for word, with only such errors as copyists ordinarily make.

The length and literalness of the codices of the second part will be discussed more fully in Chapter Six.[19] Simple arithmetic shows that the average length of the codices of the second part is 4.3 times that of the codices of the first.[20] As far as can be checked or conjectured, all the codices after 233 follow their originals closely and in order, quoting them in a condensed and occasionally paraphrased form. Hägg has distinguished two types among them, the somewhat more connected and less literal "analytical reviews" and the less coherent and more literal "excerpts." But both types, he argues with probability, must have been composed *during* Photius' readings of the books.[21] If this is right, these thirty-eight codices could not originally have been composed under the circumstances described in the preface and postface, which concur that Photius, within an extraordinarily short time, composed summaries of books that he had already read. He could hardly have read all the books which are excerpted in the second part in the time between his appointment to the embassy and his departure on it.[22]

Particularly the codices that Hägg classified as pure "excerpts," which make up most of the second part, are so unfinished and incoherent that they cannot be considered even as informal literary work. The least coherent are codices 241-43, 246-48, and 269-77. These cover: first, Philostratus' *Life of Apollonius* and Damascius' *Life of Isidore*; second, the orations of Himerius and Aristides; and third, numerous sermons, including those whose excerpts reappear in the *Amphilochia*. Most of the extracts from Philostratus and Damascius have no evident connection with each other or with Apollonius or Isidore, while the excerpts from the orations and sermons seldom permit the reader to make out a connected argument of any kind. Three of these codices include many incomplete sentences.[23] These selections are probably so incoherent because they were chosen not for their content but for their style, as several of their headings indicate.[24] But scarcely any of the selections in the second part gives

[19] See pp. 88–92 *infra*.

[20] Codd. 1–233 take up 583 Bekker cols., an average of 2.50 cols. each; codd. 234–80 cover 505 Bekker cols., an average of 10.74 each.

[21] Hägg, *Photios*, 192–94. He includes codd. 236, 237, 238, 241, 243, 245, and 246 in his sample, of which he classifies 238 as an *analytisches Referat*, the rest as *Exzerpte* (*ibid.*, 9). For a fuller discussion, see Chapter VI.

[22] For Hägg's view, see p. 82 note 3 *infra*.

[23] Cod. 241: 331b–335a *passim*, cod. 242 *passim*, and cod. 243: 353a lines 30–32, 369a line 20, 369a lines 23–24, and 371b lines 20–21.

[24] Ἐκ τοῦ αὐτοῦ βίου ὅσα παρεῖται κάλλει ῥημάτων καὶ συνθήκης διαλάμποντα (cod. 241: 331a lines 38–39). Ὅσα παρεῖται χρεὼν ταῖς ἐκλογαῖς συντετάχθαι

a coherent idea of the excerpted book as a whole, for the obvious reason that the incomplete extracts are not explained by a general summary.[25]

The peculiar use of the particle ὅτι in these codices has frequently been misunderstood. In the first part of the *Bibliotheca*, ὅτι introduces the words of authors who are quoted or summarized, but in the second part it introduces not only excerpts from the authors but also words that Photius has added to them himself. After codex 233, Ὅτι comes before seventeen comments by Photius, including three of his four critical judgments and both of his general statements about content.[26] If we include places where Photius simply writes, "That (Ὅτι) the author says" at the beginning of an excerpt, over ninety of his remarks in the second part are introduced by the particle.[27] Hägg has demonstrated that an initial Ὅτι is no indication of the beginning of a new excerpt, as several editors of individual codices have assumed.[28] And it certainly does not mean that Photius is quoting some other excerptor. It is merely a practice that Photius adopted when he took notes, usually when he was not following his author's words very closely.[29] By contrast, no such usage appears in the nine codices that are addressed explicitly to Tarasius, though these make up almost a sixth of the *Bibliotheca*.[30]

Naturally, the extracts in the second part of the *Bibliotheca* bear

---

καλλιέπειαν ἔχοντα (cod. 242: 349b lines 13–14). Cf. the beginnings of codd. 243, 246, and 269, the last of which seems to refer to all of codd. 269–77.

[25] The only exceptions are summaries in codd. 271 (502b lines 20–25) and 273 (507b line 20–508b line 9).

[26] Cod. 237: 313a lines 11–13 and 313a line 16–313b line 17; cod. 238: 313b lines 26–35; cod. 240: 322b lines 4–6; cod. 241: 328a lines 18–20; cod. 244: 377a lines 29–34, 381a lines 10–15, and 383a lines 28–30; cod. 245: 400b line 5; cod. 256: 474a lines 15–20 (a criticism); cod. 257: 477b lines 16–17 (criticism); cod. 258: 485b lines 3–4 (criticism); cod. 271: 502b lines 20–25 (a summary); cod. 273: 507b lines 19–20 (after a first-person reference and before a summary); cod. 277: 525a lines 19–29; cod. 279: 534a lines 33–37; and cod. 280: 544b lines 14–19. The other criticism is at cod. 241: 331a lines 25–37, just before the heading of the stylistic excerpts from Philostratus. Another first-person reference is at cod. 256: 469b lines 20–21; for the other two, see p. 49 *infra*.

[27] These are too numerous to list here; the first occurs immediately after the heading of cod. 234 (*Ὅτι* οὐ δεσμόν φησι τὸ σῶμα τῆς ψυχῆς εἶναι . . .). I list the codices in which the usage appears in note 44 *infra*. I have not counted any of the many cases in which the ὅτι precedes words of Photius that could be parenthetical (e.g., cod. 234: 293a line 30: *Ὅτι* ἄνθρωπός φησι λέγεται . . .).

[28] Hägg, *Photios*, 30-31.

[29] This usage is rare in codices in which Photius seems to be keeping as many of the author's words as possible, especially those on orations or sermons (codd. 243, 246-48, 269-77) and those on the lives of the ten orators (codd. 259-68). Professor L. G. Westerink has pointed out to me that such a usage occurs in some fifth-century philosophical commentaries which are written in the style of notes; e.g., Olympiodorus, *In Phaedonem*, ed. W. Norvin (Leipzig, 1913), 132-49.

[30] For these codices, see notes 9 and 10 *supra*. They total about 177 Bekker columns out of 1091.

some resemblance to the long summaries in the first part. After all, both parts were prepared by the same man, with the same interests and habits, and in both cases with the purpose of recording what the books said. What particularly characterizes the second part, and reveals that Photius was not even supervising the copying, is the variety of their peculiarities of form, which arose as the secretary copied the notes mechanically.

The reviews which are repeated a second time in the *Bibliotheca* have often been noticed and never been satisfactorily explained. They must be unintentional: not only are they counted as different books for the total in the preface, title, and postface, but none of them gives any indication that it has a double. As Hägg found when he exhaustively studied the two codices on Philostratus' *Life of Apollonius,* "Nothing in codex 241 indicates that he [sc. Photius] remembered the existence of codex 44 at all at the time."[31] It is not unreasonable to think that Photius simply forgot when he composed the five short codices that review books for a second time within the first part. But it seems very unlikely that he could have dictated all eleven second reviews in the second part, which average more than twenty-two columns in Bekker's edition and extend to forty-eight columns for codex 243, without remembering that he had already reviewed some of these books.

To suppose, as Hägg did, that Photius actually reread the eleven books in different manuscripts does not help.[32] Even in the improbable event that Photius had found two manuscripts of such lost works as Damascius' *Life of Isidore* and Agatharchides' *On the Red Sea,* he would surely have remembered the fact and reviewed them together, as he did when he found other works in more than one manuscript.[33] According to my hypothesis, however, the repeated reviews in the second part could not originally have had cross-references to the first part, because they were composed before it. Neither could their corresponding reviews in the first part have had cross-references, because they were composed before the second part was added to the *Bibliotheca.* Finally, no cross-references would have been added later, because Photius was not there to add them.

This lack of supervision is revealed most strikingly in the secretary's mechanical additions of the word Ἀνεγνώσθη at the beginnings of codices. To arrive at the original headings of Photius' notes, one

[31] Hägg, *Photios,* 39.

[32] Hägg, *Photios,* 159.

[33] Cf. codd. 48: 11b lines 14–16; 88: 66b lines 30–33; 111: 89b lines 20–27; 112–113: 90a lines 9–34 (see pp. 70–71 *infra*), 178: 124a lines 12–13, 199: 162b lines 6–11, and 200: 163a lines 23–27.

must delete the Ἀνεγνώσθη, as at the beginning of codex 234: {Ἀνεγνώσθη} Τοῦ ἁγίου Μεθοδίου ἐπισκόπου καὶ μάρτυρος, ἐκ τοῦ περὶ ἀναστάσεως λόγου, οὗ ἡ ἐκλογὴ τὰ ὑποκείμενα λέγει (From the work of St. Methodius, bishop and martyr, *On the Resurrection,* of which the selection says the following). The rather affected last phrase, which was also copied into the *pinax,* was presumably in the original abstract; Photius had no reason to add it later. The meaninglessness of the seeming construction Ἀνεγνώσθη . . . ἐκ is proved not only by Hägg's findings that the excerpts cover whole books, but by the fact that this "formula" introduces codices 240–44, whose books are introduced in earlier codices by a plain Ἀνεγνώσθη.[34]

In codex 234 it is clear, even with the interpolation, that the "selection" mentioned in the heading is simply the one given in the codex. By itself, the heading of codex 235, for example, is not as clear: {Ἀνεγνώσθη} Ἐκ τοῦ ἁγίου μάρτυρος Μεθοδίου καὶ ἐπισκόπου τοῦ περὶ τῶν γενητῶν, ἐκλογὴ κατὰ σύνοψιν (From the *On Creatures* of St. Methodius, bishop and martyr, a selection in the form of a synopsis). Here Photius has varied the form of the heading of his notes, but a comparison with the preceding codex shows that the "selection" is again the one being introduced by the heading. The word ἐκλογή is Photius' usual term for his extracts, but he also uses the words σύνοψις, συντομία, and ἐν κεφαλαίῳ.[35] These terms certainly do not mean that Photius read the books in epitomes, as many have concluded.

In the same way, if the apparent subject of such an interpolated Ἀνεγνώσθη is only a part of a book, this is no evidence that Photius read the book only in part. On the contrary, five of the codices in the second part introduce and excerpt only certain books or orations from larger works that in earlier codices are reviewed in their entirety.[36] Thus, though codices 239 and 245 introduce and excerpt only

[34] For these double reviews, see p. 41 note 13 *supra*.

[35] Photius uses ἐκλογή at the beginnings of codd. 234, 235, 238, 239 (in the plural and only in M), 243, 244, 246, 248 (see p. 47 note 40 *infra*), 252 (see p. 30 note 41 *supra*), 269 (where it probably refers to all the codices through 277), and 273 (in the plural), at the ends of codd. 256, 257, and 258, in a subordinate heading in cod. 242 (349b line 13), and in only the *pinax* for 278. He uses σύνοψις at the beginnings of codd. 235, 237, and 245, and in a subordinate heading in 234 (294a lines 22–23); ἐν κεφαλαίῳ at the beginning of 250 (in M and in the *pinax*); κεφαλαιώδης at the beginning of 253; and συντομία at the beginning of 236 and the end of 256. He says in the *pinax* under cod. 254 and at the beginning of cod. 255 that these were done "in the same way" as cod. 253, i.e., κεφαλαιώδης; he states at the beginning of cod. 248, described as an ἐκλογή, that it was done in the same way as cod. 247. Note Photius' use of the word ἔκδοσις or a similar form for his process of excerpting at the beginnings of codd. 237 (ἐξεδόθη), 245, 252, 255 (ἐκδεδομένον), 256, and 257. In the first part, Photius uses the words ἐν κεφαλαίῳ at cod. 187: 145a line 31, and ἔκλογη in cod. 223: 222a line 43, and cod. 230: 286b line 11.

[36] Cod. 238 (=76), 243 (=165), 244 (=70), 250 (=213), and 251 (=214).

two of the four books of Proclus' *Chrestomathia* and only some of Plutarch's *Lives*, this need not mean that Photius did not read all of these works. In fact, a note at the end of the extracts from Plutarch is based on a life that is not excerpted.[37] Codices 271 and 274-78 introduce only the first of the several sermons or books that they excerpt, but they have subordinate headings that clearly identify excerpts taken from the others. Codex 279 introduces only the first four books of Helladius' *Chrestomathiae* and has no subordinate headings, but later in the codex Photius mentions "the books after the fourth" and gives excerpts from them.[38] In short, the word Ἀνεγνώσθη in these codices does not necessarily indicate what Photius had read.

Although the subordinate headings are evidently Photius' own, the secretary has not always copied them correctly. He seems to have omitted or misplaced them in two codices, and quite possibly in more.[39] At codex 248, moreover, he has mistakenly turned a part of a book into a codex by adding a number and an Ἀνεγνώσθη to a subordinate heading. The heading of codex 247 introduces Aelius Aristides' four orations *Against Plato and For Rhetoric,* the fourth of which is his *For the Four,* a defense of the four statesmen criticized by Plato in the *Gorgias. For the Four* is preserved and consists of six parts: a pröoemium, individual defenses of each of the four statesmen, and finally a general defense of all four together. Probably misled because Photius' notes gave Aristides' name again in the heading of the general defense, the secretary has turned the sixth part of the fourth oration into codex 248.[40] This is hardly an error that Photius could have made himself, but the subordinate headings in his notes would have appeared much the same as the main ones to his secretary.

These peculiarities of form are fairly evenly distributed over the second part of the *Bibliotheca*. Of the forty-seven codices after codex

[37] See Henry, VI, 194 note 2.

[38] Cod. 279: 534a lines 33-37.

[39] Headings are incorrectly omitted at cod. 243: 357b line 32 and 374b line 13, and at cod. 245: 394a line 6, where the place has been taken by a heading that belongs at 393b line 30; see the apparatus to Henry's edition. There is also something wrong at the beginning of cod. 269, where a heading announcing "twenty-one" sermons introduces nine codices (269-77) with forty-five sermons, the twenty-first coming in the middle of cod. 274. Note that in cod. 271: 503b lines 13-17 Photius refers to a sermon of Asterius of Amasea (*On the Martyrdom of St. Euphemia*) for which he gives no heading or excerpts.

[40] At least MS A places the erroneous introduction correctly; M and the editors, misunderstanding the error, have transferred it to cod. 248: 423a lines 5-6, the beginning of *For the Four*. Cf. the text of the oration, in *Aristides*, ed. W. Dindorf, II (Leipzig, 1829), 156-414.

233, twenty-eight begin with the combination Ἀνεγνώσθη ἐκ, with the name of the book's author sometimes between the two words.[41] Twenty-four of the codices after 233 are labeled as a "selection," usually at the beginning.[42] Sixteen codices in the second part have subordinate headings of one kind or another.[43] Further, twenty-two codices in the second part have passages in which Photius introduces his own words with Ὅτι.[44] To sum up, all but ten codices after codex 233 have one of these indications that they were notes copied by the secretary, and almost all but those ten have more than one of these characteristics.

The ten codices without any of these characteristics are codices 259 through 268, which ostensibly review the orations of the ten Attic orators. Clearly they form a distinct group. It is not surprising that they neither begin with Ἀνεγνώσθη ἐκ, refer to themselves as selections, nor contain headings of orations, because they do not include any excerpts from the orations. Instead, they are made up of extracts from a lost work which Photius calls simply a "history" and which was plagiarized in an earlier version by the author of the Pseudo-Plutarchian *Lives of the Ten Orators.*[45] The version excerpted by Photius was edited sometime after Libanius (314–*ca.* 393), whom it quoted.[46] But it followed its archetype so closely that even a comparison of Pseudo-Plutarch with Photius demonstrates that Photius' extracts from it were fully as literal as those he made in the other codices from 234 on.[47]

Unlike all the other codices from 234 on, however, the ten codices

[41] Codd. 234-37, 239-45 (244 in M only), 247, 253-58, 269-74, 276, and 279. I leave out 250, where only A has ἐκ, probably an incorrect reading; A also has the combination in the middle of cod. 234 (294a line 22), where M omits the Ἀνεγνώσθη, leaving a heading.

[42] See note 35 *supra.*

[43] Cod. 234 (at 294a line 22 in M only; see note 41 *supra*), codd. 241–45, 247 (see note 40 *supra*), 250, 251, 271, 274–78, and 280; except for the first, all these headings are set off and italicized in the editions of Bekker and Henry.

[44] Codd. 234, 235, 237-42, 244, 245, 249, 250, 253, 254, 256-58, 271, 273, 277, 279, and 280.

[45] See A. Mayer, in *BZ*, 20 (1911), 220-23. The work by A. Vonach, "Die Berichte des Photios über die fünf älteren attischen Redner," *Commentationes Aenipontanae,* 5 (1910), 14-76, which Mayer here reviews unfavorably, makes the basic mistake of ignoring five of the ten codices and bogs down in complicated and unnecessary arguments. In 1877 R. Ballheimer, *De Photi vitis decem oratorum* (diss. Bonn, 1877), had come to essentially the same conclusion as Mayer, but he was inclined to assume some originality on Photius' part for which there is no evidence. Orth, *Photiana,* seems to be ignorant of Ballheimer's work and has gone far astray.

[46] Cod. 265: 492a line 15 and 495a line 35. See also note 53 *infra.*

[47] See Ballheimer, *op. cit.* Pseudo-Plutarch seems to have rearranged, paraphrased, and omitted parts of the material, but the verbal parallels are clear. Photius' arrangement is much more logical than Pseudo-Plutarch's and is probably the order of the original within each biography, especially since Photius was only an excerptor.

on the orators have introductory sentences that must have been composed for the *Bibliotheca* as such. These introductions do not merely describe the contents of the codices, as the other headings in the second part do. Instead they indicate which orations Photius had read. For example, he says at the beginning of codex 261, "There were read the four orations of Andocides that we have seen thus far."[48] The introductory sentence of codex 268 seems to begin at the end of codex 267: "In these things, then, is outlined the account of the nine orators whose orations we have read; 268. but there has not yet been time for us to read the orations of Lycurgus . . . ; still, we have learned from the history that fifteen by him are attested."[49]

The entries for codices 259-68 in the *pinax* are also unlike those of the other codices of the second part. As a rule, the entries for the codices after 233 quote the first sentences of the codices without the Ἀνεγνώσθη. For example, the entry for codex 234 is: "234. From the work of St. Methodius, bishop and martyr, *On the Resurrection,* of which the selection says the following." It is followed, however, by nothing but the entry for 235.[50] The entries for codices 259-68, on the other hand, read simply as follows:

259. Various orations of Antiphon.
260. Of Andocides.
261. Of Lysias.
262. Of Isocrates.
263. Of Isaeus.
264. Of Aeschines.
265. Of Lycurgus.
266. Of Demosthenes.
267. Of Hyperides.
268. Of Dinarchus.[51]

These are not the first sentences of the codices, nor is this the order and numbering of the codices in the text, which puts Isocrates second and Lycurgus last, displacing the other orators accordingly. The order of the text is attested by both manuscripts and required by the end of codex 267 and the beginning of codex 268. But the order of the *pinax* is also attested by both manuscripts, and it cannot be a

[48] Ἀνεγνώσθησαν Ἀνδοκίδου λόγοι δ´ οὓς τέως εἴδομεν. . .

[49] Τῶν μὲν οὖν θ´ ῥητόρων, οἱ λόγοι ὧν ἐποιησάμεθα τὴν ἀνάγνωσιν, ἐν τούτοις περιγράφεται ἡ μνήμη· σξη´. Λυκούργου δὲ . . . οὔπω παρέσχεν ἡμῖν ὁ χρόνος λόγους ἀναγνῶναι, φέρεσθαι δὲ αὐτοῦ ἐξ ἱστορίας ιε´ μεμαθήκαμεν. A puts the number σξη´ both here and at the head of this sentence, which is quite possibly the correct division between the codices.

[50] *Pinax,* 312 lines 31–34. The text is identical with that given on p. 46 *supra* minus the Ἀνεγνώσθη.

[51] σνθ´. Ἀντιφῶντος διάφοροι λόγοι. σξ´. Ἀνδοκίδου. σξα´. Λυσίου. κ.τ.λ. (*Pinax,* 316 lines 1-11).

simple confusion in the copying, because it is also the order of Pseudo-Plutarch and of the orators' births according to both his and Photius' versions of the history.[52] It must, therefore, have been the order of Photius' source.

To explain the difference between *pinax* and text, I conjecture that the ten sentences that begin codices 259-68 were composed by Photius specifically to adapt his notes for the *Bibliotheca* and further that the *pinax* for the second part was compiled not from the completed text of the *Bibliotheca,* as the first part plainly was, but directly from Photius' notes. If this is correct, the secretary copied the notes into the *Bibliotheca* in a modified order, putting the unread Lycurgus last so as to fit Photius' introductory sentences. These sentences seem to have supplanted whatever heading the notes had had, which may have given the author and title of the lost history.[53] But when the *pinax* was compiled from the notes, the names of the orators were copied in the original order. Though this explanation is admittedly speculative, it accounts for the otherwise unaccountable facts. Incidentally, it explains why Photius remembered that he had not read Lycurgus when he gave the number of the books that he had read in the preface, title, and postface.

Thus the principal stages of the composition of the second part of the *Bibliotheca* were probably the following. Over the years before he composed the work as such, Photius had taken notes on a number of books while he read them. After he had dictated codex 233, he simply gave his secretary a pile of his old notes with instructions to copy them and to add a codex number and an Ἀνεγνώσθη to each

[52] The history mistakenly gives Andocides' birthdate as 468/467 (cod. 261: 488a lines 20-22=Pseudo-Plutarch, 835A), before Lysias' (459), though Andocides was probably born *ca.* 440. The part of the history that is preserved gives no birthdate for Hyperides (born 389), whom it mistakenly puts after Demosthenes (born 384). I follow the dates of the *OCD.*

[53] I suppose that Photius' introductory sentences also put Isocrates second, though perhaps inadvertently. It seems possible to me that this "history" of the ten orators formed part of the missing Books III and IV of Proclus' *Chrestomathia,* of which Photius excerpts only Books I and II in cod. 239. Cod. 239: 318b lines 24-26 seems to indicate that Proclus treated both poetry and prose, and cod. 239 and the fragments of the *Chrestomathia* on Homer plainly show that Proclus concentrated on the biographies of his authors. Because the "history" quotes Libanius, my theory requires that the compiler of the *Chrestomathia* be the Neoplatonist Proclus, as the *Suda* says (IV, 210), not, as Severyns and others maintain, another Proclus who lived in the second century A.D. The textual arguments that the *Chrestomathia* was composed in the second century suggest to me only that Proclus slavishly followed earlier source material—precisely the method of the final redactor of the "history" of the orators. I can see no force whatever in the objection of Severyns (*Chrestomathie,* II, 149) that such a conclusion deprives Proclus of a "personality" of his own. But, not having made any extensive study of this very problematic work, I offer this theory only as a possibility. For the state of the "Proclus" question, see *Proclo Crestomazia,* ed. D. Ferrante (Naples, 1957), 9-14; Ferrante believes in the attribution to the Neoplatonist.

of their main headings. For the notes on the ten orators, Photius apparently composed new introductions to tell which of their works he had read, probably because he realized that his purely biographical notes did not include this information. Otherwise, Photius seems to have left his secretary completely unsupervised. The last parts of the *Bibliotheca* which Photius composed were the preface, the note at the end of the *pinax,* the title, and the postface.

Photius' reasons for following such a procedure are fairly obvious. First, having the secretary copy his old notes saved him the trouble of dictating. But more important for a man about to leave on an embassy, he needed time free from work on the *Bibliotheca* to complete the preparations for his journey. Photius does not say in codex 268, as he says of other books he had not read, that he had not found the orations of Lycurgus, but rather that he had had no time to read them. In fact, it is possible that Photius dictated codex 233, had the secretary compile the *pinax* from the notes, dictated the preface and postface, and left on the embassy at once, leaving the secretary to copy the rest and send it to Tarasius.[54] If this is what Photius did, he could have left on the embassy less than three weeks after receiving Tarasius' request. The circumlocutory wording of the preface and postface does not rule out this possibility. They give the number 279 for the books *read,* not for the books described, and what Photius says he himself has "edited" is the "summaries," which need not include the excerpts in the second part.

In any event, in codices 234 through 280 we evidently possess a word for word copy, except for a few identifiable interpolations, of Photius' reading notes. These do not date from the time of the composition of the *Bibliotheca* as we have it, but from a number of earlier occasions, while Photius was actually reading these fifty or so books. Besides explaining many peculiarities in the text, this hypothesis reduces Photius' task in producing the *Bibliotheca* for his brother to little more than half what it appears to have been at first glance.

[54] Photius would also have had to dictate the title, the introductory sentences for codd. 259–68, and the note at the end of the *pinax* before he left.

CHAPTER FOUR

The Biographical Sketches

The biographical sketches of authors that Photius includes in about sixty of his codices are the parts of the *Bibliotheca* that may properly be called literary history. Their historical value naturally depends on what Photius' sources for them were and what use he made of those sources. Because so much of the literature which Photius possessed has been lost and so little is known about the scholarly community of Photius' time, our knowledge of Photius' sources can only be approximate. The process of identifying them was well begun by Georg Wentzel, but Wentzel's work seems scarcely to have been noticed by later scholars, much less extended to the codices of the *Bibliotheca* that he did not discuss.[1]

Most scholars who have used Photius' biographies have treated them as if they had independent authority, or at least as if their sources were lost and unidentifiable. This attitude can sometimes be justified, in practice if not in theory, but it can lead imperceptibly to the undemonstrated assumption that Photius, through his teachers and colleagues, drew his information from an unbroken tradition of classical scholarship which is lost to us. Certainly Photius did know some of the other learned men of his time when he composed the *Bibliotheca*.[2] Equally certain, classical education never had broken down altogether in Byzantium, and in Photius' time it was reviving. But before we can estimate the contribution of Byzantine scholarly tradition to the literary history in the *Bibliotheca*, we must try to

[1] Wentzel's article, "Übersetzung," seems to be known to the major authorities on the *Bibliotheca* (except for Klinkenberg) only indirectly. K. Ziegler, in *RE*, XX (1941), cols. 715–16, refers only to a later article by Wentzel that asserts his thesis without giving any evidence, arguments, or reference to his earlier article. Henry (I, 101–2) refers only to the second edition of Krumbacher, 324, who accepted Wentzel's thesis without naming Wentzel.

[2] Cf. cod. 187: 145a lines 30–40, discussed on p. 28 *supra* and in Treadgold, "Photius."

identify, however tentatively, the biographical material that Photius took from specific literary sources.

Wentzel showed that much of the biographical material in the *Bibliotheca* derives from the same source as the biographical articles in the *Suda.* In its article on the sixth-century scholar Hesychius of Miletus, the *Suda* preserves a passage from this source in which the source identifies itself. Hesychius, it says, "composed an *Onomatologus, Or Index of the Famous Men in Scholarship,* of which this book is an epitome." Wentzel demonstrated that this last phrase refers not to the *Suda* but to another work (the "Hesychius Epitome"), which was the common source of the *Suda* and the *Bibliotheca.*[3]

The article adds that Hesychius did not include Christian authors. For these, Wentzel showed that the epitomator used other sources, and principally the Greek translation of St. Jerome's *Famous Men,* attributed to Jerome's friend, Sophronius.[4] "Sophronius," as this translation is conventionally called, survives *in toto* and, together with the *Suda,* makes it possible to reconstruct what is probably the larger part of this "Hesychius Epitome." According to Wentzel, the "Hesychius Epitome" presented its authors in alphabetical order.[5] I have already argued that it was probably compiled between 843 and 845, quite possibly by Ignatius the Deacon.[6]

Because the compiler used some lost sources as well as "Sophronius," while the *Suda* gives only an abridgment of the "Hesychius Epitome," the parallels between these texts and the *Bibliotheca* are not always complete. Nevertheless, the verbal parallels pointed out by Wentzel are usually beyond dispute. Compare, for example, the following passages on the works of Justin Martyr. Jerome's biography in "Sophronius" says of Justin,

> ὑπὲρ τῆς θρησκείας τῶν Χριστιανῶν πάνυ ἐκοπίασεν, ὥστε καὶ Ἀντωνίνῳ τῷ ἐπίκλην Πίῳ καὶ τοῖς τούτου υἱέσι καὶ τῇ συγκλήτῳ βίβλον κατὰ τῶν ἐθνῶν συνταγεῖσαν ἐπιδοῦναι, τὸν ὀνειδισμὸν τοῦ σταυροῦ μὴ αἰσχυνόμενος, καὶ ἄλλην βίβλον τοῖς τοῦ αὐτοῦ

[3] *Suda,* II, 594 lines 16–17. Ἔγραψεν Ὀνοματολόγον ἢ Πίνακα τῶν ἐν παιδείᾳ ὀνομαστῶν, οὗ ἐπιτομή ἐστι τοῦτο τὸ βιβλίον. This passage is discussed by Wentzel, "Übersetzung," 2–4.

[4] Wentzel, "Übersetzung," 34, listed the sources as "Sophronius," the ecclesiastical histories of Philostorgius and Eusebius, and possibly a menologion. Adler also included Theodorus Lector (*Suda,* I, xxi). This list cannot be quite complete, because it gives no source late enough for George of Pisidia (*Suda,* I, 517) and John of Damascus (*Suda,* II, 649). The compiler presumably needed no written source for his article on Ignatius the Deacon (*Suda,* II, 607–8).

[5] The order of the *Onomatologus,* however, was topical. See Wentzel, "Übersetzung," 57–63.

[6] See pp. 31–32 and 36 *supra*.

Ἀντωνίνου διαδόχοις, τουτέστι Μάρκῳ Ἀντωνίνῳ Βήρῳ καὶ Λουκίῳ Αὐρηλίῳ Κομόδῳ. Ἔστι καὶ ἄλλη αὐτοῦ βίβλος κατὰ τῶν ἐθνῶν, ἐν ᾗ περὶ τῆς φύσεως τῶν δαιμόνων διαλέγεται· καὶ τέταρτον λόγον ὁμοίως κατὰ τῶν ἐθνῶν, ὃν ἐπέγραψεν Ἔλεγχος, καὶ ἄλλον περὶ τῆς τοῦ θεοῦ μοναρχίας, καὶ ἄλλον <ὃν> ὠνόμασε Ψάλτην, καὶ ἕτερον περὶ τῆς ψυχῆς· διάλογον κατὰ τῶν Ἰουδαίων, ὃν ἔσχε κατὰ Τρύφωνος ἀρχηγοῦ τῶν Ἰουδαίων· οὐ μὴν ἀλλὰ καὶ κατὰ Μαρκίωνος ἐπίσημα τεύχη, ὧντινων καὶ Εἰρηναῖος ἐν τῷ πέμπτῳ λόγῳ τῷ κατὰ τῶν αἱρετικῶν μέμνηται· καὶ ἄλλη βίβλος κατὰ πασῶν τῶν αἱρέσεων, ἧς μέμνηται ἐν τῷ ἀπολογητικῷ ὃν ἔδωκεν Ἀντωνίνῳ τῷ Πίῳ.[7]

Copying "Sophronius" almost word for word, the *Suda* article on Justin attributed to "Hesychius" says,

> Οὗτος *ὑπὲρ τῆς θρησκείας τῶν Χριστιανῶν πάνυ ἐκοπίασεν, ὥστε καὶ Ἀντωνίνῳ, τῷ ἐπίκλην Πίῳ, καὶ τοῖς τούτου υἱέσι καὶ τῇ συγκλήτῳ* Ῥωμαίων *βίβλον κατὰ τῶν ἐθνῶν συνταγεῖσαν ἐπιδοῦναι, τὸν ὀνειδισμὸν τοῦ σταυροῦ μὴ αἰσχυνόμενος.* Ἔγραψε καὶ ἑτέραν *βίβλον,* ἣν καὶ ἐπέδωκε *τοῖς Ἀντωνίνου διαδόχοις, τουτέστι Μάρκῳ Ἀντωνίνῳ καὶ Λουκίῳ Αὐρηλίῳ Κομόδῳ. Ἔστι καὶ ἄλλη αὐτοῦ βίβλος κατὰ τῶν ἐθνῶν, ἐν ᾗ περὶ τῆς φύσεως τῶν δαιμόνων διαλέγεται· καὶ τετάρτη* βίβλος *ὁμοίως κατὰ τῶν ἐθνῶν, ἣν ἐπέγραψεν Ἔλεγχος· καὶ ἄλλην περὶ τῆς τοῦ θεοῦ μοναρχίας· καὶ ἄλλην, ἣν ὠνόμασε Ψάλτην, καὶ ἑτέραν περὶ ψυχῆς· διάλογόν τε κατὰ τῶν Ἰουδαίων, ὃν* ἐσχεδίασε *κατὰ Τρύφωνος, ἀρχηγοῦ τῶν* ἐν Ἐφέσῳ *Ἰουδαίων· οὐ μὴν ἀλλὰ καὶ κατὰ Μαρκίωνος ἐπίσημα τεύχη* ἐξέδωκε· *καὶ ἄλλην βίβλον κατὰ πασῶν τῶν αἱρέσεων, ἧς μέμνηται ἐν τῷ ἀπολογητικῷ,* ὃ ἐπέδωκεν *Ἀντωνίνῳ τῷ Πίῳ.*[8]

Photius abridges and paraphrases this slightly in his codex 125 on Justin:

> Τέσσερας δὲ πραγματείας *κατὰ τῶν ἐθνῶν συνέταξεν,* ὧν τὴν μὲν πρώτην *Ἀντωνίνῳ τῷ ἐπίκλην Πίῳ καὶ τοῖς υἱέσι* τῇ τε *συγκλήτῳ ἐπέδωκε,* τὴν δὲ δευτέραν *ὁμοίως τοῖς* ἐκείνου *διαδόχοις. Ἐν δὲ τῇ* τρίτῃ *περὶ φύσεως δαιμόνων διείλεκται.* Ὁ δὲ *τέταρτος* αὐτῷ *λόγος, ὁμοίως κατὰ τῶν ἐθνῶν* συγκείμενος, *Ἔλεγχος ἐπιγραφὴν* ἔχει. Ἔστι δὲ αὐτῷ *καὶ* ὁ *περὶ θεοῦ μοναρχίας, καὶ* ὁ ἐπιγραφόμενος *Ψάλτης, καὶ μὴν κατὰ*

7 "Sophronius," chap. 23, 22 line 31–23 line 15.

8 *Suda,* II, 645 line 26–646 line 1.

Μαρκίωνος, ἀναγκαῖοι λόγοι, *καὶ ἡ κατὰ πασῶν αἱρέσεων* χρήσιμος πραγματεία.[9]

Before this passage, Photius gives a short and somewhat vague description of the books he had read by Justin, a description he was probably only remembering, and a criticism of Justin's style. Neither of these owes anything to the "Hesychius Epitome." After the passage just quoted, Photius combines biographical material on Justin from the parts of the epitome that came immediately before and after the list of his works.[10] Thus codex 125 has four parts: a description of the books which Photius read, a criticism of them, a list of books by Justin taken from the "Hesychius Epitome," and a biographical sketch of Justin made by rearranging the information in the epitome. For the latter two parts, the *Bibliotheca* has no independent value, and researchers on Justin should go to Jerome, or preferably to Jerome's own source, Eusebius' *Ecclesiastical History.*[11]

An error made by the compiler of the "Hesychius Epitome" is further proof of Wentzel's thesis. In "Sophronius," where the biographies appear in more or less chronological order, the biography of Hippolytus of Rome is followed by a biography of a certain Ambrose, a friend of Origen. The conclusion of the article on Hippolytus and the whole article on Ambrose run as follows. Hippolytus composed many works,

> . . . προσομιλιῶν περὶ τῶν ἐπαίνων τοῦ κυρίου ἡμῶν Ἰησοῦ Χριστοῦ, ἐν οἷς παρόντος Ὠριγένους ἑαυτὸν ὡμιληκέναι κατὰ μίμησιν αὐτοῦ ἐν τῇ ἐκκλησίᾳ δηλοῖ.
>
> οα΄. Ἀμβρόσιος, ὅντινα ἀπὸ τῆς πλάνης Μαρκίωνος εἰς τὴν ἀληθινὴν πίστιν ἐπιστρέψαι προείρηται, προετρέψατο Ὠριγένει τὰς θείας ὑπομνηματίσαι γραφάς, παρεσχηκὼς αὐτῷ ἑπτὰ ἢ καὶ πλείους νοταρίους καὶ τὰς τούτων δαπάνας καὶ καλλιγράφους τὸν ἶσον ἀριθμόν, καὶ ὅπερ ἐστὶ μεῖζον, ἀνυποίστῳ σπουδῇ ἑκάστοτε ἔργον παρ' αὐτοῦ ἀπαιτῶν. Διὸ ἐν μιᾷ ἐπιστολῇ ἐργοδιώκτην αὐτὸν Ὠριγένης καλεῖ.[12]

In Photius' codex 121, the information on both men is applied to Hippolytus alone:

[9] Cod. 125: 94b line 38–95a line 5.

[10] Cod. 125: 95a lines 6–9 = "Sophronius," chap. 23, 22 lines 29–31 = *Suda,* II, 645 lines 24–26; cod. 125: 95a lines 9–16 = "Sophronius," chap. 23, 23 lines 15–20 = *Suda,* II, 646 lines 1–5.

[11] Eusebius, *Ecclesiastical History* IV.18. The translation of this passage from Greek to Latin and back again explains its lack of verbal parallels to the passages quoted.

[12] "Sophronius," chaps. 60 and 61, 39 line 20–40 line 5.

> Λέγεται δὲ οὗτος καὶ *προσομιλεῖν* τῷ λαῷ *κατὰ μίμησιν Ὠριγένους*, οὗ καὶ συνήθης μάλιστα καὶ ἐραστὴς τῶν λόγων ὑπῆρχε, ὡς καὶ *προτρέψασθαι* αὐτὸν *τὴν θείαν ὑπομνηματίσαι γραφήν*, ἐγκαταστήσας *αὐτῷ* καὶ ὑπογραφέας *ἑπτὰ* ταχυγράφους καὶ ἑτέρους τοσούτους *γράφοντας* εἰς *κάλλος*, ὧν ἦν καὶ *τῆς δαπάνης* αὐτὸς χορηγός. Καὶ ταῦτα ὑπηρετούμενος αὐτῷ *ἀπαιτεῖν αὐτὸν* ἀπαραιτήτως τὸ *ἔργον*, ἐξ οὗ καὶ *ἐργοδιώκτην ἐν μιᾷ τῶν ἐπιστολῶν* παρὰ *Ὠριγένους κληθῆναι.*[13]

Although the *Suda* article on Hippolytus consists only of two lines from the part of "Sophronius" which really does apply to Hippolytus, the mistake must have been made in the "Hesychius Epitome," because Photius could not have made it after the biographies were alphabetized.[14]

For secular writers, the only passages to compare with the *Bibliotheca* come from the *Suda* articles. For example, concerning Nicolaus of Damascus, the *Suda* records that he was a friend of the Emperor Augustus,

> οὕτως δὲ ἠσπάσατο αὐτὸν ὁ Καῖσαρ, ὡς τοὺς ὑπ' ἐκείνου πεμπομένους πλακοῦντας τῷ Καίσαρι, ἤγουν μελιττούτας, νικολάους αὐτὸν καλεῖν.[15]

In codex 189, Photius says of Nicolaus, the author of an account of curious customs,

> Ὁ ἐκ Δαμασκοῦ δ' ἐστὶν οὗτος, οἶμαι, Νικόλαος, ὁ ἐπὶ τῶν Αὐγούστου χρόνων ἀκμάσας καὶ φίλος αυτῷ χρηματίσας· ἐξ οὗ καὶ *πλακούντων* τι εἶδος, ἃ *διέπεμπε Καίσαρι*, εἰς τιμὴν τοῦ δεξιουμένου *νικολάους* ὁ Καῖσαρ *ἐκάλεσεν.*[16]

Concerning some Christian authors, the *Suda* has not included an article from the "Hesychius Epitome," and the only surviving parallel to the *Bibliotheca* is in "Sophronius." In these cases, the pattern of the other parallels makes it clear that the epitome, certainly not

[13] Cod. 121: 94a lines 34–42.

[14] The *Suda* article is at II, 662. Jerome's own source for his biography of Ambrose was again Eusebius' *Ecclesiastical History* (VI.23), but the error and lack of verbal parallels prove that Eusebius was not the direct source of either the "Hesychius Epitome" or Photius.

[15] *Suda*, III, 467 line 31–468 line 2. The rest of this article comes from the *Excerpta* of Constantine Porphyrogenitus and has nothing in common with Photius.

[16] Cod. 189: 146a lines 8–12.

"Sophronius" itself, was Photius' direct source. For example, "Sophronius" lists the following works by Clement of Alexandria:

> . . . περὶ τοῦ πάσχα εἷς, περὶ νηστείας διάλεξις, καὶ ἕτερος ἐπιγράφων Τίς ἄρα πλούσιος σωθήσεται, περὶ κακολογίας λόγος εἷς, περὶ κανόνων ἐκκλησιαστικῶν καὶ κατὰ τῶν ἀκολουθούντων τῇ τῶν Ἰουδαίων πλάνῃ λόγον, ὅντινα ἰδικῶς Ἀλεξάνδρῳ ἐπισκόπῳ Ἱεροσολύμων προσεφώνησε. . . . ἤνθησε δὲ βασιλευόντων Σεβήρου καὶ Ἀντωνίνου τοῦ υἱοῦ αὐτοῦ.[17]

In codex 111, Photius, who has just reviewed several books by Clement including the *Quis Dives Salvetur,* adds,

> Ἐπαγγέλλεται δὲ καὶ ἄλλα πεποιῆσθαι αὐτῷ συγγράμματα οὐκ ὀλίγα, καί γε καὶ ὑφ' ἑτέρων πεποιηκέναι μεμαρτύρηται, *περί τε τοῦ πάσχα καὶ περὶ νηστείας καὶ περὶ κακολογίας, περὶ κανόνων ἐκκλησιαστικῶν, κατὰ τῶν ἀκολουθούντων τῇ τῶν Ἰουδαίων πλάνῃ ὃν Ἀλεξάνδρῳ Ἱεροσολύμων ἐπισκόπῳ* προσειπεῖν. Ἤκμασε *δὲ Σεβήρου καὶ Ἀντωνίνου υἱοῦ αὐτοῦ* Ῥώμης *βασιλευόντων.*[18]

If there are no parallels to the *Bibliotheca* in either the *Suda* or "Sophronius," Photius may be the only surviving witness for a passage of the "Hesychius Epitome" where the source was not "Sophronius." He could, however, also have taken his information from a source other than the epitome. Three such passages seem to have derived from the epitome, all of them beginning with "they say" or "it is said," phrases which usually mark Photius' citations of it. First, at the end of codex 73, Photius notes that "they say" the novelist Heliodorus became a bishop after he wrote his *Aethiopica.* This is attested by Theodorus Lector, who, according to Ada Adler, was a source of the "Hesychius Epitome."[19] Thus Photius' source here was probably the epitome, which he certainly used in the following codex.[20] Photius' reference to the works of Nilus of Ancyra in codex 201 may also have come from an article of the "Hesychius Epitome"

[17] "Sophronius," chap. 38, 29 lines 19–24, 30 lines 12–13. This parallel was overlooked by Wentzel.

[18] Cod. 111: 89b line 38–90a line 3.

[19] Cf. cod. 73: 51b lines 40–41; *Theodorus Lector,* ed. G. C. Hansen, GCS, 54 (Berlin, 1971), 82 lines 28–30. See note 4 *supra* for Adler on Theodorus. Photius could also conceivably have used Socrates V.22, Theodorus' own source; Photius described Socrates' work in cod. 28.

[20] For the parallel to cod. 74, see Table VII.

derived from Theodorus Lector, though this passage is not paralleled in the surviving fragments of Theodorus.[21]

The "Hesychius Epitome" may have been Photius' source again in codex 160, where he gives biographies of Choricius of Gaza and Procopius of Gaza, neither of whom appears in the *Suda.*[22] These were well-known contemporaries of Hesychius whom he would have been likely to include in the *Onomatologus,* as he did articles on himself, Procopius of Caesarea, Agathias, John Lydus, Tribonian, John Philoponus, and even the obscure Hermolaus of Constantinople.[23] Unless biographies of Choricius and Procopius were prefaced to Photius' manuscript of their works, no other source for this material is apparent. The same is not true, however, for some other cases where Wentzel conjectured that Photius had used the "Hesychius Epitome."

The "Hesychius Epitome" was the source of biographical sketches in twenty to twenty-three codices, the earliest 13 and the latest 210. Of these, six show parallels to both the *Suda* and "Sophronius," seven to the *Suda* alone, and seven to "Sophronius" alone; codices 73, 160, and 201 have parallels in neither but may have had them in the original epitome.[24] In addition, Photius probably intended to fill two or three lacunas in the text of the *Bibliotheca* from the "Hesychius Epitome," as will be seen in the next chapter.[25]

Photius' use of the "Hesychius Epitome" in the *Bibliotheca* is not plagiarism. The words "they say" or "it is said," with which Photius marks nineteen out of a possible twenty-three citations, carry with them an acknowledgment of indebtedness.[26] Photius never claims to have read the books that he knew only from this source, and he sometimes makes it clear that he had not read them. For example, in codex 14 on Apollinarius of Hierapolis, he concludes a short biography taken from the epitome with the words, "It is said that there are also other notable works by him, which we have not yet found."[27]

[21] Cod. 201: 163b lines 14–18.

[22] Cod. 160: 102b line 37–103a line 13; 103a lines 13–16 is evidently generalized from Choricius' orations themselves, especially his orations 7 and 8, ed. R. Foerster and E. Richtsteig (Leipzig, 1929), 109–28 and 344–80.

[23] *Suda,* I, 15 (on Agathias); II, 416 (Hermolaus), 594 (Hesychius), 649 (John Philoponus and John Lydus); IV, 210–11 (Procopius of Caesarea), 588 (Tribonian). None of these articles could have come from the other, Christian sources of the "Hesychius Epitome."

[24] See Table VII for the references.

[25] See pp. 73–74 *infra.*

[26] These phrases (φασίν, λέγουσιν, λέγεται, φέρεται, etc.) appear in all the codices listed in Table VII except 34, 125, and 189.

[27] Λέγεται δὲ αὐτοῦ καὶ ἕτερα συγγράμματα ἀξιομνημόνευτα εἶναι, οἷς οὔπω ἡμεῖς ἐνετύχομεν (cod. 14: 4a lines 19–21). Photius says in cod. 58: 17b lines 22–23 that he

Moreover, Photius uses the "Hesychius Epitome" with some originality. He often rearranges and comments on its material, as he does in the case of Justin Martyr, and twice he draws on articles besides those on authors he is reviewing. In codex 60, on Herodotus, Photius relates that the young Thucydides wept when he heard Herodotus read his history, whereupon Herodotus congratulated the young man's father on his son's appreciation for scholarship. A comparison with the *Suda* shows that Photius took this anecdote from the biography of Thucydides in the "Hesychius Epitome," not that of Herodotus.[28] Second, in codex 118, on the *For Origen* of Pamphilus and Eusebius, Photius uses material from the epitome's article on Origen as well as from its article on Pamphilus.[29] Thus Photius not only looked up the alphabetical articles on his authors but checked a few related articles as well.

Notwithstanding Photius' considerable dependence on this secondary work, most of the biographical sketches in the *Bibliotheca,* like the rest of the text, come from the books which Photius reviews. Sometimes he summarizes autobiographical material by an author as part of a summary of his book's contents; such cases need no discussion here. But often Photius uses such material to make a separate sketch. These compositions, which are neither long nor elaborate, tend to be taken from titles, prefaces, and postfaces, i.e., the most accessible sources of information. Often Photius states explicitly that his source was the book itself, and at other times it is obvious that it must have been, especially when the original survives for comparison.

Codex 29, on Evagrius Scholasticus, is an example of a "biography" taken only from the title, which Photius simply paraphrases, adding the location of the author's native city. The title reads, "The Ecclesiastical History of Evagrius the Lawyer of Epiphania, Former Prefect," and Photius begins his codex, "There was read the *Ecclesiastical History* of Evagrius the lawyer, former prefect, from the city of Epiphania in Coele Syria. . . ."[30] Similarly, in codex 69 Photius

---

has not read some works by Arrian which are mentioned in the "Hesychius Epitome," and in cod. 209: 165b lines 5–7 he specifies which of the orations of Dio Chrysostom he has read. See the parallels in Table VII.

[28] The *Suda* gives the anecdote twice, once under Thucydides (II, 721 lines 16–21) and once to illustrate the use of the verb ὀργάω (III, 552). The second entry must be the work of the *Suda,* since the "Hesychius Epitome" was not lexical. This parallel was not noticed by Wentzel, "Übersetzung." The source of the "Hesychius Epitome" was no doubt Hesychius, who, in turn, depended on Marcellinus' *Life of Thucydides* chap. 54 (*Thucydides,* ed. O. Luschnat, I [Leipzig, 1954], 12).

[29] For the references, see Table VII.

[30] Cf. Evagrius Scholasticus, *Historia Ecclesiastica,* ed. J. Bidez and L. Parmentier (London, 1898), 1 (Κεφάλαια τοῦ πρώτου τόμου τῆς ἐκκλησιαστικῆς ἱστορίας Εὐαγρίου

gives the title (ἐπιγραφή) of Hesychius' general history as his source for the author's birthplace and his parents' names.[31] Wentzel pressed his argument too far when he tried to draw a parallel between this statement and the *Suda*.[32]

Gelasius of Cyzicus' preface to his history and an anonymous preface to John Moschus' *Pratum Spirituale* closely parallel Photius' short biographical sketches of these authors found in codices 88 and 199, and obviously served as his sources.[33] In codex 57, Photius took his biographical information on Appian from Appian's own preface, and Wentzel's conjecture that the source was a lost article of the "Hesychius Epitome" is mistaken.[34] In codex 61, Photius probably took his account of the orator Aeschines from a lost biography appended to his manuscript, which was similar to three other such biographies preserved in existing manuscripts.[35] In codex 213, Photius takes part of his biography of Agatharchides from that historian's postface to his *On the Red Sea* and part from what seems to have been an anonymous biography appended to the manuscript.[36]

In other codices, Photius takes information from the body of the book but usually from just one place. Codex 26 on several works by Synesius of Cyrene, for instance, summarizes a part of a letter by him, in which he describes how he did not believe in the resurrection of the dead when he first became a Christian and a bishop.[37] In

σχολαστικοῦ καὶ ἀπὸ ὑπάρχων τοῦ Ἐπιφανέως) with cod. 29: 6a lines 25–27 (Ἀνεγνώσθη Εὐαγρίου σχολαστικοῦ ἀπὸ ὑπάρχων, πόλεως δὲ Ἐπιφανείας τῆς κατὰ τὴν κοίλην Συρίαν, ἐκκλησιαστικὴ ἱστορία . . .). For Ἐπιφανείας A reads Ἐπιφανέως, which may be a misinterpretation of Evagrius' title by Photius himself. Henry's translation "érudit" is incorrect.

[31] Cod. 69: 34a lines 37–41.

[32] Wentzel, "Übersetzung," 43–44.

[33] Cf. cod. 88: 67a lines 16–25 with Gelasius, I, preface and chap. 4 (PG, 85, cols. 1192–97 and 1208). Cf. cod. 199: 162a line 29–162b line 5 with the anonymous preface to Moschus in H. Usener, *Der Heilige Tychon* (Leipzig-Berlin, 1907), 91–93.

[34] Wentzel, "Übersetzung," 56. Cf. cod. 57: 17a line 13–15 with Appian's preface, section 15.

[35] Cod. 61: 20a line 5–20b line 8. For the other biographies, see *Eschine*, ed. V. Martin and G. de Budé (Paris, 1927), 3–7. The biography used in cod. 61 cannot be from the lost history of the ten orators from which Photius excerpted the life of Aeschines in cod. 264, because the two lives have no verbal parallels, even when they deal with the same subjects.

[36] Cod. 213: 171a lines 11–19 is certainly from Agatharchides' postface, which Photius excerpts in cod. 250: 460b lines 3–16. There is no reason to think that Photius had read the histories of Asia and Europe, because he mentions reading only one ἱστορικόν, evidently the *On the Red Sea*. Cod. 213: 171a lines 6–11 and 19–27 must come from a *vita* of some sort (so *FGrHist*, 86: II C, 151).

[37] Cf. cod. 26: 5b line 34–6a line 4 with Synesius, letter 105, ed. R. Hercher, in *Epistolographi Graeci* (Paris, 1873), 705–6. Therefore, at 5b line 35 read φησι with M instead of the φασι of A and the editors, which is presumably a corruption, and translate "He says," not "On dit" (Henry, I, 15). Photius seems simply to have assumed that Synesius later came to believe in the resurrection of the dead.

codices 28 and 30, the single sentences which Photius devotes to biographies of the ecclesiastical historians Socrates and Sozomen are based on short passages in their histories which Photius might even have remembered.[38] Photius' biography of Dionysius of Halicarnassus in codex 83 is a paragraph in length and, as Photius says, derives from that author's *Roman Antiquities.*[39]

The history of Olympiodorus is lost, but there is no reason to doubt Photius when he says that he took his information about that writer from his history.[40] Photius likewise gives Praxagoras' *History of Constantine* as his source when he says that the author wrote the book at age twenty-two, adding that Praxagoras also wrote other books when he was nineteen and thirty-one, books which Photius makes no claim to have read.[41] If the thirty-one of the text is emended to twenty-one, which fits the other two remarkable ages better, the *History of Constantine* may be presumed to be the source for all this information. Photius' words are ambiguous in codex 118, on the *For Origen* of Pamphilus and Eusebius, where he evidently uses "they say" to mean both the "Hesychius Epitome" and the two authors. Probably the book, not the epitome, was the source of some of the material in the codex for which Wentzel found unconvincing parallels in different parts of "Sophronius" and the *Suda.*[42]

Because Photius frequently does not say that he is taking biographical material from a book he reviews when he can be proved to have done so, his source for several biographies of authors of lost books may also have been these books themselves. For example, although Photius used the "Hesychius Epitome" for a biographical sketch of Arrian that appears at the end of codex 58, his source for the beginning of the codex, which has no parallel in the *Suda,* was probably the preface of Arrian's lost *Parthica,* the book under review.[43] Lost parts of the books themselves were probably also Pho-

[38] Cf. cod. 28: 5b lines 16–20 with Socrates, *Ecclesiastica Historia* V.16, ed. R. Hussey, II (Oxford, 1853), 706–8. Cf. cod. 30: 6a lines 40–41 with Sozomen, *Kirchengeschichte* II.3, 10, ed. J. Bidez, GCS, 50 (Berlin, 1960), 53.

[39] Cf. cod. 83: 65a lines 2–10 with *Roman Antiquities* I.7; note Photius' phrase ὥς φησιν in line 6.

[40] Cod. 80: 56b lines 12–21.

[41] Cod. 62: 21b lines 9–15.

[42] Wentzel, "Übersetzung," 49–51. Cod. 118: 92b lines 19–22 and 93a lines 26–29 are definitely from the "Hesychius Epitome" (cf. the parallels in Table VII); but φασί and λέγουσιν seem to mean the authors at 92b line 7 and 92b line 34, as Wentzel notes. The passage in question is 92b lines 24–33, introduced by φασίν, for which Wentzel's parallels (*Suda,* III, 616 line 24, "Sophronius," chap. 63, p. 35 line 5 and chap. 48, p. 29 lines 13–14) seem too remote and diverse to reflect the mechanical copying and alphabetization characteristic of the "Hesychius Epitome."

[43] Cod. 58: 17a lines 24–28. Photius was able to criticize Arrian's *Anabasis* because he had read it (cod. 91). For the parallels to the end of the codex, see Table VII.

tius' sources for biographical sketches of Dio Cassius in codex 71, Himerius in codex 165, and Damascius of Damascus in codex 181. These have no real parallels in the *Suda*, though Wentzel argued unconvincingly for a parallel to the article on Himerius.[44] The biographical sketches in three other codices also seem to have come from parts of the books being reviewed, i.e., the lost history of Amyntianus and lost treatises by Eulogius of Alexandria and Ephraem of Amida.[45]

Besides the texts of the books he reviews, Photius could use scholia in his manuscripts as sources. In codex 48, he says that he read a work *On the Universe* which his manuscript attributed to Josephus, "but I found in scholia" that the author was not Josephus, but Gaius of Rome. The scholia went on to observe that Gaius' other works were variously misattributed to Josephus, Justin Martyr, Irenaeus, and Origen.[46] Johann Klinkenberg has discovered that in codex 91 Photius used scholia on Arrian's *Anabasis* that survive in some of our manuscripts.[47] Lost scholia seem the probable source of passages in three additional codices. In codex 63 on Procopius' *Wars*, Klinkenberg has shown that Photius' epitome includes a sentence and a half borrowed from Agathias. Though Klinkenberg conjectured that Photius had read Agathias and reviewed him in a codex that dropped out in the lacuna following codex 63, the absence of such an entry in the *pinax* rules out his theory.[48] Especially because Photius earlier quotes what is evidently a scholion on Procopius' use of the word μαργαρίτης, his source is more likely to have been a scholion based on Agathias than to have been Agathias himself.[49] Likewise, scholia were probably the sources of short passages in Photius' summary of Herodotus and the epitome of George of Alexandria that

[44] Wentzel, "Übersetzung," 53. Cod. 71: 35b lines 14–23 is not parallel to *Suda*, II, 116 line 30–117 line 3; nor cod. 165: 109a lines 2–4 to *Suda*, II, 633 lines 25–28; nor cod. 181: 126b line 40–127a line 14 to *Suda*, II, 3 line 28–4 line 2.

[45] Cod. 131: 97a lines 18–22 (Amyntianus), cod. 226: 244a lines 3–7 (Eulogius), cod. 228: 245a lines 21–29 (Ephraem). In this last codex, where Photius uses the word φασί, I suspect that his source was a preface not by Ephraem; cf. note 33 *supra* on cod. 199 (John Moschus).

[46] . . . εὗρον δὲ ἐν παραγραφαῖς . . . (cod. 48: 11b line 40–12a line 6). The author of *On the Universe* was actually Hippolytus of Rome; see p. 68 *infra*. The paragraph at the end of the codex is from the "Hesychius Epitome"; see Table VII.

[47] Klinkenberg, 37–40.

[48] *Ibid.*, 40–42. The passages are cod. 63: 21b lines 35–36 and 22a lines 8–9, which correspond to Agathias IV.27.

[49] Though the editors have printed this scholion at cod. 63: 22a lines 12–17, it appears in both MSS just before cod. 62 (Praxagoras): 20b line 28 (see Henry's apparatus), to whom the scholion also explicitly refers. Perhaps Photius had a MS with scholia that included both codd. 62 and 63.

are not in our manuscripts of their works.[50] Other material from scholia, still unidentified, may well be imbedded in other codices.

Although Photius did little that could properly be called research for the *Bibliotheca,* he did take some information for several codices from books that he reviews in other codices. In three codices he says he is doing this, apparently only from memory. In codex 60, he cites Diodorus Siculus, reviewed in codex 70 and excerpted in codex 244, along with "others" as an authority for the assertion that Herodotus had lived through the Persian Wars.[51] Diodorus does corroborate this fact, which Photius could easily have remembered, since it makes Herodotus' history the earliest book in the *Bibliotheca.*[52] In codex 61, Photius mentions "Phrynichus and others" who attest that there were two writers named Aeschines, the orator and Aeschines Socraticus.[53] Here Photius is presumably referring to the lost *Preparation for the Sophist* of Phrynichus the Arab, reviewed in codex 158, and again he could easily have remembered this fact. In codex 196, Photius must be working from memory when he says that Eusebius attests that Ephraem the Syrian had written a thousand books, because such a statement is not in Eusebius, who died more than thirty years before Ephraem, presumably before Ephraem had reached that figure.[54] Photius probably had read this in Sozomen's ecclesiastical history, which he reviews in codex 30.[55]

Twice Photius gives references so vague that the books cannot be identified. In codex 89, on the continuation of Eusebius' ecclesiastical history by Gelasius of Caesarea, Photius says that he has found "by reading elsewhere" that this history is merely a translation of the Latin history of Rufinus of Aquileia.[56] This seems to be chronologically impossible, and in any event Photius' half-remembered reference is insufficient to prove it.[57] Similarly, in codex 189 Photius says of Nicolaus of Damascus, "This man also left a history of Assyria in

[50] Herodotus (cod. 60: 19b lines 32–34); see Klinkenberg, 42–43, who thinks that Photius' source may have been Nicephorus' *Chronicle.* But why then is it not reviewed in the *Bibliotheca,* like his *Breviarium* (cod. 66)? On George of Alexandria (cod. 96: 81a lines 35–40), see Henry, II, 56 and supplementary note on p. 209.

[51] Cod. 60: 19b lines 36–38.

[52] Diodorus Siculus, II.32, 2.

[53] Cod. 61: 20b lines 23–27.

[54] Cod. 196: 160b lines 35–38. Eusebius died about 340, Ephraem in 373; *ODCC, s.vv.* Cf. cod. 177: 123a lines 23–26, where Photius misremembers the number of books (28 for 25) in Theodore of Mopsuestia's *Against Eunomius,* reviewed in cod. 4.

[55] Cf. Sozomen III.16, 3–4, *op. cit.* (*supra,* note 38).

[56] . . . ἀνεγνωκότες ἐν ἄλλοις . . . (cod. 89: 67a lines 35–39).

[57] See Henry, II, 15, note 1.

a large book, as far as we can remember reading long ago."[58] The book Photius remembered seems to be Nicolaus' voluminous universal history, which began with the Assyrians.[59] Perhaps Photius had found a reference in another book to what Nicolaus said about the Assyrians and assumed that Nicolaus had written about the Assyrians alone; or perhaps he simply made a mistake. No doubt Photius had many foggy memories of things that he had read during his twenty years or more of reading since his school days.

Besides citing from memory, Photius sometimes refers in some detail to a book that he reviews in another codex, and for which he apparently had a text or notes. In codex 33, he cites Josephus as his source for a paragraph on Josephus' enemy, Justus of Tiberias; a comparison of texts shows that the source was Josephus' autobiography, which Photius includes in codex 76.[60] This paragraph seems too detailed to have been composed from memory.

Though Photius leaves a blank for the title of Eunomius' *Apologeticus* in codex 137, and seems not to have had the book at hand, he gives a paragraph of information on it. Close parallels show that Photius took this paragraph, which is mostly polemic against Eunomius and does not resemble Photius' usual style, from Book I of Gregory of Nyssa's *Against Eunomius,* reviewed in codex 6.[61] Next, in codex 138, Photius avoids giving the title of Eunomius' *Apologia Pro Apologia* but gives a paragraph describing its publication and refutation, again in a polemical style that is not Photian. Here the source is not Gregory's refutation, which dealt only with the *Apologeticus,* nor a later work of Gregory that Photius describes in codex 7. At the end of the paragraph, Photius mentions that Eunomius' second work was refuted by "Theodore, Gregory of Nyssa, and Sophronius, whom we have reviewed above."[62] I therefore conjecture that Photius' source in codex 138 was either one or both of the refutations by Theodore of Mopsuestia and by Sophronius, reviewed in codices 4 and 5.[63]

[58] Οὗτος καὶ Ἀσσυριακὴν ἱστορίαν ἐν πολυστίχῳ βιβλίῳ, ὅσα παλαιὰν μνήμην ἀναγνωσμάτων ἔχομεν, καταλέλοιπεν (cod. 189: 146a lines 12–14).

[59] *FGrHist,* 90: IIA, 328 lines 2–4; cf. 328–35.

[60] Cf. cod. 33: 6b line 38–7a line 5 with Josephus, *Life,* chaps. 174–78 and 336–67. As Henry observed (I, 157 note 3), Photius reviews Josephus' *Jewish Antiquities* and *Life* as one book in cod. 76, since the end of the former introduces the latter.

[61] Cf. cod. 137: 97b lines 1–10 with Gregory, *Contra Eunomium* I, ed. W. Jaeger in *Gregorii Nysseni Opera,* 2nd ed., I (Leiden, 1960), 23–24.

[62] . . . Θεόδωρος καὶ ὁ Γρηγόριος Νύσσης καὶ Σωφρόνιος, ὧν ἐμνήσθημεν ἄνωθεν (cod. 138: 97b lines 15–34). Theodore's work is mentioned again in cod. 177: 123a lines 23–26 (see p. 63 note 54 *supra*).

[63] This is possibly the same Sophronius who may have translated Jerome's *Famous Men*; see A. Puech, *Histoire de la littérature grecque chrétienne,* III (Paris, 1930), 549.

According to Wentzel, Photius used the "Hesychius Epitome" for his very full account of Theopompus in codex 176. But the only information in this codex that is paralleled in the *Suda*'s biography is Theopompus' birthplace, Chios, and his father's name, which Photius gives as Damostratus and the *Suda* as Damasistratus.[64] This "parallel" proves nothing. Besides, Photius' biography of Theopompus, unlike any of the articles of the "Hesychius Epitome," cites other sources specifically. These are three historians: Menophanes of unknown date, Duris of Samos who lived from about 340 to 260 B.C., and Cleochares of Smyrlea, born about 300 B.C.[65] All three are lost, none of them is reviewed in the *Bibliotheca*, and to judge from his habits in other codices, Photius is not at all likely to have consulted them in the original when he composed codex 176. Klinkenberg conjectured that Photius' source was a biography of Theopompus attached to his manuscript.[66] This may be correct, but another possibility is that these historical extracts on Theopompus were recorded by Pamphila of Epidaurus, who during the reign of Nero compiled a collection of historical extracts, now lost, which Photius had just reviewed in the preceding codex, no. 175. Photius praises her book for its usefulness and seems to have had it at hand, because he quotes from her preface and even models part of his own preface to the *Bibliotheca* upon it.[67] All Photius would have had to do was keep Pamphila's book by him when he composed his next codex.

In one codex only does Photius give bibliographical information which he seems to have learned by word of mouth. When he reviews Ephraem the Syrian in codex 196, he notes that, though the style of the Greek translation is poor, "those who have an exact knowledge of Syriac" say that the style of the original is excellent. Later in the same codex, Photius notes that, agreeing with Eusebius, the Syrians report that Ephraem wrote more than a thousand works.[68] Presumably Photius had met Syrians in Constantinople or elsewhere from whom he had learned these things.[69] But otherwise, Photius does not appear to have drawn any identifiable information for his biographies from his teachers, colleagues, or other contemporaries.

[64] Wentzel, "Übersetzung," 53; *Suda*, II, 698 lines 14–20. "Damasistratus" is the accepted form.

[65] Cod. 176: 120a lines 11–13, 121a line 41–121b line 3, and 121b lines 9–15. On Menophanes, see *RE*, Menophanes 2; on Duris, see *OCD*, *s.v.*; and on Cleochares, see *RE*, Kleochares 5.

[66] Klinkenberg, 45–46.

[67] It is the passage from Pamphila that makes a reconstruction of the lacuna in the preface possible. See Treadgold, "Preface."

[68] . . . οἵ γε τῆς Σύρας φωνῆς τὴν ἀκρίβειαν ἠσκημένοι . . . (cod. 196: 160b lines 1–5 and 35–36).

[69] Perhaps including the mysterious Berzelis; see p. 29 *supra*.

As he was dictating the first part of the *Bibliotheca,* then, Photius kept a manuscript of the "Hesychius Epitome" by his side and looked up its alphabetical articles on approximately twenty of the authors he was reviewing. More often, he looked for autobiographical material in the authors' own books. He might also use a book he reviewed in one codex as a source for the literary history of another codex. Once or twice his use of additional sources may have affected the order of the codices. Thus, Photius treats Theopompus after Pamphila, who may have excerpted biographical material on Theopompus; he describes works by Clement of Rome after works by Clement of Alexandria, who would have preceded Clement of Rome in the alphabetical "Hesychius Epitome," consulted by Photius on both writers. But these are exceptions, since passages based on the epitome are distributed over the whole first part of the *Bibliotheca* and almost all of the biographies are simply supplementary notes at the ends of codices.

To judge from this survey, the contribution of Byzantine scholarly tradition to these biographies was close to zero. If Photius' teachers and colleagues taught him anything about literary history, the *Bibliotheca* shows no traces of it. Photius took his biographical sketches from the books that he had read. He did so in haste, but with evident interest in the life, times, and literary production of his authors. Though his search for sources was not at all systematic, it was surprisingly wide. In fact, Photius cites so many parts of so many books that he seems to have been composing the first part of the *Bibliotheca* not merely from notes but from the resources of a sizable library.

CHAPTER FIVE

Errors and Omissions

The *Bibliotheca,* like any large encyclopedic work, contains mistakes. These may be the fault of Photius, of his secretary, or of his sources. In fact, examples of each of these three kinds of errors have already been given in the preceding chapters. In his biography of Ephraem the Syrian, Photius cited the wrong ecclesiastical historian as his source, confusing Eusebius with Sozomen.[1] While copying Photius' notes for the second part of the *Bibliotheca,* the secretary mistook the heading of a part of an oration by Aristides for a new speech and incorrectly wrote it down as a new codex.[2] In taking a biography of Hippolytus of Rome from the "Hesychius epitome," Photius repeated a mistake that the epitomator had made while copying and alphabetizing his own source, "Sophronius."[3]

As a rule, the mistakes made by Photius' sources are more appropriate material for a study of each source than for a study of the *Bibliotheca.* Further, the problem of errors in the transmission of texts in the *Bibliotheca,* which could be the fault of either Photius, his secretary, or his original manuscript, is too large to treat here with any thoroughness. The notes to Henry's edition give the most comprehensive picture of Photius' process of transmission and his errors in executing it, while the works of Klinkenberg and especially of Hägg provide more detailed treatment of selected codices.[4] They have shown that, as a transmitter of texts, Photius made occasional careless errors, but few irresponsible ones.[5] What I have attempted here is a survey of Photius' errors as a literary historian, as far as these can be detected in the present state of our knowledge.

[1] See p. 63 *supra.*

[2] See p. 47 *supra.*

[3] See pp. 55–56 *supra.*

[4] See Klinkenberg, 53–56, and Hägg, *Photios, passim.*

[5] Perhaps the worst transmission is in cod. 73 on Heliodorus; see Hägg, *Photios,* 199, and H. Gärtner, "Charikleia in Byzanz," *Antike und Abendland,* 15 (1969), 50–54.

The errors in the *Bibliotheca,* both textual and analytic, were probably accidental. Admittedly, Photius was not always above deception in his scholarship, as he proved *circa* 872 when he plagiarized Peter the Sicilian's account of the Paulicians but claimed that his sources were converted Paulicians whom he had met.[6] In the *Bibliotheca,* however, Photius seems to have been consistently candid. In particular, he was willing to admit his ignorance or uncertainty about many points, often mentioning that he has not seen or read certain books or parts of books, or that he did not know the answer to some bibliographical problem.[7] Besides this, the second part of the *Bibliotheca* is presumably free from any intent to deceive, simply because it is a transcription of Photius' notes. In any case, no demonstrably deliberate deception seems ever to have been found in the *Bibliotheca.*

Like any scholar who makes conjectures, Photius occasionally made wrong ones. He is, however, reasonably careful about labeling his conjectures as such and giving his reasons for them. Thus, in codex 48, he describes the various conflicting indications of the authorship of the treatise *On the Universe,* rejects its attribution to Josephus, and hesitantly follows a scholion in his manuscript that ascribed the work to Gaius of Rome. The scholion should have said Hippolytus of Rome, who is now believed to be the author, but Photius cannot be blamed for this; on the contrary, when Photius observes that the doctrine in the book was not compatible with the ideas of Josephus or Judaism, he is perfectly right.[8] Similarly, in codex 88 Photius confuses Gelasius of Cyzicus, who wrote about 475, with Gelasius of Caesarea, who died in 395. But Photius realizes that the one must have been a good deal earlier than the other and, almost correctly, postulates two Caesarean Gelasii.[9] In codex 129 Photius may be wrong to think that the author of the *Metamorphoses* which he is reviewing was named Lucius of Patrae and that this man

[6] See P. Lemerle, "L'Histoire des Pauliciens d'Asie Mineure d'après les sources grecques," *TM,* 5 (1973), 31–47.

[7] Photius mentions books that he has not read at codd. 14: 4b lines 19–21, 35: 7a lines 32–33 (part of book, implied), 41: 9a lines 15–19 (part), 42: 9a lines 35–40 (part), 58: 17b lines 21–22, 62: 21b lines 10–15, 78: 54b lines 32–35 (part), 97: 84a lines 34–35 (part), 98: 84b lines 32–36 (but see p. 69 *infra*), 111: 89b line 38–90a line 1, 158: 100b lines 10–15 (part), 176: 120a lines 8–10 (part), 209: 165b lines 5–7 (implied), 213: 171a lines 19–21, 224: 240a lines 9–11 (part), 228: 245a lines 28–29 (implied), 261: 488a lines 15–16 (implied), 268: 496b lines 38–41, and 273: 507b lines 15–20 (part). He admits ignorance or uncertainty at codd. 48: 12a lines 9–10, 51: 12b lines 3–5, 88: 66b line 35, 95: 78b lines 21–23, 96: 78b line 27, 115: 91a lines 28–29, 129: 96b lines 20–22, 150: 99b lines 11–15, 166: 112a lines 2–3, 170: 117b lines 27–32, 172: 119a lines 15–19 and 41–42, 177: 121b lines 35–36, 186: 138b lines 39–40, 213: 171a lines 27–28, and 256: 469b lines 21–22.

[8] See Quasten, II, 195–96, and cod. 48: 11b lines 31–34.

[9] Cod. 88: 66b line 30–67a line 1.

was in earnest; but, with the text lost and the author still in doubt, we should not criticize Photius too sharply for failing to recognize a parody.[10] On the basis of the information available to him, he does not seem to have drawn unreasonable conclusions in these cases.

With somewhat less care, in codex 98 Photius interprets the title of Zosimus' *New History* (Ἱστορία Νέα) to mean a new edition (νέα ἔκδοσις) of a history whose old edition he had not found. Here Photius was led astray by the close similarities he saw between Zosimus and Eunapius of Sardis, who wrote a history that Photius had indeed found in old and new editions.[11] Zosimus' title actually means *History of Recent Times*.[12] In codex 166, Photius almost fancifully conjectures that Antonius Diogenes' *The Wonders Beyond Thule* was written not long after Alexander, simply because it mentions that Alexander's troops discovered the coffins of the novel's heroes.[13] A date some four centuries later is now accepted.[14] Again, in codex 180, Photius guesses from John Lydus' interest in myths that the writer was a pagan, which he was not.[15]

Another, self-contradictory conjecture has caused scholars trouble. In codex 41, Photius reviews the *Ecclesiastical History* of a certain John, a Monophysite. This John denounced the Council of Chalcedon in his history, "from which," Photius writes, "it is possible to conjecture that John, the author of this book, is the priest of Aegeae who, heretic that he was, also composed a separate book against the Council of Chalcedon."[16] Photius reviews this second book in codex 55, where he says that the author was John of Aegeae, but this time calls him a Nestorian, not a Monophysite.[17] Fortunately, fragments of the *Ecclesiastical History* of codex 41 are preserved under the name of John Diacrinomenus, which means "John the Monophysite"; this work seems to have been written after 526.[18] But John of Aegeae was

[10] On cod. 129, and the novel's author and date, see H. Van Thiel, *Der Eselsroman*, I, Zetemata, 54 (Munich, 1971), 1–7 and 36–42. I am not completely convinced by Van Thiel's assertion (p. 3) that no one would write such a work about himself.

[11] Cod. 98: 84b line 27–38; cf. cod. 77: 54a line 26–54b line 4.

[12] See Zosimus, *Histoire nouvelle*, ed. F. Paschoud, I (Paris, 1971), xxi.

[13] Cod. 166: 111b line 42–112a 4, cf. 111a line 41–111b line 24.

[14] Antonius Diogenes flourished *ca.* A.D. 100 (*KP*, Diogenes 17, *Nachträge*).

[15] Cod. 180: 125b lines 24–28; cf. Henry, II, 224.

[16] Ἐξ ὧν ἔστι συμβαλεῖν Ἰωάννην εἶναι τὸν πατέρα τοῦ βιβλίου τὸν πρεσβύτερον τὸν Αἰγεάτην, ὃς καὶ ἰδίως ὡς αἱρετικὸς κατὰ τῆς ἐν Καλχηδόνι συνόδου βιβλίον συνέταξε.

[17] Cod. 55: 15b lines 1–5.

[18] *Theodorus Lector*, ed. G. C. Hansen, GCS, 54 (Berlin, 1971), 152–57. Evagrius Scholasticus, *Historia Ecclesiastica*, ed. J. Bidez and L. Parmentier (London, 1898), 155–56, mentions that a history by John "the Rhetor," whose subject and time period fairly securely identify it as this history, ended with an eyewitness account of the Antioch earthquake of 526. Cf. *KP*, Iohannes 9, which does not, however, note this last point.

certainly a Nestorian, as Photius says he was in codex 55, because he and his work against the Council of Chalcedon were condemned for Nestorianism in 511, and again in 680.[19] In fact, since John of Aegeae corresponded with Theodoret of Cyrus, who died about 466, he would have been very old indeed after 526.[20] In this case Photius' facts were right, but his conjecture that the two anti-Chalcedonian Johns were the same was wrong, as he would have seen himself if he had rechecked what he had said. The conjecture should be discarded without misgivings.[21]

Besides these more or less reasonable conjectures, Photius makes some simple factual mistakes. In codex 26, he calls Synesius the bishop of Cyrene, thus confusing Synesius' home town with his see, Ptolemaïs. In codices 44, 150, and 241, Photius seems to think that the first two Philostrati were one man, an easy error, and that this Philostratus came from Tyre, though both were from Lemnos. How Photius made the error about Tyre is obscure.[22] At codex 95, he confuses Maximus Confessor's letter to Marianus with his treatise *To Marinus*.[23] In codex 212, he refers to Aenesidemus of Cnossus as Aenesidemus "of Aegae," a slip evidently connected with the Dionysius of Aegeae whose book Photius has just reviewed in the preceding codex.[24] Further, in codex 240 Photius states that the Sergius to whom John Philoponus dedicated his *On the Hexameron* was Sergius of Constantinople, who lived a century after John; in fact, the dedication is to Sergius of Antioch.[25] But these are all understandable and easily identifiable errors.

In the combined codex 112-13, however, Photius' confusion is more complex and difficult to unravel. This double codex may be summarized as follows. Photius says that he has read two volumes by Clement of Rome, of which one is his *Apostolic Constitutions*. The second volume is introduced by a letter to St. James the Greater and describes the acts of St. Peter, including Peter's disputation with Simon Magus and St. Clement's recognition of his own father and

[19] Mansi, VIII, cols. 512A-B and XI, col. 567A.

[20] *Patrologia Orientalis*, XIII (Paris, 1919), 188–91. The fragments by John attack Chalcedon and could conceivably come from the work read by Photius.

[21] *RE*, Ioannes 46, at least notes that Photius must be wrong; Beck (393) and Henry (I, 25) have been misled by him.

[22] Photius' mistake does not come from the "Hesychius Epitome," which distinguished the two and noted that both were Lemnians (*Suda*, IV, 734). Though Henry (I, 28 note 1) thinks that Photius has confused Philostratus II with the Philostratus of cod. 150 who supposedly was from Tyre, the work in cod. 150 looks very much like the Ζητούμενα παρὰ τοῖς ῥήτορσι that the *Suda* assigns to Philostratus I.

[23] Henry, III, 88 note 1.

[24] Cod. 212: 170a line 41; cf. cod. 211 and Henry, III, 242.

[25] Cod. 240: 322b line 4; cf. Henry, V, 226.

brothers. Because of this last description, some manuscripts give this whole work on Peter the title, *The Recognition of Clement of Rome.* In some manuscripts the letter to St. James which introduces the work on Peter is attributed to Peter himself, and in others a different letter is given and attributed to Clement, but all the numerous manuscripts which Photius has seen give after the letter the same work, which begins with the words "I, Clement" (Ἐγὼ Κλήμης). Photius compares this work on the acts of Peter to the *Apostolic Constitutions* and finds the *Constitutions* somewhat less heretical than the acts of Peter but much inferior to them in prose style. He concludes with a biographical sketch of Clement, taken from the "Hesychius Epitome."[26]

Though here Photius is obviously alluding to the Pseudo-Clementine literature, it is difficult to determine precisely which of the Pseudo-Clementines he is referring to at which times.[27] I conjecture that Photius has confused the Pseudo-Clementine *Homilies* with the *Recognitions.* Only manuscripts of the *Recognitions,* which now survives solely in the Latin translation of Rufinus of Aquileia, have that title and include the recognition scenes of Clement and his father and brothers; only manuscripts of the *Homilies* contain the introductory letter of Peter to James.[28] But both the *Homilies* and the *Recognitions* begin with the words "I, Clement" (*Ego Clemens* in Rufinus' translation) and the same first few pages of text, as far as the Latin translation can show; both include closely comparable descriptions of the acts of Peter and of his disputation with Simon.[29] Apparently Photius read the *Recognitions* but only glanced at manuscripts of the *Homilies,* whose title he does not mention. Though he noticed the difference in the introductory letters, he concluded from the identical beginnings that the two works were the same throughout and did not continue reading a book that he thought he had already read. This would both be a natural mistake and account for the discrepancies between codex 112-13 and the Pseudo-Clementines as they are preserved.

Finally, though Photius is usually correct when he gives a number for the parts into which a book is divided, three times he gives a

[26] For the parallels to the biographical notice, see Table VII.

[27] Henry (II, 83 and notes 1 and 2) considers the second work mentioned by Photius to be a collection of three works entitled *Acts of St. Peter, Disputations with Simon Magus,* and *Recognition of Clement of Rome;* but this is not supported by the text, which refers to them as one work.

[28] See *Die Pseudoklementinen,* ed. B. Rehm, I, *Homilien,* 2nd ed. (Berlin, 1969), and II, *Rekognitionen* (Berlin, 1965). Rufinus believed that the letter of Clement to James did not belong to the *Recognitions* (see his preface, *ibid.,* II, 4) and translated it separately (*ibid.,* II, 5–22); but it seems to have been in his Greek MS.

[29] *Pseudoklementinen,* I, 23–35, and II, 6–18.

wrong number, as his own descriptions prove. In codex 46, he says that Theodoret's *Eranistes* has three books, but then he describes four books, the number it actually has.[30] He reports in codex 190 that Ptolemaeus Chennus' *New History* had six books, then epitomizes seven.[31] He mentions eight books by Mark the Hermit in codex 200, then summarizes nine.[32] These errors seem to form a pattern. Consider codex 165; here Photius says that Himerius' orations were "about seventy in number," though he has just listed seventy-two, a total that itself leaves out three which he excerpts in codex 243.[33] In all these cases, I suspect that Photius, finding no number for the books or orations in the title of his manuscript, quickly leafed through the text to count them, missing one or more in the process. Such are the different kinds of mistakes in the *Bibliotheca* that can be attributed to Photius himself. They are no doubt the result of haste, but not of excessive carelessness.

This haste must also be the cause of a number of gaps in the *Bibliotheca* which Photius left to be filled in later and then forgot. Not every gap in the text is of this sort; a few are the result of damage to our manuscripts or to their archetype. But when the lacunae are considered all together, such a large majority represent specific facts—numbers, titles, and the like—that they can hardly have been the result of accidental damage.

Six of these lacunae are obviously the result of Photius' working from memory at the time and forgetting certain specific information. In codices 11 and 12, he leaves blank spaces for the numbers of books in Eusebius' *Praeparatio Ecclesiastica* and *Demonstratio Ecclesiastica*. In codices 19 and 20, he omits the numbers of acts of the Sixth and Seventh Ecumenical Councils, and in codex 21 the number of parts in John Philoponus' *On the Resurrection*. None of these codices is longer than six lines in Bekker's edition nor includes anything that Photius would have had to look up besides the numbers. Photius' most striking lapse of memory is at codex 124, where he forgets the title of the last of three works by Epiphanius of Salamis that he had read. The codex reads in full, "There was read by the same author ***" (Ἀνεγνώσθη τοῦ αὐτοῦ ***).[33a]

In some other codices, Photius could not have been working entirely from memory, but he leaves blank spaces nonetheless. He

[30] Cod. 46: 11a lines 6–13.

[31] Cod. 190: 146a line 42, cf. 152b line 26 and 153b line 28.

[32] Cod. 200: 162b line 16, cf. 163a line 19.

[33] Cod. 165: 108b line 29. For a comparative list of Himerius' orations, see the table in A. Colonna, *Himerii Declamationes et Orationes* (Rome, 1951), facing p. x (Colonna's Φ = cod. 243, Φκ = cod. 165).

[33a] Here and later three asterisks denote lacunae in the text.

leaves a gap at the end of codex 216 for the number of books in Oribasius' *Excerpts from Galen,* though he has just quoted the work's whole first paragraph. The easiest explanation is that Photius had the manuscript, intended to leaf through it and count the books later, but forgot to do so. In codex 68, Photius begins to give the numbers of the books and authors cited by the historian Cephalion in the nine books of his *Muses;* but he leaves blanks for the number of works and their authors cited in Books VI through VIII and of the works cited in Book IX, though there he gives a figure for the authors.[34] If, as Henry suggests, Photius' manuscript of Cephalion had lacunae, he would have had no reason to leave gaps that he would be unable to fill later on.[35] I conjecture rather that Cephalion did not number his sources but offered unnumbered lists; Photius began to count these but tired of the task, leaving it to be finished later, perhaps by his secretary.[36] Photius did, however, count the thirty authors cited in Book IX, though not the number of works, which probably ran into the hundreds as it did in the other eight books.

At the end of codex 203, Photius states that he will list the points on which Theodoret's *Commentary on Daniel* disagrees with that of Hippolytus, reviewed in the preceding codex. He then leaves a lacuna, evidently intending to go back and compile the list.[37] At the end of codex 231, gaps indicated in our manuscripts show that Photius had not finished recapitulating the citations from a pro-Chalcedonian anthology but that he did plan to do so.[38] The process of listing examples seems to have particularly bored Photius, because in codex 78 he leaves a blank even for a single example of the style of Malchus of Philadelphia.[39]

At the ends of codices 74 and 85, Photius begins to give biographical sketches of Lesbonax of Mytilene and Heraclianus of Chalcedon, only to stop with the words "This Lesbonax ***" and "This most pious Heraclianus was in the times ***" Because Photius had just used the biography of Themistius from the "Hesychius Epitome" in the preceding paragraph, he presumably intended to complete the

[34] Cod. 68: 34a lines 29–33.

[35] Henry, I, 101 note 1. The few preserved fragments of Cephalion (*FGrHist,* 93) seem to be of no use in solving this problem.

[36] Cf. the long list of authors excerpted by John Stobaeus, cod. 167: 114a line 14–115b line 17.

[37] Henry (III, 103) notes the lacuna in both MSS in his apparatus, but he ignores it in his text, mistranslating the last sentence accordingly. Translate not "ceux que j'ai dits," but "the following: ***."

[38] The lacuna after cod. 231 is one line in A, no gap but the marginal note λείπει in M; see T. Hägg, review of *Photius Bibliothèque,* ed. R. Henry, vols. I–VII, in *Göttingische Gelehrte Anzeigen,* 228 (1976), 41.

[39] Cod. 78: 54b line 41. The lacuna is about eight letters in A.

first lacuna from its biography of Lesbonax, which is preserved in the *Suda.*[40] Photius does not use the "Hesychius Epitome" again until codex 90, apparently leaving this research on codices 74 and 85 to be done later.[41]

The last sentence of codex 168 on Basil of Seleucia seems also to be incomplete: "And other writings by him ***" with a gap of one line in M.[42] Just before this, Photius says that Basil wrote a work "in verse" on St. Thecla, which he makes no claim to have read. Since the work by Basil on St. Thecla that has been preserved is in prose, here Photius seems to have been relying on his imperfect memory of what he had read or heard about this work; to conclude that Basil wrote another, lost and unattested verse work on Thecla is to overvalue this testimony.[43] Though no article on Basil of Seleucia has survived from the "Hesychius Epitome," Photius probably meant to look up more about Basil's works there or elsewhere.

Both manuscripts have considerable lacunae at the ends of codices 219 and 229 which seem to represent whole books that Photius has left out.[44] At the beginning of codex 216, he says, "There were read four books which contain the medical work composed by Oribasius, plus another seven books, by the same man and published in a very similar form."[45] Photius remarks at the beginnings of the codices that codex 216 is the first of these books, 217 the second, 218 the third, and 219 the fourth. In the last part of codex 219 he describes another book, entitled *Euporista,* which was a mere transcription of the fourth book with a different dedication.[46] At the end of this codex comes the lacuna, which was evidently supposed to be filled by

[40] Cod. 74: Οὗτος δὲ ὁ Λεσβῶναξ ***. Cod. 85: Ἦν δ᾽ οὗτος ὁ θεοσεβέστατος Ἡρακλειανὸς κατὰ τοὺς χρόνους ***. Cod. 74: 52a lines 15–21 parallels *Suda,* II, 690–91; *Suda,* III, 252 is on Lesbonax. No biography of Heraclianus from the "Hesychius Epitome" is preserved.

[41] For the uses of the "Hesychius Epitome," see the parallels in Table VII.

[42] Καὶ ἄλλα δὲ αὐτοῦ γράμματα ***. Only the rest of the line is blank in A. The sentence could conceivably be complete, but such an abrupt omission of εἰμί is not typical of Photius. The συγγράμματα φέρονται printed by Bekker is a completion by the scribe A² (see Henry's apparatus) and has no authority.

[43] Cf. Quasten, III, 528, and Henry, II, 221. Neither should Photius be relied on when he says that Hippolytus of Rome was a student of Irenaeus (cod. 121: 94a lines 24–25), which is chronologically possible but unsupported in "Sophronius" or elsewhere; cf. Quasten, II, 164, and Henry, II, 217. Coming after the series of teachers and pupils mentioned in codd. 118, 119, and 120, Photius' statement is a little too tidy.

[44] At the end of cod. 219, 28 lines and 1 folio side in A, 3 lines in M; at the end of cod. 229, 4 lines and 1 page in A, no gap but the marginal note λείπει in M.

[45] Ἀνεγνώσθησαν βιβλία δ´ ἃ τὴν πραγματείαν ἰατρικὴν Ὀρειβασίῳ συντεταγμένην περιεῖχε καὶ ἔτι ἕτερα ζ´ ἀνδρός τε τοῦ αὐτοῦ καὶ εἰς παραπλήσιον ἐξενηνεγμένην τύπον. Cod. 216: lines 173b. 34–37.

[46] Cod. 219: 176b lines 11–15.

reviews of the six remaining "very similar" books by Oribasius. This would fit the description of these codices in the *pinax*: "216, 217, 218, 219. Eleven [4 + 7] books of Oribasius."[47] But Photius seems to have forgotten to go back and add reviews of these six books.

The lacuna at the end of codex 229 is of a similar kind but has caused a further error. Near the beginning of codex 228, Photius says of Ephraem of Amida, "The man thus composed various books, of which three have come to us so far." At the end of the same codex, Photius says, "Thus the first volume that has come into our hands contained these things." Then codex 229 describes another volume of the works of Ephraem. After it is a lacuna, which was presumably left for a codex on the third volume, because codex 230 describes a volume of the works of Eulogius of Alexandria. But near the end of codex 230, Photius concludes his description of a council held by Eulogius with the surprising statement, "And thus he dissolved the council, and with that there end the summary and the proclamation, and the third volume which has come into our hands."[48]

Here Photius has confused Ephraem, Patriarch of Antioch from 527 to 545, with Eulogius, Patriarch of Alexandria from 580 to 607. This was an easy mistake, because in his codices before those on Ephraem Photius had reviewed some anti-Monophysite works by Eulogius that closely resembled Ephraem's. Photius' chronological confusion is evident when he dates Eulogius' council to the seventh year of Marcian (i.e., 457), too early even for Ephraem, rather than to the seventh year of *Maurice* (589/90), which is presumably right.[49]

[47] σις΄, σιζ΄, σιη΄, σιθ΄. Ὀρειβασίου βιβλία ια΄. So M, evidently correctly. The copyist of A has tried to divide the codices and blundered: σιε΄. Ὀρειβασίου. σις΄. Τοῦ αὐτοῦ. σιζ΄. Τοῦ αὐτοῦ. σιη΄. Ὀρειβασίου βιβλία ια΄. (A's numbers are one short here because it has omitted cod. 185). Martini's apparatus is incomplete, and his conjecture ἰα⟨τρικά⟩ is unhappy (*Pinax*, 312 lines 5–6).

[48] Συνέταξε μὲν οὖν ὁ ἀνὴρ διαφόρους βίβλους, ὧν εἰς ἡμᾶς τέως τρεῖς περιῆλθον (cod. 228: 245a lines 28–29). Τὸ μὲν οὖν πρῶτον περιελθὸν εἰς τὰς ἡμετέρας χεῖρας τεῦχος ταῦτα περιεῖχεν (cod. 228: 249a lines 29–30). Καὶ οὕτω τὸν σύλλογον διαλύει, συντελευτώσης αὐτῷ καὶ τῆς ὑποθέσεως καὶ τῆς ἐκφωνήσεως καὶ τοῦ περιελθόντος εἰς τὰς ἡμετέρας χεῖρας τρίτου τεύχους (cod. 230: 285b lines 23–26). The "summary" and "proclamation" refer back to 285a lines 24–26. Henry (V, 62 note 1) is understandably confused by this, "que je traduis tant bien que mal" following a highly creative effort in Schott's Latin translation (PG, 103, col. 1086C).

[49] Cod. 230: 285b lines 13–15; see Henry's apparatus and Henry, V, 206. As the reading of both MSS, Μαρκιανός should be printed in the text. Cod. 230 cannot be assigned to Ephraem, because it repeatedly mentions Eulogius by name and epitomizes a letter from Eulogius to Domitianus of Melitene (280b lines 37–38), who lived from *ca.* 564 to 602 (*Dictionary of Christian Biography,* ed. W. Smith and S. Cheetham [London, 1877–87], Domitianus 15) and to whom Eulogius dedicated the work Photius reviews in cod. 225 (240a lines 20–21). Henry (V, 204–5) has identified this bishop with another Domitianus to whom Ephraem did write (cod. 228: 247a line 21), but, unless something even worse than I suppose has gone wrong in codd. 225–30, the identification is chronologically impossible.

Apparently, Photius, who had spent at least three days composing codices 225–30 on very similar works by Eulogius and Ephraem, lost track of which author had composed which volumes.[50]

Running short of time to work on the *Bibliotheca* before his embassy left, Photius never returned to his text to fill any of these lacunae. But when he told his secretary to leave the gaps in the first place and did not avoid the question or admit ignorance, Photius must have expected to be able to fill them in later. This means that he had in his possession either copies of the original books or extensive notes on them. The notes would have had to be so complete that it was laborious to count lists and sections in them, to find examples of various kinds in them, and to keep their parts in order. They would have had to be at least as long as those transcribed in the second part of the *Bibliotheca* and to have included many specific facts, such as book divisions, which those notes mostly omit. All of this seems quite improbable. On the whole, it seems more likely that Photius had with him complete manuscripts of the books in question.

Such are the factual mistakes and omissions that are attributable to Photius alone, and though the list is doubtless not complete, its relative shortness is to Photius' credit. A few more errors are attributable to Photius' secretary, or rather to misunderstandings between author and secretary for which neither need be blamed. While the secretary was a competent copyist—if he had not been, the *Bibliotheca* would be much more disorganized and corrupted than it is—in the absence of proofreading he made some highly misleading errors.

The first such error seems to occur in codices 9–13, which read as follows in our manuscripts:

> 9. There were read the fifteen books of Eusebius' *Praeparatio Evangelica,* in which he says that he refutes the vain doctrine of the pagans completely and that they disagreed with each other all along. He notes at the beginning of the fifteenth book and at the end of another book, which he entitles *Demonstratio Evangelica* and which is a sequel to the *Praeparatio Evangelica,* that the former is for the most part a refutation of the error of the pagans and the latter is a confirmation of the message of the Gospel.
>
> 10. There was read Eusebius' *Demonstratio Evangelica* in twenty books.
>
> 11. There was read Eusebius' *Praeparatio Ecclesiastica* in *** books, in which there are excerpts.
>
> 12. There was read Eusebius' *Demonstratio Ecclesiastica* in *** books.
>
> 13. There were read Eusebius' two works of refutation and defense, and another two, which, though differing from the first two in certain

[50] On copying time, see pp. 23–25 *supra.* Codd. 225–30 consist of 92 Bekker columns.

respects, in the others are the same both in expression and in content. He brings forward questions on the part of the pagans against our blameless religion and resolves these well, if not in all cases.

Continuing codex 13, Photius notes that Eusebius is a poor stylist, learned but unintelligent and heretical: "Even in these works he can be seen blaspheming against the Son in many places, calling him 'second cause,' 'captain of the host,' and some other excrescences of the Arian madness." Photius concludes with some biographical material on Eusebius, taken from the "Hesychius Epitome," making codex 13 slightly longer than codices 9–12 combined.[51]

The *Praeparatio Evangelica* and the first ten books of the *Demonstratio Evangelica* are preserved, and contain what Photius says they do. Eduard Schwartz has attempted to identify the *Praeparatio Ecclesiastica* with Eusebius' fragmentary *General Elementary Introduction,* because this work contained a section of excerpts from the Prophets (*Eclogae Propheticae*).[52] This identification seems a feeble one, however, because almost all Eusebius' works contain excerpts of one kind or another, while Eusebius repeatedly refers to his *General Elementary Introduction* by that title alone.[53] The *Praeparatio Ecclesiastica* does not seem to be attested anywhere else under that title, and Eusebius' *Demonstratio Ecclesiastica* is mentioned only in one late source.[54] The

[51] θ'. 'Ανεγνώσθη εὐαγγελικῆς προπαρασκευῆς Εὐσεβίου λόγοι ιε', ἐν οἷς ὡς ἐπίπαν τὴν 'Ελλήνων ματαιολογίαν ἐλέγχει, καὶ ὡς ἀσύμφωνοι αὐτοὶ πρὸς ἑαυτοὺς διετέλεσαν. Μέμνηται δὲ ἐν ἀρχῇ τοῦ πεντεκαιδεκάτου λόγου καὶ ἐν τῷ τέλει ἑτέρας πραγματείας, ἣν εὐαγγελικὴν ἀπόδειξιν ἐξονομάζει, ἀκόλουθον οὖσαν τῇ εὐαγγελικῇ προπαρασκευῇ, ὅτι ἡ μὲν ἔλεγχός ἐστι σχεδὸν τῆς 'Ελλήνων πλάνης, ἡ δὲ βεβαίωσις τοῦ κηρύγματος τοῦ εὐαγγελικοῦ.

ι. 'Ανεγνώσθη Εὐσεβίου ἡ εὐαγγελικὴ ἀπόδειξις ἐν βιβλίοις εἴκοσιν.

ια'. 'Ανεγνώσθη Εὐσεβίου ἐκκλησιαστικὴ προπαρασκευὴ ἐν βιβλίοις ***, ἐν οἷς ἐκλογαί.

ιβ'. 'Ανεγνώσθη Εὐσεβίου ἐκκλησιαστικὴ ἀπόδειξις ἐν βιβλίοις ***.

ιγ'. 'Ανεγνώσθη Εὐσεβίου ἐλέγχου καὶ ἀπολογίας λόγοι δύο, καὶ ἕτεροι δύο, οἵτινες πρὸς τοὺς προτέρους δύο ἔν τισι ῥητοῖς παραλλάσσοντες ἐν τοῖς ἄλλοις τῇ τε λέξει καὶ τῇ διανοίᾳ οἱ αὐτοί εἰσιν. Εἰσάγει δὲ ὡς ἀπὸ τῶν 'Ελλήνων τινὰς ἀπορίας κατὰ τῆς ἀμωμήτου θρησκείας ἡμῶν, καὶ ταύτας καλῶς, εἰ μὴ καὶ ἐν πᾶσιν, ἐπιλύεται. ...καὶ γὰρ κἂν τούτοις ἐν πολλοῖς ἔστιν αὐτὸν ἰδεῖν τὸν υἱὸν βλασφημοῦντα, καὶ δεύτερον αἴτιον καλοῦντα καὶ ἀρχιστράτηγον καὶ ἄλλα τινὰ τῆς ἀρειανικῆς λύσσης βλαστήματα. Though Henry indicates a lacuna at the end of cod. 11, it is not indicated in the MSS. For the parallels between the end of cod. 13 and the "Hesychius" texts, see Table VII.

[52] In *RE,* Eusebios 24, col. 1386.

[53] In the surviving parts of the *Introduction* itself (PG, 22, cols. 1120D; 1261B-C; 1272B-C; and 1273A) and in the *Praeparatio,* ed. K. Mras, I (Berlin, 1954), 8.

[54] PG, 119, col. 908D. This is a twelfth-century elaboration of what seems to have been a considerably earlier document; see *Le Patriarcat byzantin,* ser. I, vol. I, fasc. 3 (Istanbul, 1947), no. 991. It is conceivable that the title is a confusion of the *Demonstratio Evangelica* and the *Historia Ecclesiastica,* mentioned just before this in the text.

two editions of the "refutation" and "defense" are considered to be completely lost works, known only from the *Bibliotheca.*[55]

I conjecture that the "refutation" (ἔλεγχος) and "defense" (ἀπολογία) are in fact the *Praeparatio Evangelica* and *Demonstratio Evangelica* themselves, of which the *Praeparatio Ecclesiastica* and *Demonstratio Ecclesiastica* mentioned in the *Bibliotheca* were slightly different editions. In codex 9 Photius refers to these works as a "refutation" (ἔλεγχος) and "confirmation" (βεβαίωσις). The *Praeparatio* and *Demonstratio* treat the very themes attributed in codex 13 to the "refutation" and the "defence," as Schwartz also noticed, suggesting that the works of codex 13 were either earlier or later treatments of material in the *Praeparatio* and *Demonstratio,* or excerpts from them.[56] In addition, the *Praeparatio* and *Demonstratio* contain the references to Christ as "second cause" (δεύτερον αἴτιον) and "captain of the host" (ἀρχιστράτηγος) which Photius condemns in codex 13.[57] As for the "excerpts" mentioned in codex 11, because the *Praeparatio Evangelica* is mostly made up of excerpts from pagan writers, its slightly different edition would also have contained excerpts.[58] It does not necessarily follow that Eusebius himself prepared these other editions of his two works, which Photius is the first to mention. But the supposed six lost works and editions of works by Eusebius in these codices can be reduced to two lost editions of works that are well-known and for the most part preserved.

Evidently Photius first dictated codices 9–12, then dictated codex 13 in such a way as to mislead his secretary. Though in their present form these codices constitute a sort of double recension, Photius probably did not mean simply to cancel codices 9–12, so as to omit the titles of the books altogether. Adding a word such as "Thus" to the beginning of codex 13 and omitting a codex number would have made everything clear. Codices 9–13 would then resemble codex 112–13 on the Pseudo-Clementines and several other combined codices which do not divide up neatly by codex numbers.[59] In a work as long and complicated as the *Bibliotheca,* such a mistake is not surprising, especially at the start, when Photius was not yet accustomed to his process of composition. A similar double recension may

[55] See, e.g., Quasten, III, 334.

[56] *RE,* Eusebios 24, col. 1394.

[57] *Praeparatio, I,* 391 line 12, and II (Berlin, 1956), 34–46 *passim; Demonstratio,* ed. I. Heikel (Berlin, 1913), 206 lines 10 and 38.

[58] Since practically nothing but the *Eclogae Propheticae* survives of the *Introduction,* it cannot be proved that the rest of it was not an edition of the *Praeparatio,* but this seems very improbable.

[59] Cf. codd. 88–89, 109–11, 132–35, 154–55, 172–74, 216–19, and 228–29.

even occur later, where the lexica reviewed in codices 146–48 bear a suspicious resemblance to the multivolume lexicon of codex 145.[60]

Three lacunae also seem to have been left in the process of composition. At the ends of codices 63 and 64, both manuscripts include considerable gaps.[61] Though Photius says in the first sentences of these codices that he read all eight books of Procopius' history and ten of Theophanes', they epitomize only Book I and some of Book II of each work, with the gap presumably left for the rest.[62] Likewise, a considerable gap in manuscript A follows codex 94 on the *Babyloniaca* of Jamblichus.[63] Whereas the *Suda* records that this novel had thirty-nine books, a note at the end of Photius' codex marks the end of only Book XVI, with the gap presumably accounting for the others.[64] If Photius was merely tired of epitomizing these works, however, why did he not simply end the codices, as he did many other partial summaries in the first part of the *Bibliotheca*?

Codices 63, 64, and 94 strongly resemble the codices of the second part. Having demonstrated that codex 63 follows Procopius' *Wars* closely and comprehensively, Hägg concluded that, unlike his other examples of the first part but like all of those from the second, it was composed while Photius read the book.[65] Codices 64 and 94 are similarly comprehensive. The only parts of these three codices that must have been composed for the *Bibliotheca* are the introductions.[66] I therefore conjecture that Photius dictated these prefaces and then, as in the second part, had his secretary copy the epitomes from notes

[60] Thus the lexicon of Helladius of cod. 145 could be identical with the λεξικὸν καθαρᾶς ἰδέας, λεξικὸν σεμνῆς ἰδέας, and λεξικὸν ἰδίως (leg. ἰδέας) λόγου πολιτικοῦ of codd. 146–48. Photius seems to say that Helladius' lexicon existed in five or seven volumes, while the other lexica consisted of, respectively, one, one or three, and three volumes, totaling five or seven. If these lexica were anonymous, one would expect Photius to say so (cf. codd. 115, 116, 117, and 170), but he does not always repeat an author's name if it is the same as in the preceding codex (cf. codd. 104, 144 [just before the codd. in question], and 184). Further, Photius describes all the lexica of codd. 145–48 as voluminous, alphabetical, and useful. Finally, the *Suda*, II, 238 line 6 refers to Helladius' lexicon by the title Λέξεως παντοίας χρῆσις κατὰ στοιχεῖον ("alphabetical usage of all sorts of style"), which could fit the three lexica of codd. 146–48. But the complete loss of Helladius' lexicon makes it impossible to confirm this conjecture.

[61] At the end of cod. 63, 2 lines and 3 cols. in A, 4½ lines and 1 folio side in M; at the end of cod. 64, 15 lines in A, 24 lines in M. Neither lacuna is noted in Henry's apparatus; see Hägg, review (*supra*, note 38), 40–41.

[62] Cod. 63 epitomizes as far as Procopius, *De bellis* II, 19, as a comparison with the text shows. In cod. 64, the beginning of Book II is marked with a β′ at 26b line 31 in both MSS, but not in Henry's edition; see Hägg, review (*supra*, note 38), 58.

[63] The lacuna is 12 lines and 1 col.; see Henry's apparatus.

[64] *Suda*, II, 603 lines 18–21; cf. *Iamblichi Babyloniacorum Reliquiae*, ed. E. Habrich (Leipzig, 1960), 70.

[65] See pp. 88–90 *infra* and notes 31–39.

[66] At cod. 94, the beginning includes a criticism (73b line 24–74a line 3).

taken while reading the books at an earlier time. But in these cases the secretary seems to have copied only a portion of the notes and left a gap for the rest, which he never returned to copy.

Finally, two short blanks were left for a quotation and a proper name among a great many names and quotations in the long codices 229 and 230; these seem likely to have been caused by some kind of confusion in the composition.[67] A few other lacunae must postdate the composition. Only two, one in the middle of a sentence and the other in the middle of a word, seem to represent damage done to the archetype of our manuscripts.[68] A corner missing from the first folio of A and rips in the last few folios of M account for the lacuna in the preface and a few short lacunae near the end of the *Bibliotheca*.[69] Further, four blanks in M and two in A appear to have been left accidentally by copyists.[70]

Besides their intrinsic importance for the history of the books, authors, and subjects that Photius reviews, the mistakes and omissions made by him and his secretary in the first part of the *Bibliotheca* give substantial evidence about the methods of the *Bibliotheca*'s composition. They seem to show that at times he worked from memory or from copies of the books, and sometimes had his secretary copy his notes. A more complete picture of how and when he applied these methods will be attempted in the next chapter.

[67] Cod. 229: 259b line 31; cod. 230: 281b line 5.

[68] At the end of cod. 225 (the copyist of A has probably completed M's ἀναληφ to ἀναληφθέντα on his own initiative) and the end of cod. 244 in the second part.

[69] See Treadgold, "Preface," 343–49.

[70] After cod. 168, 1 line is blank in M; after cod. 175, 2½ lines are blank in A and 1 in M; after cod. 176, 1 line is blank in A (Hägg, review [*supra,* note 38], 41). After cod. 215, 2½ lines are blank in M (Henry's apparatus).

CHAPTER SIX

The Descriptions of the Texts

Among the descriptions of books in the *Bibliotheca* several different types of presentation and methods of composition can be distinguished. The codices after codex 233 all give epitomes and excerpts from their texts and, I have argued, were copied from Photius' reading notes by his secretary without Photius' supervision. The descriptions in the codices as far as 233 differ from these, but they also differ from one another both in their form and in their relation to their original texts. A definitive classification of all these descriptions is impossible, because their types shade into each other and their original texts often have not survived for comparison. A sure explanation of the methods by which each was composed is also impossible; too much guesswork is involved. But, imperfect though it must be, only a classification of the descriptions can clarify how the *Bibliotheca* was composed and how it presents its texts.

Working from the relation of the codices to their subjects, and leaving Photius' criticisms and biographical sketches aside, Tomas Hägg, following Jonas Palm, distinguished three broad categories of descriptions: the "short review" (*Kurzreferat*), "analytical review" (*analytisches Referat*), and "excerpts" (*Exzerpte*). Hägg classified the ten codices on which he concentrated his study as follows: codices 44 and 209 as "short reviews," codices 63 and 238 as "analytical reviews," and codices 236, 237, 241, 243, 245, and 246 as "excerpts."[1] Hägg defined the "short reviews" as brief and free summaries of the originals in Photius' own words, the "analytical reviews" as long epitomes with many literal borrowings and occasional excerpts from the originals, and the "excerpts" as selections of passages from the originals with some transitional passages by Photius. Hägg concluded that Photius had composed the "short reviews" after he had

[1] Hägg, *Photios,* 9; cf. J. Palm, *Über Sprache und Stil des Diodoros von Sizilien: Ein Beitrag zur Beleuchtung der hellenistischen Prosa* (Lund, 1955), 16–26.

read the texts, and the "analytical reviews" and "excerpts" while he read them.[2] These conclusions, however, apply only to the original composition of the epitomes and extracts and not necessarily to their inclusion in the *Bibliotheca.*[3]

In order to distinguish plainly the methods by which the descriptions were included in the *Bibliotheca,* in the present study I have combined two of Hägg's classes and added another class to them. The three different classes that result will be distinguished here by Roman numerals. Class I are the descriptions that, because of their vagueness and liability to error, Photius seems to have composed from memory for the *Bibliotheca.* This class is not represented in Hägg's sample. Class II are the descriptions that Photius seems to have composed for the *Bibliotheca* by referring back to manuscripts of books which he had already read or to notes on them. These correspond to the "short reviews" of Hägg, though a few of them are quite long. Class III are the descriptions that Photius seems to have composed while reading the books. These include both the "analytical reviews" and the "excerpts" of Hägg, which do not differ in this respect. Such descriptions, I have argued, were reading notes taken earlier by Photius and later copied into the *Bibliotheca* by his secretary.[4]

For greater precision, I have divided Classes II and III into subclasses. Class I, which does not need to be subdivided, is completely composed of short and imprecise references to the books. An example of this class is codex 105 on Philo. The first subclass of Class II, Class IIA, also consists of short references, but these are precise and accurate; e.g., codex 29 on Evagrius Scholasticus. Class IIB consists of sets of short references to the different parts of composite works, such as codex 209 on the various orations of Dio of Prusa. In contrast to all these mere references, Class IIC are precise summaries, which give some idea of the contents of the whole book. Codex 44 on Philostratus' *Life of Apollonius* is an example of such a summary. The last subdivision, Class IID, consists of lengthy epitomes which are addressed to Tarasius in the second person, such as codex 222 on Jobius the Monk. Under Class III, Class IIIA are those of Hägg's "analytical reviews" which include additions that Photius composed specifically for the *Bibliotheca,* such as codex 63 on Procopius' *Wars.*

[2] Hägg, *Photios,* 197–203.

[3] As Hägg has written to me in one of his many helpful letters, ". . . that the Procopius codex [cod. 63] was made during the reading of course does not mean that it passed into the *Bibliotheca* at that time—the composition of the *Bibliotheca* is another thing . . . ."

[4] On those in the second part, see Chapter III; on those in the first part, see pp. 79–80 *supra.*

Class IIIB are the rest of the "analytical reviews," which were simply copied by the secretary without Photius; e.g., codex 238 on the *Jewish Antiquities* of Josephus. Finally, Class IIIC are Hägg's "excerpts," all of which seem to have been copied without Photius' supervision—for example, codex 241, again on Philostratus' *Life of Apollonius*. Thus the full number of divisions that I use here is eight.

This classification applies only to the parts of codices which actually describe the texts. If Photius gives a detailed biography of a book's author from the "Hesychius Epitome," this does not prove even that Photius had read the book and has nothing to do with the method that he used to describe its contents. For purposes of classification, codices that cover more than one work are considered work by work, since Photius could have described the different works in different ways. Naturally, some of the descriptions border on two classes so that assigning them to one or the other is a somewhat arbitrary process, particularly when the original text is lost. Still, in order to give some kind of general picture, I have tentatively assigned all the descriptions to one of the eight groups, which I indicate by a I, IIA, IIB, IIC, IID, IIIA, IIIB, or IIIC in the right-hand margin of Table I. Table V is an index to the descriptions by groups. Whenever possible, I have used examples studied by Hägg; more detailed descriptions of these will be found in his book. The total number of classified descriptions, which of course counts each of the double and triple descriptions separately, is an even four hundred.

Class I, the imprecise references that Photius seems to have composed from memory, is represented in Tables I and V by ninety-one descriptions from codex 2 to codex 229. These are often only a sentence giving the author and title, and they never have more than a brief note on the general subject of the book. There are many imprecisions in the titles and the authors' names, a number of outright errors and blank spaces, and never any specific information, such as numbers, which Photius could not have remembered easily. Undoubtably, at least the great majority of these descriptions were composed from memory alone, or, in the case of gaps, never composed because of a lapse of memory.

In codex 105, for example, Photius gives little to compare with two works by Philo besides the titles, which he reports as *Gaius Reproved* and *Flaccus (or Flacco) Reproved.* These must be references to Philo's *Embassy to Gaius* and *Against Flaccus,* also known as *Flaccus Reproved.* Here Photius is evidently working from memory, since he is even unsure of the correct form of Flaccus' name.[5] His criticisms

[5] Cf. Photius' Γάϊος ψεγόμενος and Φλάκκος ἢ Φλάκκων ψεγόμενος with Philo's Πρεσβεία πρὸς Γάϊον and Εἰς Φλάκκον or Φλάκκος ψεγόμενος (see *Philonis Alexandri*

of Philo's style, which he praises for its power and beauty, and of his doctrines, which he disapproves of because they presuppose the Platonic Ideas and other non-Jewish conceptions, are short and general. Most of the codex is a long biographical sketch from the "Hesychius Epitome," which of course indicates nothing about Photius' reading in Philo's own works.[6] Though Photius' criticisms show that he had in fact read these books and the four others by Philo which he refers to vaguely in codices 103 and 104, he seems to have read them a long time before and had neither texts of them nor notes on them when he compiled the *Bibliotheca*.

Class IIA, the precise references, is the first subclass of Class II, the descriptions composed by referring back to texts or notes. IIA includes 104 descriptions from codex 4 to the last sentence of codex 227. Like the imprecise references, these generally consist of just a sentence or two, but these report the authors and titles with precision and accuracy. In particular, if a book is divided into parts, the precise references give the exact number or numbers of them. The few errors in these numbers seem to result not from Photius' misremembering but from his miscounting the parts when he recorded them.[7] Photius does not seem to have had a phenomenal memory for such figures, since he had to leave blanks for them in six codices outside this class.[8] Therefore he probably composed these descriptions either from a reading record or from copies of the original texts. Like the imprecise references of Class I, the precise references can include criticisms, passages from the "Hesychius Epitome" or other outside sources, and a further note or two on the contents. As a rule, however, such notes are taken from just the beginnings and ends of the books.[9]

An example of this kind of reference, codex 29, has already been described as a biographical sketch.[10] This codex accurately reports the profession and home town of Evagrius Scholasticus, as well as the number of books in his history (six) and its chronological limits (from the end of the histories of Socrates and Theodoret to the twelfth

Opera Quae Supersunt, ed. L. Cohn and S. Reiter, VI [Berlin, 1915], 120, apparatus). Photius is evidently trying to give the title (ἐπιγραφή) but misremembering it slightly.

[6] Cod. 105: 86b lines 2–4 may be translated, "He errs in many matters, presupposing the [Platonic] Ideas and writing other things foreign to the Jewish philosophy." Henry's translation (II, 71) fails to make the sense clear. For the parallels in this codex to the "Hesychius" texts, see Table VII.

[7] See pp. 71–72 *supra.*

[8] Numbers are left blank at codd. 11, 12, 19, 20, 21, and 216.

[9] Klinkenberg, 27–28, discusses codd. 27–31 and 66, which are of this class.

[10] See pp. 59–60 *supra.*

year of the Emperor Maurice). This information was presumably gathered from a look at the first and last pages of the book and particularly from its title. Photius also observes that Evagrius' style is not bad, that he is perfectly orthodox, and that he includes some passages on icons.[11] Though these observations are exactly the sort of thing that Photius would have been likely to remember from his reading without the aid of a text or notes, he must have used one of the two to refresh his memory about the bibliographical specifics. Such material, taken exclusively from the book's beginning and end, seems more likely to have come from a glance back at the book than from notes.

Class IIB, the references by parts, is the class of twenty-seven descriptions in codices from 1 to 232. Although these descriptions range in length from a paragraph to about nine Bekker columns, they are rather references than summaries.[12] Referring to each part of collections of letters, orations, or other works with divisions, they tell only the subjects of the various parts and little or nothing of what the author has to say on the subjects. Where these tables of contents can be checked, they are quite accurate. In short, they seem to show the application of the method of the specific references of Class IIA to each part of a book. This could mean either that Photius was working from notes which contained such information or that he had manuscripts of the books from which he consulted the tables of contents or subordinate headings.

An example of this class, codex 209 on the orations of Dio of Prusa, has been studied by Hägg. This codex begins with a biography of Dio from the "Hesychius Epitome" and a favorable to mixed judgment on Dio's style. In the actual description of the orations, which takes up about five Bekker columns, Hägg found that Photius quotes or paraphrases the titles of all eighty orations in their correct order. In some cases, Photius gives only the title, but in the majority he tells something more about the speech and sometimes quotes short portions of the text. Hägg observed that Photius must have referred to the headings of the orations, not just to a table of contents, and concluded that Photius had read the orations some time before he composed the codex but refreshed his memory either by skimming the manuscript or by looking at notes on it.[13] Though Hägg conjectured that two errors in the codex were the result of Photius' mis-

[11] On the icons, cf. Evagrius Scholasticus, *Historia Ecclesiastica* IV.7, ed. J. Bidez and L. Parmentier (London, 1898), 175.

[12] Cod. 232 (Stephen Gobar) is the longest.

[13] Hägg, *Photios,* 160–83, especially 182–83.

reading his notes, the mistakes seem easy to explain without that assumption.[14] The simpler explanation is that Photius returned to the original manuscript, looked at its headings, and passed his eyes over the text.

Class IIC, the precise summaries, is composed of ninety-nine descriptions, the first in codex 3 and the last in codex 233. These summaries vary in length from a paragraph to six Bekker columns, but most are shorter than two Bekker columns.[15] They include the specific information on the author, title, and divisions of the book that are given in the precise references of Class IIA, and they often indicate the divisions in the appropriate places, as do the references by parts of Class IIB.[16] They differ from those two classes in giving a better, though still haphazard, overview of what the author of the book says. Often this is based only on the beginning or on one or two other parts of the book, but at least these parts are summarized in detail, or even quoted.[17]

Of this class, Hägg has studied codex 44, the first of the two codices on Philostratus' *Life of Apollonius of Tyana.* After giving the correct title and number of books (eight), and praising Philostratus' style in one sentence, Photius summarizes the book in a little over one Bekker column. He briefly describes what Philostratus says, first about Apollonius' life, then about his beliefs, and finally about his miracles, which Photius ridicules. Hägg found that this summary ranges over the whole work but includes only a few subjects that interested Photius. It follows the order of the text, but only within each subject, and is accurate even in detail, with one minor exception. Though Photius' wording is mostly his own, he has taken over a few words from the original.[18] As with codex 209 on Dio, Hägg concluded that Photius had composed codex 44 some time after having read the book but had refreshed his memory either from notes or by looking over the manuscript again.[19] Although Hägg preferred the former alternative, the freedom with which Photius cites subjects and quotes words suggests rather that he had the whole text in front of him. He

[14] Hägg, Photios, 170. I suspect that the mistake at Oration 18 was a corruption in Photius' MS, that at Oration 19 simply a misreading of the text by Photius.

[15] Only cod. 166 (Antonius Diogenes) and cod. 187 (Nicomachus of Gerasa) are longer than four Bekker columns.

[16] Cod. 192A first gives a summary of the preface of Maximus Confessor's *Questions to Thalassius,* then a table of contents of the type of Class IIB.

[17] Klinkenberg, 28–34, discusses codd. 76, 71, 79, 88, 47, and (at length) 57, which are all of this class.

[18] On the whole codex, see Hägg, *Photios,* 15–24 and 119–22. At 10a lines 6–9, Photius reports that the soul of King Amasis of Egypt inhabited a lion as a punishment for the King's sins, though Philostratus does not mention this edifying reason.

[19] Hägg, *Photios,* 193–94.

certainly did not use the long notes on the same book that were transcribed in codex 241, whose independence from codex 44 Hägg has amply demonstrated.[20] I therefore conjecture that Photius, after reading Philostratus and taking those notes, returned to the text when he prepared codex 44 for the *Bibliotheca*.

As Hägg has convincingly argued, Photius probably composed all the references and summaries classified so far after he had read the books, and not during the reading, as he did the notes that were transcribed for the codices after 233. But the codices up to 233 include twenty-two descriptions that are more than references or summaries and reproduce their texts at lengths comparable to those of the codices of the second part, ranging from nine to fifty-four Bekker columns.[21] These descriptions could have been composed in two possible ways. First, Photius could have dictated from his texts or notes at the time the *Bibliotheca* was compiled, but more extensively than he did in his references and summaries. Second, he could have given his reading notes to his secretary to copy, as he did in the second half of the *Bibliotheca*—though here he would have had to dictate at least the beginnings of the codices for the occasion, since they tell what he had read and display none of the peculiarities of the second part. While there are signs that Photius used both methods for different codices of the first part, to distinguish those composed by each method is a treacherous undertaking. Accordingly, several of my assignments of descriptions between the next two classes—IID and IIIA—are very tentative.

Class IID, the epitomes apparently addressed to Tarasius, includes perhaps thirteen descriptions from codex 92 to codex 230. Because codices 186, 228, and 229 include both epitomes of this type and precise summaries of works that were bound in the same volumes with them, this class seems to be closely related to Class IIC. In codex 186, where Photius says that he is "almost transcribing" his text, he implies that he had the manuscript before his eyes.[22] Moreover, five of these codices have commentary by Photius that he addresses to Tarasius in the second person.[23] Strikingly, the originals of all but

[20] Hägg, *Photios*, 15–42, especially 39–41.

[21] These descriptions are listed as Classes IID and IIIA in Tables I and V. The shortest is cod. 92 (Arrian's *After Alexander*), the longest cod. 222 (Jobius the Monk). I do not count the lengths of codd. 63, 64, 94, and 225, which end in lacunae and would be much longer if they were completed in anything like their original proportions.

[22] . . . μικροῦ μεταγράφειν . . . (cod. 186; 131b line 19).

[23] Codd. 222, 223, 225, 229, and 230; for the references, see p. 40 notes 9 and 10 *supra*.

one of these thirteen descriptions are lost.[24] The reason is probably that Photius, who in his preface tells Tarasius that he has treated summarily books that Tarasius had probably seen, described at length for him books that were very rare in his day and are lost altogether in ours.

Because it is particularly doubtful whether the only one of these codices with a surviving original was addressed to Tarasius, I shall take as an example codex 222, on Jobius the Monk's lost *On the Incarnation.*[25] At fifty-four Bekker columns, this is technically the longest codex in the *Bibliotheca.*[26] Photius must have read the treatise before he composed the beginning of the codex, where he says that Jobius has chosen excellent questions to answer and that he has answered some well but others superficially; Photius then illustrates these judgments in the rest of the codex.[27] He epitomizes each of the forty-five chapters in the work's nine books, labeling each division as he goes along. To judge from the accuracy with which he reproduces Jobius' Scriptural quotations, Photius followed his original closely.[28] Eight times in his epitome he addresses comments to Tarasius, usually calling his attention to an observation of Jobius' that seemed particularly apt.[29] Despite its length, therefore, codex 222 was evidently dictated for Tarasius from Photius' manuscript or notes, just as the precise references and summaries were. Notes, however, seem much less likely than a manuscript, because if Photius had had notes he could have saved himself some two days' work by having his secretary copy them. This guess is confirmed by the fact that in his later *Amphilochia* Photius gives more complete extracts from two parts of Jobius' treatise.[30] This was evidently a book that Photius owned.

Class IIIA, the first of the classes probably copied from notes, are the epitomes that seem not to be addressed to Tarasius. These include

[24] Only the original of cod. 96 (George of Alexandria) is preserved; some fragments survive for codd. 92 (Arrian's *After Alexander*) and 222 (Jobius the Monk). Cod. 96 includes only a little commentary at its end (83b lines 19–21) and could also reasonably be assigned to Class IIIA.

[25] I am inclined to agree with Henry (III, 245) that the scraps in PG, 86, cols. 3313A–20C are parts of a description of the work, not of the original. I have found them of no use in my analysis here. For fragments of Jobius in the *Amphilochia,* see note 30 *infra.*

[26] But if cod. 247–48 had not been mistakenly divided by the secretary (see p. 47 *supra*), it would be longer, with over 58 Bekker columns.

[27] Cod. 222, 181a line 39–181b line 4. A passage in which Photius likes Jobius' formulation of a problem but not his solution is discussed below, pp. 105–6.

[28] Cf. the notes to Henry's edition. Henry has omitted the first ten divisions from his text, though they are found in both MSS.

[29] For the references, see p. 40 note 9 *supra.*

[30] *Amphilochia,* PG, 101, no. 188, cols. 909A–913B and no. 191, cols. 924C–929B.

perhaps nineteen descriptions in codices from 63 to 268, the only ones in the second part being Photius' extracts from the lost history of the ten Attic orators. I have already suggested that the gaps which end codices 63, 64, and 94 are the result of the secretary's failing to finish copying Photius' notes.[31] Further, four codices of this class are the only ones in the first part in which Photius uses Ὅτι to introduce his own words, in the manner of his notes that are transcribed in the second part.[32] The beginnings of these codices, five of which even include stylistic criticisms, seem to be of the ordinary kind and were presumably composed for the *Bibliotheca*.[33] But nowhere else in these very long codices is there any commentary by Photius, much less any addressed to Tarasius. I have already conjectured that codices 259-68 on the ten orators were notes that Photius had taken on his lost history which were copied by the secretary after Photius had dictated new introductions for them.[34] Therefore, descriptions of this class in both parts seem to come from Photius' notes.

Hägg has studied one of the descriptions of this class, codex 63 on Procopius' *Wars,* which he classified along with the second-part codex 238 as a type "between reviewing and excerpting." Codex 63 is only nine Bekker columns long, but it ends in a gap after covering only one and a half of the eight books of the *Wars* which it announces at the beginning. If it had continued epitomizing in the same proportion, about 1:20, it would have extended to nearly fifty Bekker columns. This proportion is comparable to those of the "excerpts" that Hägg studied, which range from 1:3 to 1:50.[35] Codex 63 includes only one long textual excerpt, but many excerpted words and phrases, along with summarizing by Photius that follows the original text closely. Comparing this codex to a "pure" excerpt-codex, Hägg summed up the difference: "literal excerpts with short introductions from Plutarch, a compressed epitome with isolated pure excerpts

[31] See pp. 79–80 *supra*.

[32] This usage appears 18 times: cod. 63; 24b line 27; cod. 72: 47a line 11, 49b line 5; cod. 80: 57b line 1, 58b line 35, 60a line 23, 60b line 6, 61a line 12, 62a line 1, 62a line 9, 62a line 27, 63b line 5; cod. 190: 146a line 36, 151b line 9. Cod. 3: 2b line 35, where the usage appears in A only, is probably just a copyist's confusion. Klinkenberg (pp. 44–45) explained this usage in cod. 80 by supposing that Photius is quoting chapter headings in his MS of Olympiodorus, but this is an *ad hoc* solution that cannot cover the other 25 codices with this construction.

[33] The criticisms begin cod. 65, the second description in cod. 72 (45a lines 5–19), and codd. 80, 94, and 190. Cod. 65 could also reasonably be assigned to Class IID.

[34] See pp. 48–51 *supra*. Note that these ten codices do not come from notes on the orations themselves. The introductions give specific information only on the orations of Andocides (cod. 261) and the orations and letters of Aeschines (cod. 264), the latter of which is mentioned in a precise reference in cod. 61.

[35] Hägg, *Photios,* 142; cf. *ibid.,* 184.

from Procopius."[36] Hägg concluded that Photius had composed both types during his reading of the books.[37] Though Hägg found that Ὅτι is used without consistency in this codex, he did not specifically mention the one passage in which it introduces Photius' words: *Ὅτι* ἐν τῷ δευτέρῳ λόγῳ διέξεισιν ὅπως. . . (*That* in the second book he [sc. Procopius] narrates how . . .).[38] This is clearly the usage of Ὅτι that characterizes the transcribed notes of the second part.[39] Thus the epitome in codex 63 probably was composed when Photius originally read Procopius, but some time before he composed the *Bibliotheca*; that Photius decided to read Procopius while he was composing his work for Tarasius seems improbable.

Class IIIB, the epitomes copied without Photius' supervision, is practically indistinguishable from Class IIIA, except for beginning with the peculiar introductions in Ἀνεγνώσθη ἐκ. Nineteen descriptions belong to this class, the first in codex 238 and the last in codex 279. The longest is over thirty-two Bekker columns and ends in a lacuna that appears to have been the result of damage to the archetype; the shortest five are a sentence or less.[40] Of these nineteen, twelve begin with Ἀνεγνώσθη ἐκ, two have subordinate headings, and ten have remarks by Photius introduced by Ὅτι.[41] I have included in this class the five short references to works by Egyptian poets that were bound in the same volume with Helladius' *Chrestomathiae* in codex 279, because they presumably formed part of Photius' notes on Helladius.

Among this class, Hägg found codex 238, on Josephus' *Jewish Antiquities*, similar in method to codex 63.[42] The principal difference is that at the beginning of codex 238 Photius observes that his selection (ἐκλογή) covers only the part of Josephus' work that concerns Herod the Great: Books XIV through XX. The proportion of epitome to original, as in codex 63, is about 1:20. As I have already argued, all the codices in this class were entirely copied by the secretary from notes that Photius had made earlier while he read the books.

Class IIIC, the selections of excerpts, includes twenty-eight de-

[36] Hägg, *Photios*, 193, and, on the whole codex, 185–92.

[37] *Ibid.*, 193–94.

[38] *Ibid.*, 185; cod. 63; 24b line 27.

[39] See p. 44 *supra*.

[40] The longest is cod. 244 (Diodorus Siculus); the five shortest are at the end of cod. 279 (Egyptian poets). On the lacuna at the end of cod. 244, see p. 80 and note 68 *supra*. Aside from the five references at the end of cod. 279, the shortest is cod. 254 (*Martyrdom of Timothy*), about a Bekker column.

[41] All but codd. 238 and 252 have ἐκ, codd. 244 and 278 have subordinate headings, and all but codd. 239, 252, 255, and 278 have the peculiar Ὅτι. Cf. the complete list of descriptions of this class in Table V.

[42] Hägg, *Photios*, 192.

scriptions in twenty-two codices—the first, codex 234 and the last, 280. These descriptions differ from Class IIIB only in being more literal and less coherent. They vary in length from the accidentally divided codex 247–48, with fifty-eight Bekker columns, to codex 270, a bit less than one Bekker column. Sixteen of these twenty-two codices begin with Ἀνεγνώσθη ἐκ, fourteen have subordinate headings, and eleven have the Ὅτι before Photius' words.[43] As has already been noted, this class presents literal or almost literal excerpts, often joined by short summarizing passages. Photius uses the same words for these selections as for those of Class IIIB, most commonly the word ἐκλογή.[44]

Among his six examples of this class, Hägg described codex 241, the second codex on Philostratus' *Life of Apollonius,* in the most detail. This codex is a little less than twenty-three Bekker columns long, with the last ten or so columns introduced by the heading, "From the same *Life*: whatever was put aside as distinguished by beauty of words and composition."[45] Hägg found that this heading separates two series of excerpts, each covering the whole work and each in almost exactly the order of the original. Those of the first series, which Hägg called "substantive excerpts" (*Sachexzerpte*), omit almost all the facts about Apollonius and give extracts and some summarizing on the geography and ethnography of India, Spain, and Ethiopia, with a few quotable sayings by Apollonius thrown in. These evidently interested Photius more than the beliefs, virtues, and exploits of Apollonius, which are dismissed in a disdainful note.[46] The excerpts after the heading Hägg called "stylistic excerpts" (*Stilexzerpte*). These are very short samples of Philostratus' style, quoted out of context and often in incomplete sentences.[47] Though Hägg thought that Photius had composed the substantive excerpts during his original reading and the stylistic excerpts while looking over the manuscript after the reading, Photius' heading could also mean that he had taken both kinds of notes on different pages during the same reading.[48] Therefore Photius sometimes took notes in different ways

[43] All but codd. 246, 249, 250, 251, 275, and 280 have the ἐκ. Codd. 234, 241, 242, 243, 245, 247–48, 250, 251, 271, 274, 275, 276, 277, and 280 have subordinate headings, and codd. 234, 235, 237, 241, 242, 245, 249, 250, 271, 277, and 280 have the peculiar Ὅτι. For these purposes I count cod. 247–48 as one codex. Cf. the complete list of descriptions of Class IIIC in Table V.

[44] For the references, see p. 46 note 35.

[45] Ἐκ τοῦ αὐτοῦ βίου ὅσα παρεῖται κάλλει ῥημάτων καὶ συνθήκης διαλάμποντα (331a lines 38–39).

[46] 328a lines 18–20. Hägg, *Photios,* 24–35.

[47] *Ibid.*, 35–39.

[48] Of course, the notes themselves may also have been dictated in the first place.

according to his interests. While he seems to have included only notes of the more coherent kind in the first part of the *Bibliotheca* (Class IIIA), he let even very rough notes be copied for the second part, e.g., those on Damascius' *Life of Isidore* in codex 242.

The question remains whether the descriptions in Class II were composed from notes, from the original manuscripts, or from a combination of the two methods. Evidently Photius did have his reading notes on hand when the *Bibliotheca* was compiled, because they were used for Class III. At the same time, Photius certainly had many books of his own. In two letters that date from his first exile, Photius complains bitterly that he has been deprived of his much-prized library.[49] In a passage from his *Amphilochia,* quoted above, Photius laments that he has had to compose his answer to a question from notes because the books on which he had depended have been taken away.[50] Nicetas the Paphlagonian, speaking of the time before Photius' first patriarchate, says of Photius, "Everything joined in him—natural aptitude, application, wealth—to make every book flow to him also." Nicetas then rails against him for his "hard-to-count swarm of books" with anti-intellectual indignation.[51] This large private library is the first place one would expect Photius to turn to refresh his memory about his reading.

Most of the specific information in the descriptions of Class II is of exactly the sort that a man would find by picking up each volume and giving it a cursory look: the author, the title, the dedication, the number of parts in the work, the number of works in the volume, the table of contents, the chapter headings, and a few facts from the first page, the last page, or a page in the middle to which he happened to open the book. This is not, however, the information from all over the book that one would expect from notes taken during a complete reading. In fact, the reading notes that Photius had his secretary copy for the *Bibliotheca* mostly pass over such bibliographical details and give substantive facts or quotable phrases.

This does not mean, of course, that Photius had not read the books that he describes in Classes IIA, IIB, and IIC, whose general style and content he usually indicates faithfully enough, but only that he had read most of them some time ago and had only the texts, and no notes, to refresh his memory about them. Because Photius

[49] *Letters,* no. 211, p. 526; no. 218, pp. 531-32; cf. also *Amphilochia,* PG, 101, no. 180, col. 880B.

[50] See p. 39 *supra.*

[51] Πάντα γὰρ συνέτρεχεν ἐπ' αὐτῷ, ἡ ἐπιτηδειότης τῆς φύσεως, ἡ σπουδή, ὁ πλοῦτος, δι' ὃν καὶ βίβλος ἐπ' αὐτὸν ἔρρει πᾶσα. Nicetas Paphlago, PG, 105, col. 509B. . . . ὁ δυσαρίθμητος τῶν βιβλίων ἑσμός . . . (*ibid.,* col. 532D).

had little reason to bother dictating material that was in his notes and ready to be copied, Class IID would also seem to be descriptions of books for which Photius had no notes; thus he had to compose epitomes for Tarasius from his manuscripts. As a general rule, therefore, though it would be rash to say always, the descriptions in Classes IIA, IIB, IIC, and IID were probably composed from Photius' own books.

If this explanation is fundamentally sound, Photius would have had to own a minimum of about 150 volumes, many containing several works bound together.[52] This figure would include the "Hesychius Epitome," probably a few mislaid books which he expected to find and use to fill blanks in some codices, and some school texts and volumes of Scripture which he left out of the *Bibliotheca.*[53] Admittedly, this would have been an enormous library by Byzantine standards. Among the small number of other private libraries that have been identified, the best-attested and probably the largest is that of the provincial magnate Eustathius Boilas, who died in 1059, leaving a will that lists some seventy-eight volumes among his bequests.[54] And Boilas was a wealthy man; even noted scholars like Arethas of Patras seem to have owned fewer books.[55] But Photius, as few if any other private citizens did, combined the resources of a rich man with the interests of a scholar. That he owned 150 or more volumes, even at age thirty-five, is certainly not impossible, and, given what Nicetas says, even seems likely.[56]

Naturally, Photius need not have owned the books that he described from memory or from his notes; these he had probably bor-

[52] The number of *works* in all of Class II is 243 by my count. From what Photius says of how they were bound, this would be about 150 volumes, probably over half the volumes described in the *Bibliotheca.*

[53] On the school texts, see pp. 6–7 *supra.*

[54] Sp. Vryonis, "The Will of a Provincial Magnate, Eustathius Boilas (1059)," *DOP,* 11 (1957), 269–70.

[55] N. G. Wilson, "Books and Readers in Byzantium," *Byzantine Books and Bookmen,* (Washington, D.C., 1975), 7-8. But I cannot accept Wilson's apparent assumption that the 24 volumes that survive from Arethas' library are all that ever existed.

[56] According to Mango's valuation ("Books," 39) 150 books would have cost about $450,000 in 1971 dollars (3,000 nomismata). This does not seem beyond the means of a wealthy Byzantine of the ninth century; the *Strategi* of the Anatolic, Armeniac, and Thracesian Themes made almost that much in a year (40 pounds of gold = 2,880 nomismata; see Bury, *Eastern Roman Empire,* 225 note 2). Further, Photius probably inherited a number of books from his wealthy and educated father. What became of Photius' library is an interesting problem. The fact that we cannot identify any surviving books from it (Lemerle, *Humanisme,* 190–91), combined with the fact that so many of the texts that seem to have been in it are lost, suggests to me that Photius' books were somehow destroyed as a collection. But how or when this could have happened, except that it was no earlier than his first exile, I would not venture to guess.

rowed or read in other libraries.[57] But the double reviews seem to show that he had taken notes on eleven books that he owned, five of which form a special section in the second part, codices 240-44. Though he presumably took such notes for purposes of reference, substantial differences in content prove that no second-part description could have been used to compose any description in the first part.[58]

The five double reviews that occur within the first part are not hard to explain. In four cases, Photius seems to have picked up again a book that he had already used for a review and absent-mindedly dictated another review from it.[59] In the other case, St. Basil's *Ascetica,* he seems first to have dictated codex 144 from memory and then to have found the book and dictated codex 191 from it. Thus, that Photius used his memory or notes to review a book does not always mean that he did not own it.

The references to books in Photius' later writings show how he continued to consult the books that he owned and even some of his reading notes. In his letters and the *Amphilochia,* Photius quotes or paraphrases ten books that are also described in the *Bibliotheca.* Of these, seven are of Class II, for which Photius probably owned the books.[60] As noted above, the excerpts in the *Amphilochia* from two more books are textually identical with excerpts from them in the *Bibliotheca;* here Photius simply had his notes copied once again.[61] Though the last book quoted in Photius' later works, Theodoret's *Commentary on the Octateuch,* seems to be reviewed from memory in

[57] The suggestion of Mango ("Books," 43) that Photius used the Patriarchal Library is possible but does not seem to be demonstrable. The writings of the iconoclasts were deposited there, but Photius does not review any of those. The one heretical book reviewed by Photius which Mango cites (cod. 114 on Pseudo-Leucius Charinus) was ordered to be *burned,* not put in the Patriarchal Library.

[58] Note that John Philoponus' *On the Hexameron* and Philostratus' *Life of Apollonius* appear one after another in codd. 43 and 44, and again in codd. 240 and 241; similarly, Agatharchides' *On the Red Sea* and Hierocles' *On Providence* appear one after another in codd. 213 and 214, and again in codd. 250 and 251. I conclude from this that Photius owned each pair bound together in one volume, and consulted and took notes on them together.

[59] Codd. 15 (=88), 49 (=169), 182 (=208), and 185 (=211). Though Photius lists 100 chapters of Dionysius of Aegeae in cod. 181 and 50 propositions in cod. 211, he makes it clear in both codices that his MS had 100 chapters (cod. 211: 168b lines 23–24), which he resolved into 50 propositions and their contraries in cod. 211. Because five of the original chapters had no corresponding contraries, Photius had to omit five to arrive at the number 50 in cod. 211; but this need not mean that Photius had two MSS of this book. It must have been very rare, since it is known only from him.

[60] Of Class IIA, cod. 31 (Theodoret's *History*); of Class IIB, cod. 232 (Stephen Gobar); of Class IIC, codd. 112-13[1] (*Apostolic Constitutions*), 52 (Council of Side), 182 and 208 (Eulogius' *On Dispensation*), and 195 (Maximus Confessor's *To Marinus*); of Class IID, cod. 222 (Jobius the Monk). For the references, see Table VI.

[61] See pp. 38–39 *supra.*

the *Bibliotheca,* Photius could have mislaid it then or have acquired it after he had composed the *Bibliotheca.*[62]

Mango has identified ten sources of the homilies that Photius delivered in 867 on the Arian heresy. Though two of these are not mentioned in the *Bibliotheca* and had presumably not yet been read when it was composed, eight of them are reviewed in codices. Of these eight sources, five are described in classes for which Photius probably owned the books. The parallels that Mango has found between the homilies and the other three works appeared in the notes that were transcribed in codices 256, 257, and 258, which Photius would naturally have kept and continued to use.[63] Consequently, such correspondence as there is between the *Bibliotheca* and Photius' later writings seems to be due less to his remembering his earlier reading than to his referring back to the texts and notes that he still possessed.

Although I believe that these explanations of the composition of Classes I, II, and III are correct in general, they may well have gone wrong in various specific cases. While Photius seems to have composed the bulk of the descriptions of Class II with copies of the books at hand, a more thorough study than I have made might well show that some are different from the rest in ways that would make it probable that they were composed from notes. The most likely candidates are among the summaries of Class IIC, some of which are considerably more careful than others. Then too, certain of my assignments of descriptions to one class or another are doubtful, since it is sometimes hard to tell whether Photius could have composed a given description from memory or not, or whether a given description was transcribed from notes or composed specifically for the *Bibliotheca.* But such adjustments would not greatly alter the theory I propose.

This is, in sum, as follows. When Photius received his brother's request, he sat down with his secretary among his books, picked up a volume, and began to dictate with the text before his eyes. Besides dictating from books he owned, he also dictated from memory on other books. From time to time, he consulted his "Hesychius Epit-

[62] Cod. 204. Besides these, in his later works Photius seems only to be remembering St. Basil's letters (cod. 143) and Demosthenes' orations (cod. 265). For the references, see Table VI.

[63] *Homilies,* 237 and notes to 244-78. The codices are 15 (Gelasius), 28 (Socrates), 30 (Sozomen), and 31 (Theodoret) of Class IIA; 40 (Philostorgius) and 88 (Gelasius again) of Class IIC; and 256 (*Life of Metrophanes and Alexander*), 257 (*Life of Paul of Constantinople*), and 258 (*Life of Athanasius*) of Class IIIB. Athanasius' *Apologia Contra Arianos* and *De Synodis* seem to be sources of the homilies but are not reviewed in the *Bibliotheca.*

ome" on the authors. He also had his file of reading notes beside him, from which, after dictating an appropriate beginning, he sometimes had the secretary copy a codex. The order in which Photius kept his books, the associations of his memory, and his own choice would have determined the order of the codices. Beginning with codex 222, Photius dictated several particularly long descriptions for Tarasius. But after codex 233, he simply left the remainder of his file of notes to be copied by the secretary. In all, Photius probably dictated a little less than half the work, and had his secretary copy the rest without him.

CHAPTER SEVEN

Photius' Literary Interests

Photius was interested in nearly everything. Nicetas the Paphlagonian, meaning no compliment, observes that before 858 Photius was famous for his learning "in grammar and in poetry, in rhetoric and in philosophy, and even in medicine, and in nearly every secular discipline. . . ."[1] This is the breadth of interest that appears in the *Bibliotheca,* minus the material in standard texts that Photius deliberately omitted, plus much theological knowledge that Nicetas was reluctant to record to Photius' credit. Though naturally Photius was not equally interested in everything, it would be dangerous to assert that there was any branch of learning that did not interest him at all.

Because Photius' reading must have been determined less by what he found interesting than by what he was able to find to read, the number of titles in the *Bibliotheca* on different subjects is not a reliable indication of his interest in them. Neither are his criticisms necessarily a reliable guide. He could, and apparently did, criticize the style and presentation of books on subjects which interested him greatly and praise the style and presentation of books on subjects that interested him much less. A better guide is the amount of space that the *Bibliotheca* devotes to certain subjects, because Photius would hardly have noted down at length material that he did not find interesting. On the other hand, cursory treatment need not mean that Photius did not care for the subject; it *could* mean only that he was working from memory or in haste, or thought that Tarasius would already have read the book. The best evidence that Photius was interested in a subject is his explicit expression of interest in it,

[1] Γραμματικῆς μὲν γὰρ καὶ ποιήσεως, ῥητορικῆς τε καὶ φιλοσοφίας, ναὶ δὴ καὶ ἰατρικῆς, καὶ πάσης ὀλίγου δεῖν ἐπιστήμης τῶν θύραθεν . . . Nicetas Paphlago, PG, 105, col. 509B. Nicetas considered this learning too worldly. On Nicetas himself, see R. Jenkins, "A Note on Nicetas David Paphlago and the *Vita Ignatii,*" *DOP,* 19 (1965), 241–47.

and especially his making one of his relatively few extended comments on it.

Of Photius' interests, the one most readily apparent from the pages of the *Bibliotheca* is his interest in books, which Nicetas says "made every book flow to him."[2] To judge from the sixteen times that Photius lists books or parts of books which he has not found—"as yet," he adds in half the cases—he was always looking for books.[3] Sometimes the *Bibliotheca* almost takes on the character of a book collector's inventory of his findings. For example, Photius notes in codex 176 that Books VI, VII, XXIX, and XXX of Theopompus' *Philippica* are lost, as ancient authorities say, "but a certain Menophanes (the man is an ancient and not to be lightly dismissed), writing on Theopompus, says that the twelfth book is also lost; yet *we* have read it along with the others." Photius goes on to devote a column in Bekker's edition to summarizing Book XII; he concludes proudly, "These are the things included in the twelfth book, lost to Menophanes."[4]

Likewise, Photius explains in codex 40 how, shortly after reading a volume containing six books of Philostorgius' ecclesiastical history, he found another volume containing six books to complete the set, with the first letters of the twelve books forming an acrostic of the author's name.[5] As we have already seen, Photius also made an epitome of the whole twelve books which is preserved outside the *Bibliotheca*.[6] In other codices, Photius records that he had found more than one manuscript of a number of works.[7] He often mentions which of his books were large or small and which were multivolume or bound together with other works, though, somewhat surprisingly, he describes only three books as "old." No doubt many of the books that Photius read were "new"—that is, copied in minuscule after it was invented at the end of the previous century—and a number of them may well have been copied for Photius himself.[8]

[2] See p. 92 note 51 *supra*.

[3] The list of citations of books that Photius had not seen is the same as that of those that he had not read cited on p. 68 note 7 *supra*, excepting codd. 97, 158, and 268; Photius adds "as yet" in codd. 14, 35, 58, 213, 224, 228, 261, and 273.

[4] . . . Μηνοφάνης δέ τις τὰ περὶ Θεοπόμπου διεξιών (ἀρχαῖος δὲ καὶ οὐκ εὐκαταφρόνητος ὁ ἀνήρ) καὶ τὴν δωδεκάτην συνδιαπεπτωκέναι λέγει· καίτοι αὐτὴν ἡμεῖς ταῖς ἄλλαις συνανέγνωμεν (cod. 176: 120a lines 11–14). Ἃ μὲν οὖν ὁ ἠφανισμένος Μηνοφάνει δωδέκατος λόγος περιέχει, ταῦτά ἐστιν (cod. 176: 120b lines 17–18).

[5] Cod. 40: 8b lines 27–28.

[6] See p. 39 *supra*.

[7] Codd. 48: 11b lines 14–16, 88: 66b lines 30–33, 111: 89b lines 22–27, 112–13: 90a lines 18–21, 178: 124a lines 12–13, 199: 162b lines 6–11, and 200: 163a lines 23–27.

[8] He mentions two "old" books at cod. 77: 54a lines 36–37 (Eunapius of Sardis), and another at cod. 111: 89b line 22 (Clement of Alexandria). On the minuscule hand, see Lemerle, *Humanisme*, 109–28.

Photius has much to say in codex 187 about his discovery of the "celebrated and hard to find" *Arithmetical Theology* of Nicomachus of Gerasa. This was, he says, "a title suited to astonish and to excite a keen desire, but the treatise—not to call it a work of computations that are based on air and are a waste of time—falls far short of its title."[9] At the end of the codex, Photius observes to Tarasius that the books that have been lost over the course of time include both useful and useless ones; "and even the treatise of Nicomachus would have profited by its being generally believed to have been destroyed among many useful things. It does exist, however, and is studied, shearing itself of no small renown. . . ."[10] Though Photius passes this harsh judgment on Nicomachus' catalogue of identifications of pagan gods with numbers, he devotes more than four Bekker columns to summarizing and disparaging it. The work did have its points, he says, because it presupposed an acquaintance with the subtleties of geometry, arithmetic, and astronomy, and even with music and musical instruments.[11] In short, despite his objections to the book, Photius was taken with its subject, which was practically pure erudition.

The length of this codex on Nicomachus shows that Photius could give an extended review of a book even if he found it mediocre, as long as he was interested in the subject. If the length of his reviewing is any guide, the fact that he devotes 57% of the bulk of the *Bibliotheca* to secular books must be significant, especially because only 38% of the titles are secular. Even this high proportion of secular material may have been lowered by Photius to fit Tarasius' tastes; only 48% of the first part of the *Bibliotheca* is secular, compared to an astonishing 67 percent of the reading notes that were copied for the second part. Apparently Nicetas had some justification for emphasizing that Photius' learning was largely profane. By contrast, only eight of the seventy-eight books in Eustathius Boilas' library were not religious, though Boilas, like Photius before 858, was a layman.[12] At the time Photius compiled the *Bibliotheca,* then, his scholarly interests were not primarily theological.

[9] . . . πολυθρύλητος καὶ δυσεύρετος . . . (Cod. 187: 145a lines 31–32). Ἡ μὲν οὖν ἐπιγραφὴ οὕτω θαυμάσαι καὶ δριμὺν ἔρωτα κινῆσαι ἀξία, ὁ δὲ πόνος, ἵνα μὴ λέγω λογισμῶν κενεμβατούντων καὶ ματαιοσχόλων ἔργον, πόρρω τῆς ἐπιγραφῆς διερριμμένος (cod. 187: 142b lines 17–21).

[10] . . . καὶ ἐκέρδανεν ἂν καὶ ἡ Νικομάχου σπουδὴ τῷ μετὰ πολλῶν χρησίμων μικροῦ νομίζεσθαι διεφθάρθαι. Ἀλλ' ἔστι καὶ πράττεται, οὐκ ὀλίγην δόξαν . . . ἀποκειραμένη (cod. 187: 145b lines 3–7). On the text and its interpretation, see Treadgold, "Photius," 172–74.

[11] Cod. 187: 143a lines 2–19.

[12] Cf. Sp. Vryonis, "The Will of a Provincial Magnate, Eustathius Boilas (1059)," *DOP*, 11 (1957), 269–70.

Among secular books, Photius shows a preference for plain, readable historical narrative. Though the codices include only thirty-seven titles of secular histories, among them are the multivolume compilations of Appian, Dio, Diodorus Siculus, and Dionysius of Halicarnassus, all of which Photius seems to have read in full. In the first quarter of the *Bibliotheca* histories are generally described at greater length than other books. The first seven lengthy epitomes cover the histories of Procopius, Theophanes of Byzantium, Theophylact Simocatta, Ctesias, Olympiodorus, and Arrian.[13] Prominent among the very short theological codices at the beginning is the longer, secular codex 3, on Nonnosus' history of his embassy to the Himyarites and Ethiopians; Photius may well have thought of it in connection with his own prospective embassy.[14] To judge from the subjects that he describes in most detail, Photius had a long-standing interest in the history and ethnography of non-Byzantine regions, particularly those to the East.[15]

In historiography, Photius especially valued readability. Perhaps his warmest critical judgment in the *Bibliotheca* is in praise of Arrian: "This man is second to none of those who compose the best works of history, for he is the best at narrating with conciseness, never damaging the continuity of history with untimely digressions and additions. . . ." Photius concludes that "even many of the ancients stand below his rank."[16] By contrast, in his three incidental references to Thucydides, Photius points out that his history is not as clear as those of Dio, Dexippus, and Agatharchides.[17] Clarity is admittedly not one of Thucydides' virtues.

What Photius most objected to in historical works was excessive detail and documentation that made boring reading. He roundly condemns Cephalion for listing too many sources, and Olympiodorus for merely assembling "materials for a history."[18] Photius blames Phlegon of Tralles for including too many athletic and historical

[13] Codd. 63, 64, 65, 72 (Ctesias' two works), 80, and 92.

[14] Cf. πρεσβεύειν ἡμᾶς . . . αἱρεθέντας (preface, *Bibliotheca*: 1 line 1) with Νόννοσον πρεσβεύειν αἱρεθῆναι (cod. 3: 2a line 38).

[15] Klinkenberg, 21–26, argues that Photius deliberately composed his reviews to cover various periods of history in a comprehensive fashion; but, though practically all history does happen to be touched upon somehow and somewhere in the 45 codices cited by Klinkenberg, I fail to see a real pattern. I conclude only that Photius had wide-ranging tastes.

[16] Ἔστι μὲν οὖν ὁ ἀνὴρ οὐδενὸς τῶν ἄριστα συνταξαμένων ἱστορίας δεύτερος· ἀπαγγεῖλαί τε γὰρ καὶ μετὰ συντομίας κράτιστος, καὶ παρεκτροπαῖς ἀκαίροις οὐδὲ παρενθήκαις τὸ συνεχὲς τῆς ἱστορίας οὐδαμοῦ λυμαινόμενος. . . . (cod. 92: 72b line 40–73a line 3). . . . πολλοὺς καὶ τῶν ἀρχαίων . . . τῆς αὐτοῦ τάξεως ἱσταμένους ταπεινότερον (cod. 92: 73a lines 28–30).

[17] Cod. 71: 35b lines 30–32, cod. 82: 64a lines 17–20, and cod. 213: 171b lines 9–12.

[18] Cod. 68 and cod. 80: 56b lines 12–29.

events in his chronicle; these seem to have bored Photius so much that he stopped reading in the middle.[19] Though such an attitude may seem somewhat unscholarly, Photius was after all not a political historian himself, but simply a man who liked to read political history.

Not only in his reviews of histories but in other places, Photius shows a love of the strange and exotic. The marvels he enjoyed, however, were only those that he thought were true or, in works of fiction, that he thought seemed true. He was obviously fascinated by the strange men and beasts described in the histories of Nonnosus, Ctesias, and Agatharchides, and in Philostratus' *Life of Apollonius.* His excerpts from Diodorus begin with detailed reports, which Photius considers trustworthy, of men born with the physical characteristics of women.[20] Although Photius makes fun of Olympiodorus' stories of pagan magic, he noted them down at length.[21] In codices 188 and 189, his critical comments on five works of paradoxography are surprisingly favorable. He has high praise for Antonius Diogenes' novel, *The Wonders Beyond Thule,* which included journeys to the North Pole and the moon and cases of suspended animation. Antonius' writing, says Photius, "has particular charm in his ideas, since it puts material that is near to being myths and wonders into the most believable form and construction."[22]

At the end of his review of Antonius' novel, Photius recommends all novels that are morally edifying as well as diverting: "Especially in this, in comparison with other fictions and fables of the same sort, two things are most useful to follow: first, how the author brings the evildoer, even though he may appear to escape a thousand times, to pay the penalty nevertheless, and second, how he shows many innocent characters, who are brought into great danger, saved repeatedly contrary to expectation."[23] Photius praises Heliodorus' *Aethiopica* on similar grounds.[24] But he condemns Achilles Tatius' *Leu-*

[19] Cf. cod. 97: 83b lines 32–35 and 84a line 34–84b line 2. This is the interpretation of Mango, "Books," 39, though Photius could conceivably have had an incomplete MS.

[20] Cod. 244: 377a line 29–379a line 33.

[21] Cf. cod. 80: 58a lines 20–31 (μυθολογεῖ), 62a lines 1–5 and 62a lines 25–36 (τερατολογεῖ), etc.

[22] Ταῖς δὲ διανοίαις πλεῖστον ἔχει τοῦ ἡδέος, ἅτε μύθων ἐγγὺς καὶ ἀπίστων ἐν πιθανωτάτῃ πλάσει καὶ διασκευῇ ὕλην ἑαυτῇ διηγημάτων ποιουμένη (cod. 166: 109a lines 10–12).

[23] Ἔστι δὲ ἐν αὐτοῖς καὶ μάλιστα, ὡς ἐν τηλικούτοις πλάσμασί τε καὶ μυθεύμασι, δύο τινὰ θηράσαι χρησιμώτατα· ἓν μὲν ὅτι τὸν ἀδικήσαντά τι, κἂν μυριάκις ἐκφυγεῖν δόξῃ, εἰσάγει πάντως δίκην δεδωκέναι, καὶ δεύτερον ὅτι πολλοὺς ἀναιτίους ἐγγὺς μεγάλου γεγονότας κινδύνου, παρ' ἐλπίδας δείκνυσι πολλάκις διασωθέντας (cod. 166: 112a lines 6–12).

[24] Cod. 73: 50a lines 9–12.

cippe and Clitophon, despite finding it well written, because of its obscenity, which "makes reading it, for those who wish to read it, disgusting and to be avoided."[25] It is plain, however, from the rest of his review that Photius did read the book through with some pleasure, as he did some other novels which he criticizes for indecency.[26]

Photius had a more serious interest in intellectual history, to which, indeed, he contributed in the *Bibliotheca* itself. He took some care to assemble biographical materials from the "Hesychius Epitome," the lost history of the ten orators, and the autobiographical parts of the books which he reviews. In eleven codices Photius makes judgments on the authorship of various books on the basis of their style and content, and he chose a book on the authenticity of Pseudo-Dionysius to begin the *Bibliotheca*.[27] Using internal evidence, he conjectures in codex 129 that Lucian copied his *Lucius or the Ass* from Lucius of Patrae's *Metamorphoses,* rather than the reverse. The conjecture is now generally accepted.[28]

Photius' lively, if not very discriminating, interest in the history of scholarship shows when he reviews and makes long excerpts from the biographies of the philosophers Apollonius, Isidore, and Pythagoras, and the literary histories of Ptolemaeus Chennus, Proclus, and Helladius.[29] He seems to have liked Pamphila's collection of historical extracts largely because he was able to use it as a source for literary history.[30] No doubt the interest he shows in the lives of philosophers and poets reflects an interest in philosophy and poetry that is disguised by his omission of school texts from the *Bibliotheca,* but mentioned by Nicetas the Paphlagonian.

Photius' philological interests are further demonstrated by his fondness for reference works. Of his thirteen criticisms of lexica, all are favorable, and all but two unreservedly so.[31] Besides the literary

[25] . . . τοῖς ἀναγινώσκειν ἐθέλουσι κατάπτυστον τὴν ἀνάγνωσιν ποιεῖται καὶ φευκτήν (cod. 87: 66a lines 23–24).

[26] Cf. cod. 94: 73b lines 25–27 and cod. 129: 96b lines 27–28.

[27] Photius' judgments on authorship are in codd. 48: 11b line 40–12a line 10, 61: 20a lines 5–6, 88: 66b line 30–67a line 1, 89: 67a line 33–67b line 9, 184: 128a lines 32–35, 196: 160b lines 13–14, 197: 161a lines 33–34, 203: 164a lines 32–33, 204: 164b lines 15–17, 271: 503b lines 13–20, and 274: 510b lines 9–13. He does not give a judgment on the authenticity of Pseudo-Dionysius in cod. 1, but in cod. 222 (189b lines 32–33) he seems to accept Jobius the Monk's opinion that it is authentic, and a passage in the *Amphilochia* (PG, 101, no. 119, cols. 697D–700A) implies the same.

[28] H. Van Thiel, *Der Eselsroman*, I, Zetemata, 54 (Munich, 1971), 1–7; cf. pp. 68–69 *supra*.

[29] Codd. 44 (=241), 181 (=242), 190, 239, 249, and 279.

[30] See cod. 175 and p. 65 *supra*.

[31] Codd. 145–48, 150 (three judgments, one with reservations), 152 (two judgments), 153, 154–55, 156, and 158 (with reservations).

histories just mentioned, he gives long accounts of the anthologies of Sopatrus of Apamea and John Stobaeus in codices 161 and 167, and of Conon's manual of mythology in codex 186. He praises the usefulness of Sopatrus, Stobaeus, and Pseudo-Apollodorus, whose *Bibliotheca* he reviews briefly at the end of codex 186. When he stresses how useful these reference works are, Photius implies that he has used them himself in his teaching and writing, and presumably in compiling his own lexicon when he was younger.[32]

Photius had also read widely in the orators, including nine of the ten Attic orators and several representatives of the second sophistic. He seems rather to have preferred Hellenistic orators to classical ones. Though the reason he had nothing of his own to say about Demosthenes' orations was presumably that they were school texts, his codices 61 and 159 on the orations of Aeschines and Isocrates are not particularly long or enthusiastic, and he gives only biographies of the other eight Attic orators. Considerably longer and more detailed reviews cover Himerius and Dio Chrysostom, and very long extracts are given from the speeches of Himerius and Aristides, both of whom Photius praises in the headings of his notes.[33]

As Nicetas says, Photius' knowledge of medicine was substantial, and practically professional. That Photius practiced medicine is plain from four of his letters, which prescribe medicines and accept thanks for a successful cure.[34] In the *Bibliotheca* he reviews eighteen medical texts, usually in technical detail, evaluating their usefulness and efficacy in practice, and once criticizing the carelessness of the doctors of his own day.[35] In his review of Vindanius Anatolius' agricultural manual, Photius implies that he even had some personal acquaintance with agriculture: "This book is useful, as we have seen in many cases even from experience, for tilling the land and for agricultural projects. . . ."[36]

Nevertheless, mathematics and the natural sciences, apart from medicine, were not Photius' strong points. The *Bibliotheca* does include works by John Lydus, Nicomachus of Gerasa, and Theo-

[32] *Amphilochia,* PG, 101, no. 21, col. 153C. On the question of whether this is Photius' *Lexicon* as we have it, see p. 4 note 15 *supra*.

[33] Codd. 165, 209, 243, and 246–48. Though secular epistolography is scarcely represented in the *Bibliotheca,* in one of his letters Photius expresses a preference for Hellenistic models for letter writing rather than classical ones (*Letters,* no. 233, p. 545).

[34] *Letters,* no. 131, p. 450; no. 228, pp. 542–43; no. 230, pp. 543–44; and no. 231, p. 544.

[35] Cf. cod. 178: 123b line 31–124a line 11 and cod. 221: 181a lines 1–32. On Photius' low opinion of the doctors of his time, cf. also *Letters,* no. 231, p. 544.

[36] Χρήσιμον δὲ τὸ βιβλίον, ὡς καὶ διὰ πείρας αὐτῆς ἐπὶ πολλῶν εἴδομεν, πρὸς τὰς κατὰ γῆν ἐργασίας καὶ τοὺς γεωργικοὺς πόνους. . . . (cod. 163: 107a lines 4–6). Photius may have become familiar with farming while in exile before 842 (see pp. 2–3 *supra*).

phrastus on these subjects, and Photius had naturally read the standard scientific and mathematical texts that the *Bibliotheca* omits.[37] But it is difficult to class Ptolemy and Strabo as standard texts, not to speak of less common works of geometry, astronomy, and so on that are also absent from the *Bibliotheca*.[38] Photius seems simply not to have read them. He seldom discusses the non-medical sciences in either his letters or the *Amphilochia*, and they are not mentioned as interests of his by Nicetas.[39] At the end of his codex on Nicomachus, Photius notes that there are many expert mathematicians among his acquaintances, but he does not count himself as one.[40] Here he is evidently thinking of Leo the Mathematician and John the Grammarian, who had both attained such preeminence in mathematics and the sciences at this time that Photius may well have been discouraged from challenging them. With these exceptions, however, the *Bibliotheca* reveals no significant gaps in Photius' interests in secular subjects.

On the other hand, the *Bibliotheca* contains only a little less evidence of interest in religious subjects. According to one of his letters, Photius had wanted to become a monk when he was young, before worldly thoughts and government appointments changed his mind.[41] Like most Byzantine laymen, he was interested in religion, but his interest, unlike that of most, was intellectual as well as spiritual. Nearly a third of the religious books he read were at least slightly heretical or Jewish, and, though he read them partly in order to refute them, others tried to refute them without reading them.[42] Since he had read even the works of gnostics and Manichaeans, it would be surprising if he had not read iconoclasts as well, though he might well have preferred not to mention them after their works were banned in 843. As it was in secular matters, Photius' learning in religious matters was wide-ranging.

The attention he pays to Christology is not unusual for a Byzantine scholar, but his extensive acquaintance with the writings of Arians, Nestorians, and Monophysites must have been exceptional. Though as a rule conciliar acts were seldom read, he had read acts of all seven Ecumenical Councils except for the Second.[43] He also

[37] See codd. 180, 187, and 279; on the standard texts, see pp. 6–7 and note 31 *supra*.

[38] Cf. the scientific library of Photius' contemporary, Leo the Mathematician, described by Lemerle, *Humanisme*, 169–72.

[39] Cf. the citations of books in Table VI, and the quotation from Nicetas, p. 97 *supra*.

[40] See p. 28 *supra*, and Treadgold, "Photius," 172–74.

[41] *Letters*, no. 2, p. 145.

[42] Of 239 religious books, he read 64 heretical and 10 Jewish ones; see Table III.

[43] Codd. 15–20. Cod. 15 is not on the actual *acta* of the First Council but rather on a history of the council by Gelasius of Cyzicus.

devotes codices to many works that attack the Christological heresies, particularly the anti-Monophysite works of Eulogius of Alexandria and Ephraem of Amida; Photius epitomizes these for Tarasius in codices 225-30, which make up more than a fifth of the *Bibliotheca*. Because Monophysitism was the final Christological heresy, and the only one that still had a sizable following in the ninth century, both in the Caliphate and in Armenia, it is natural that Photius should have given most attention to it; but the absence of Arians did not make him neglect Arianism.

One of Photius' two longest passages of exposition in the *Bibliotheca* concerns a Christological point in Jobius the Monk's lost work, *On the Incarnation*. Jobius discusses an anti-Arian argument of Gregory of Nyssa: if God is not dumb or irrational (ἄλογος), He must have a Word (Λόγος), namely the Son, who, like Him, must be wholly God. A friend of Jobius has objected that then not only the Father but also the Son and Spirit must have divine words, which must themselves have more divine words, so that God must be not merely a Trinity, but an infinity of persons. Jobius seems to have become hopelessly entangled in his thirteen arguments against this, which Photius thought less likely to lead a skeptic to piety than to laughter. Without repeating these unfortunate arguments, Photius presents an argument of his own, based on the nature of the Trinity:

> . . . if one first considers the Father, then asks about Him whether He is irrational (ἄλογος) or rational, and only then proposes that a Son must also be attributed to the Father, perhaps this over-subtle objection has some application and force. But if one does not do this (for it should not be done, and the admirable Gregory did not present his statement in this way), but considers first the concept of God, which is the common and indivisible name of the Divine Persons, and then asks about *His* Word—or Fatherhood, and, if one wishes, His Spirit also—this man will represent the mystery of the Trinity, and will not give an opportunity to one who wishes to make the representation over-subtle.

Thus it is the whole Godhead, not only the Father, that has a Word, and this one Word is enough for all three Persons. Photius spends more than a Bekker column discussing this problem, which evidently interested him very much.[44]

[44] . . . εἰ μέν τις τὸν πατέρα προτίθησιν, εἶτα περὶ αὐτοῦ διερωτᾷ πότερον ἄλογον ἢ λογικόν, κἀκεῖθεν κατασκευάζει τῷ πατρὶ δεῖν προσεῖναι καὶ υἱόν, τῆς ἀνθυποφορᾶς τὸ περιέργον ἴσως ἔχει πάροδον καὶ ἰσχύν. Εἰ δὲ τοῦτο μὲν οὐ ποιεῖ (οὔτε γὰρ δεῖ, οὔτε ὁ θαυμαστὸς Γρηγόριος οὕτω τὸν λόγον προήνεγκεν) αὐτὸ δὲ τὸ θεὸς προβαλλόμενος, ὃ κοινόν ἐστι καὶ ἀμέριστον τῶν θεαρχικῶν ὑποστάσεων ὄνομα, ἐπ' αὐτοῦ δὴ καὶ τὸν λόγον ἢ τὸ γόνιμον, εἰ βούλει δὲ καὶ τὸ ἔμπνουν, ἐπερωτᾷ, κατασκευάσει μὲν τὸ τῆς τριάδος μυστήριον οὗτος, οὐ μήν γε χώραν ἐνδώσει τῷ βουλομένῳ

The nature of the Trinity was to be one of Photius' major concerns during his patriarchate, when he attacked the Western form of the Creed that said the Holy Spirit proceeded from both the Father "and the Son" (*filioque*). A recent study of Photius' triadology has suggested that he attacked the *filioque* because his idea of the Trinity "begins not with the oneness of the Divine Essence but with the personal reality of God the Father. . . ."[45] But this generalization, which seems to oversimplify even Photius' arguments against the *filioque*, is very hard to reconcile with Photius' comments on Jobius.

Another particular interest of Photius was the problem of original sin. Among the short, theological codices of the first thirty Bekker columns, Photius devotes one column to the Ecumenical Councils but almost six columns to councils that condemned Messalianism and Pelagianism.[46] After describing a colorful Messalian priest who found holiness in fornicating and condemned psalm-singing as subservience to the Law, Photius mentions his own effort to convert similar heretics, meaning, I believe, the first edition of his *Against the Manichaeans*.[47] In the next codex, Photius notes that the Pelagians, much like the Messalians, denied the significance of Adam's sin and consequently saw no need for infant baptism.[48] Photius shows an interest in Manichaeanism in three other codices, including one on Agapius, himself a Manichaean.[49] On the general subject of free will, he reviews three more works at length, and one of them twice: Hierocles' *On Providence and Fate*, Diodorus of Tarsus' *Against Fate*, and Methodius of Olympus' *On Free Will*.[50]

Photius' interest in free will is most evident in the other of his two extended expository passages in the *Bibliotheca*, which concerns Theodore of Mopsuestia's lost work, *Against Those Who Say That Men Sin By Nature and Not by Intention*. Though he generally approves of Theodore's arguments, Photius considers his denial of the significance of Adam's sin erroneous and Origenistic. He goes on to say, "And this also I do not admit among the teachings of truth, as an excessive statement, unknown to the Church of God: to say that there are two remissions of sins, one of sins committed, and the other (I do not know how one could call it a 'remission' too, as he

τὴν κατασκευὴν περιεργάζεσθαι (cod. 222: 199a lines 14–25). Photius' argument extends from 198b line 30 to 199a line 35.

[45] R. Haugh, *Photius and the Carolingians* (Belmont, Mass., 1975), 17. This is Haugh's formulation of the "Greek triadological model" to which Photius supposedly subscribed.

[46] Codd. 52–54.

[47] Cod. 52: 13a line 38–13b line 16. On this passage, see pp. 28–29 *supra*.

[48] Cod. 53: 14a lines 4–12.

[49] Cod. 81, 85, and 179 (Agapius).

[50] Cod. 214 (=251), 223, and 236.

does) sinlessness, or rather the condition of no longer sinning."[51] According to Theodore, this condition of no longer sinning became possible at Christ's incarnation, was fully bestowed at the time of His resurrection, and is confirmed in baptism, with the effect that we shall no longer sin after our own resurrection. Photius rejects this, pointing out that not even the unbaptized and those who died before Christ could commit sins after their death—after all, he says, what worse punishment than damnation could be found for them? Observing that Theodore is trying to answer those who ask why infants need baptism, Photius says that this problem must be resolved in another way. Again, Photius' comments take up more than a Bekker column.[52]

This idea of the "two remissions" curiously resembles the doctrine of the "two souls" which, according to three sources, Photius facetiously proposed as a layman to see if the Patriarch Ignatius could refute it without the aid of the philosophical reasoning that Ignatius disdained.[53] The proposal was that "each man has two souls, and the one sins, but the other does not sin."[54] Fr. Dvornik rejected this account on the ground that the Eighth Council, in condemning this heresy, did not say that Photius held it.[55] But the sources themselves do not say that Photius held it, and in fact say that he denied it, as he does Theodore's similar doctrine. He was only interested in the argument as an idea, and, according to contemporary reports, as a means of embarrassing Ignatius. Anastasius Bibliothecarius dates this proposal of Photius's "some years before" Photius became patriarch in 858, apparently soon after Ignatius became patriarch in 847.[56] The *Bibliotheca,* probably composed in 845, is evidence that Photius was interested in a similar idea only a few years earlier.

Photius' interests in Christology and free will naturally carried over into another interest of his, ecclesiastical history. Though his treatment of the fifteen religious histories in the *Bibliotheca,* except for Josephus' *Jewish Antiquities,* is fairly cursory, his treatment of conciliar acts has already been noted, and he also epitomizes eight

[51] Ἔτι δὲ κἀκεῖνο οὐκ ἐγκρίνω ἔγωγε τοῖς τῆς ἀληθείας δόγμασι, περιέργως τε εἰρημένον καὶ οὐδὲ γνώριμον τῇ ἐκκλησίᾳ τοῦ Θεοῦ, τὸ δύο ἀφέσεις ἁμαρτιῶν εἶναι λέγειν, τὴν μὲν τῶν πεπραγμένων, τὴν δὲ οὐκ οἶδ' ὅπως εἴποι τις ἂν καὶ ἄφεσιν, ὡς ἐκεῖνος λέγει, αὐτὴν τὴν ἀναμαρτησίαν ἤτοι τὸ μηκέτι ἁμαρτάνειν (cod. 177: 122b lines 19–24).

[52] Cod. 177: 122b line 10–123a line 22.

[53] See Mansi, XVI, cols. 5E–6A (Anastasius Bibliothecarius) and 456A (synodical letter of Pope Hadrian); and Pseudo-Symeon, Bonn ed. (1838), 673–74.

[54] . . . ἕκαστος ἄνθρωπος δύο ψυχὰς ἔχει, καὶ ἡ μὲν μία ἁμαρτάνει, ἡ δὲ ἑτέρα οὐχ ἁμαρτάνει (Pseudo-Symeon, Bonn ed. [1838], 673).

[55] F. Dvornik, *The Photian Schism, History and Legend* (Cambridge, 1948), 32–34; cf. Mansi, XVI, cols. 166D–67A and 404D–E.

[56] . . . ante annos aliquot . . . (Mansi, XVI, cols. 5E–6A).

saints' lives and shows a historical interest in many theological works.[57] When he became patriarch, Photius drew on some of the books reviewed in the *Bibliotheca* to prepare a sort of history of Arianism in several of his homilies.[58] He concerns himself with the development of doctrine in, for example, what he says about the third-century theologian Pierius: "He honors the Father and the Son in an orthodox manner, except that he speaks of 'two substances' and 'two natures,' using the words 'substance' and 'nature,' as is obvious from what follows and precedes the passage [in question], for 'person,' and not as the followers of Arius do."[59] Photius knew that Pierius lived before Arius from the "Hesychius Epitome," which he consulted for fourteen other religious writers as well.[60]

Of course, as a believing Christian, Photius also read religious books simply for spiritual benefit. To judge from the more than fifty-five Bekker columns of excerpts from forty-five sermons that appear in codices 269-77, sermons were his favorite kind of devotional reading. But in codices 191-208 he also presents a section of twenty-three Bekker columns on a wide variety of devotional works. He praises almost all these books for their usefulness in leading a Christian life, not excepting those whose style and even argumentation he found deficient. About half of this section reviews works by Maximus Confessor, praising his piety and deploring his style. When he reviews John Cassian's monastic rules, Photius' praise seems to reflect his youthful ambition to become a monk. Their usefulness for ascetics, he declares, is so great that even in Photius' own time monasteries thrive according to whether they follow or reject Cassian's rules; "it is therefore necessary to disregard none of the things handed down in them, for they are an unrolling and unfolding of the Law of the Lord and the life of the Gospel."[61]

Photius' theological, historical, and spiritual concerns come together in his admiration for John Chrysostom. The *Bibliotheca* describes more works by Chrysostom, including spurious ones, than by any other author, secular or religious. Codices 270, 274, and 277 excerpt nineteen of his sermons, codices 96 and 273 epitomize biographies of him, and codex 59 gives a full summary of the Council

[57] The epitomes of hagiography are codd. 96 and 252–58.

[58] See p. 95 *supra*.

[59] Ἀλλὰ περὶ μὲν πατρὸς καὶ υἱοῦ εὐσεβῶς πρεσβεύει, πλὴν ὅτι οὐσίας δύο καὶ φύσεις δύο λέγει, τῷ τῆς οὐσίας καὶ φύσεως ὀνόματι, ὡς δῆλον ἔκ τε τῶν ἑπομένων καὶ προηγουμένων τοῦ χωρίου, ἀντὶ τῆς ὑποστάσεως, καὶ οὐχ ὡς οἱ Ἀρείῳ προσανακείμενοι, χρώμενος (cod. 119: 93a line 42–93b line 4). Cf. cod. 202: 163b line 38–164a line 2, on Hippolytus of Rome.

[60] As usual, see Table VII for the references.

[61] Διὸ χρεὼν ἐστι μηδὲν τῶν ἐν αὐτοῖς παραδεδομένων παρορᾶν· δεσποτικῆς γὰρ ταῦτα νομοθεσίας καὶ τῆς εὐαγγελικῆς πολιτείας ἐστὶν ἀνάπτυξίς τε καὶ ἐξάπλωσις (cod. 197: 161a lines 17–20).

of the Oak, which deposed the saint from the patriarchate. In the combined codex 172-74 on four collections of Chrysostom's homilies, Photius uses internal evidence and his knowledge of the saint's life to conjecture the dates at which the homilies were delivered. At the end of the codex, he even finds a sort of merit in the roughness of Chrysostom's style and the occasional superficiality of his treatment: "This is why I always find myself even marveling at this thrice-blessed man, because, always and in all his works, he makes the profit of his hearers his aim, and considers other things either not at all or as little as possible."[62] Presumably Photius found much in Chrysostom to emulate when he himself became Patriarch of Constantinople.

In connection with Photius' patriarchate, it is of interest that in his excerpts of Eulogius of Alexandria's *On Dispensation* we find a note taking exception to Eulogius' statement that Christ gave the power of the keys to St. Peter alone. Though Eulogius does not seem to have been stressing the Pope's succession from Peter in this passage, Photius is obviously thinking of it when he observes that the power of the keys and of binding and loosing was given to all the disciples, who transmitted it to their successors.[63] Defense of the prerogatives of the Eastern patriarchates, here presented in a moderate way, became particularly associated with Photius during the Photian schism.

The preceding discussion has centered on Photius' interests in the content of his books, though for the great majority he pays attention to their style as well. His nearly two hundred stylistic criticisms are an almost inexhaustible subject, because, as George Kustas has pointed out, Photius judges each author and book originally and as an individual case. Though he seems to have omitted rhetorical manuals from the *Bibliotheca* along with the school texts, Photius' rhetorical vocabulary shows that he knew the manuals of Hermogenes and Dionysius of Halicarnassus, and probably some others. Still, Kustas found that Photius does not adopt the rhetorical systems of these authorities along with their terminology.[64] While he generally shows a preference for a clear and somewhat innovative style that resembles the ideal of the second sophistic, Photius often observes that different styles are appropriate to different subjects, and my examples here have shown how he distinguishes and ad-

[62] Διό μοι καὶ ἀεὶ θαυμάζειν ἔπεισι τὸν τρισμακάριστον ἄνθρωπον ἐκεῖνον, ὅτι ἀεὶ καὶ ἐν πᾶσιν αὐτοῦ τοῖς λόγοις τοῦτο σκοπὸν ἐποιεῖτο, τὴν ὠφέλειαν τῶν ἀκροατῶν, τῶν δ' ἄλλων ἢ οὐδ' ὅλως ἐφρόντιζεν ἢ ὡς ἐλάχιστον. . . (cod. 172–74: 119b lines 7–11).

[63] Cod. 280: 537a lines 29–35.

[64] See G. L. Kustas, "The Literary Criticism of Photius: A Christian Definition of Style," *Hellenika,* 17 (1962), 132–69.

mires a variety of styles. A far more thorough discussion of Photius' literary criticism will be found in the studies of Orth and especially of Kustas.[65]

Such are the principal interests that Photius displays in his *Bibliotheca*. He was interested in political history, paradoxography, novels, and oratory simply as a reader, and in devotional works as a Christian. He made a practice of book collecting and medicine. As a scholar, and no doubt as a teacher, he was interested in intellectual history, reference works, theology, church history, and literary criticism, to all of which he contributed before, after, or while he composed the *Bibliotheca*. This combination of serious secular and religious interests was an extraordinary one in Byzantium. Even Leo the Mathematician, the greatest scholar of his time except for Photius, seems to have surpassed Photius only in science and mathematics and had no such competence in theological subjects.[66] As Nicetas the Paphlagonian says, only the ancients really rivaled Photius in learning.[67]

Comparing the *Bibliotheca* to Photius' later *Amphilochia*, Paul Lemerle concluded that Photius' interests became more exclusively religious over the years and with his accession to the patriarchate.[68] Though allowances must be made for the fact that Photius wrote the *Amphilochia* to answer questions put to him by an archbishop, such an evolution in Photius' interests would have been perfectly natural under the circumstances. But at the time Photius composed the *Bibliotheca*, his interests seem to have tended somewhat toward the secular. Often making no particular distinction between Christian and profane learning, he applied historical, logical, and stylistic analysis to both religious and non-religious books. When the *Bibliotheca* was written, probably in 845, Photius could still have had a brilliant career either as a scholar and government official or as a theologian and ecclesiastic. In the end, of course, he had both brilliant careers.

[65] See Orth, *Photiana; idem, Die Stilkritik des Photios*, Rhetorische Forschungen, II (Leipzig, 1929); Kustas, "Criticism," 132–69; *idem*, "History and Theology in Photius," *Greek Orthodox Theological Review*, 10 (1964), 37–74; and *idem*, *Studies in Byzantine Rhetoric*, Analekta Vlatadon, 17 (Thessalonica, 1973). Orth often assumes that Photius himself composed material in codd. 259–68 that I attribute to the lost history of the ten orators (see pp. 48–50 *supra*). Kustas also does this in "Criticism," 139 note 1, and in "History," 54–58, he attributes to Photius material in cod. 242 that I would attribute to Damascius.

[66] Photius is probably expressing respect for Leo's mathematical knowledge in cod. 187 (see p. 28 *supra*). On Leo's knowledge, see Lemerle, *Humanisme*, 148–76, particularly 157 on Leo's competence in theology.

[67] Nicetas Paphlago, PG, 105, col. 509B.

[68] Lemerle, *Humanisme*, 202. Though I consider Lemerle's date for the *Bibliotheca*, 838, somewhat too early, the date I propose, 845, still leaves about 25 years between the *Bibliotheca* and the *Amphilochia*, which dates from 868–72.

Conclusion

Thus the evidence of the text of the *Bibliotheca* can be combined with that of its preface and postface to give a consistent and plausible picture. From the time that Photius considered himself to have some literary discrimination, presumably in his teens in the 820's, he began to read voraciously.[1] His reading continued during his exile with his family during the 830's, and after he returned to Constantinople about 842, when he embarked on a career in teaching and in the civil service.[2] Many of the books that he read were his own, either inherited, purchased second hand, or copied for him. He read the others in libraries or on loan.[3] Often, especially when he did not own the book, he took long notes in the form of excerpts or epitomes while he was reading and saved them for future reference.[4] He read the books known to the well-educated men of his time, but he also sought out and read very rare books.[5] He pursued interests in almost everything, though the natural sciences and mathematics seem to have interested him less than theology, history, and philology.[6] Though he generally read alone, his favorite brother Tarasius, who shared some of his enthusiasm and respected his judgment, joined him in studying at least the lengthy orations of Himerius, which he read aloud while Photius listened.[7]

Then, probably in the spring of the year 845, Photius was chosen to accompany some Byzantine ambassadors to the court of the Caliph at Samarra.[8] The embassy was to take several months, and there was always the chance that Photius would not return. At this news, Tarasius asked Photius to put together some sort of inventory of all the books that he had read by himself, both as a remembrance of

[1] See quotation on p. 18 *supra*.
[2] See pp. 2–3 *supra*.
[3] See pp. 92–95 *supra*.
[4] See Chapter III.
[5] See pp. 6–7 and 98–99 *supra*.
[6] See Chapter VII, esp. pp. 103–4.
[7] See p. 22 *supra*.
[8] See pp. 26–36 *supra*.

Photius during his absence and as a guide to Tarasius' future reading, some of which might even be done in Photius' own library.[9] Photius evidently liked the idea, and he agreed. He had considerable time, a month or two, before the embassy was to depart, and he set about reconstructing the course of his reading over the preceding twenty years or more.[10] To assist his memory, he had his large private library and the notes that he had taken over the years. He engaged a secretary to copy down his account of his reading.[11]

Photius began to compose an inventory of substantial but not staggering proportions, which would have taken about five days of steady work and amounted to some seventy folios.[12] His method was simple enough. He worked quickly through the books that he had at hand, dictating to his secretary a brief notice on each; these notices generally gave the author, the title, a brief outline of the contents (for which he used the preface or table of contents if the book had one), and the opinion of the book that he remembered having formed when he read it.[13] He also tried to remember what he could about the books that he had read but did not have at hand.[14] To supplement this material, Photius referred to a copy of the biographical dictionary known to us as the "Hesychius Epitome," which was conveniently arranged in alphabetical order. As he dictated a notice on a book, Photius would often look up its author in the dictionary and paraphrase the short biography of him to round off the notice.[15] The result of this sort of work was a series of brief and modest notices. Those that Photius composed only from memory were naturally imprecise and occasionally erroneous, and those done with the book at hand were not much better, being compiled hastily and still largely on the basis of memory.[16] Photius realized how imperfect these reviews must be, as he told Tarasius in his preface, observing that "for a man who reads many books together to come to an exact recollection of them, especially when some time passes in the interval, is not, I think, an easy thing."[17]

As Photius dictated, however, he warmed to his task. He began

[9] See quotations on pp. 16 and 18 *supra*.

[10] See pp. 23–25 and 35–36 *supra*.

[11] See quotation on p. 17 *supra*.

[12] If completed in proportion to the first 56 codices, which may well represent Photius' first day's work, the full 280 codices would take up 70 Bekker pages or folios. See pp. 24–25 *supra*.

[13] See pp. 84–87 and 92–93 *supra*.

[14] See pp. 83–84 *supra*.

[15] See pp. 53–59 *supra*.

[16] On Photius' errors and omissions, see Chapter V.

[17] See p. 17 *supra*.

to have more to say about the books that he looked over; sometimes he would summarize the texts at some length; and the fullness and extent of his summaries expanded to such a degree that once he admitted he was practically transcribing.[18] Further, he began to make efficient use of the body of reading notes that he had accumulated. To save himself time and trouble, he dictated appropriate introductions and then simply gave his secretary the notes to copy.[19] Thus the summaries that Photius was composing for Tarasius became fuller, though they still suffered from being hastily compiled. The material that came from Photius' notes had, on the contrary, been composed at the very time he had read the books, some time before the embassy and the inventory; but these notices had the defects of most personal notes, being more or less disorganized and rough. Finally, Photius left his secretary to copy the remainder of his notes without supervision, with the result that almost the last half of the work, beginning with codex 234, is in very rough shape.[20] Some peculiarities in the form of the *pinax* may indicate that Photius actually departed on his embassy at this point, entrusting the secretary with finishing the copying for delivery to Tarasius.[21]

The *Bibliotheca,* therefore, is a private and informal compilation of literary memoirs, summaries, and reading notes, composed for the author's brother and for the author's own satisfaction, probably with the thought that it might be circulated among a few friends or students, but not with the idea of having it copied and distributed. Despite its immense length, the *Bibliotheca* really is a sort of letter, prepared and largely composed to be sent to one man. In its preface, postface, and passages of commentary it is a fairly formal sort of letter, and in its descriptions of texts it is a simple communication, while the reading notes may almost be thought of as added enclosures. The *Bibliotheca* was meant, as Photius says with a play on words in his postface, as "a summary and memory of love and of consolation," summing up and recording both his reading and his affection and concern for Tarasius.[22] Though after it was sent this private work eventually became known to a number of Byzantine

[18] See p. 23 *supra.*

[19] See pp. 88–90 *supra.*

[20] See Chapter III.

[21] See pp. 49–51 *supra.*

[22] φιλίας τε ἅμα καὶ παραμυθίας ὑπόθεσιν καὶ ἀνάμνησιν (postface, *Bibliotheca*: 545 lines 18–19). Cf. Photius' use of the words ὑπόθεσις in the preface, *Bibliotheca*: lines 2, 8, 13, and 14, and ἀνάμνησις in the preface, *Bibliotheca*: 15 and 20 and postface, *Bibliotheca*: 545 line 13 to mean summaries and memories of the books reviewed in the *Bibliotheca.*

scholars, complete manuscripts of it can never have been numerous, and its currency can easily be exaggerated.[23]

The private and informal character of the *Bibliotheca,* like that of Photius' other great compilation, the *Amphilochia,* seems to reflect the immaturity of Byzantine scholarly literature at the time. A work which before the seventh century, or later than the ninth century, would have been composed in the form of a regular commentary or encyclopedia was here composed in the form of a letter. Part of the reason is no doubt that the tradition of writing encyclopedias and commentaries had died out in Byzantium for the time being, while the tradition of writing private letters was alive and highly adaptable. As we can see from the collected correspondence of Theodore of Studium, Ignatius the Deacon, and Photius himself, ninth-century Byzantine letters could include extensive scholarly discussions and, no less than the *Bibliotheca,* could be circulated to persons other than the addressee.[24] But, tradition aside, there was a practical reason for writing scholarly letters rather than long philological works in the mid-ninth century. In this period, the reading public for scholarly literature in Byzantium was still quite small, and particularly small for a work as long, erudite, and secular as the *Bibliotheca.*[25] Theological works, read by monks and the clergy, and short manuals and works of reference, used in schools, could reasonably be copied and distributed, but it is not surprising that Photius did not think of copying and distributing the *Bibliotheca.* When Photius said that he wrote for Tarasius it was no literary fiction, but if he had said that he wrote for many people it would have been. Because Photius was mainly composing for himself and his brother, he consciously worked in a quick, careless, and offhand manner; to criticize the *Bibliotheca* for its carelessness or superficiality would be to misunderstand the nature of the work.

Despite its relatively primitive form, however, the *Bibliotheca* is proof of the vast progress made by the ninth-century revival of learning in discovering, circulating, and studying books of all kinds.

[23] On later uses of the *Bibliotheca* in Byzantium, see A. Diller, "Photius' *Bibliotheca* in Byzantine Literature," *DOP,* 16 (1962), 389–96; and I. Ševčenko, *Etudes sur la polémique entre Théodore Métochite et Nicéphore Choumnos,* Corpus Bruxellense Historiae Byzantinae, Subsidia, 3 (Brussels, 1962), 172 note 2.

[24] The letters of Theodore are edited in PG, 99 (Paris, 1860), and by G. Cozza-Luzi, in *Nova Patrum Bibliotheca,* VIII, 1 (Rome, 1871), 1–244. The letters of Ignatius are edited by G. Gedeon, Νέα βιβλιοθήκη ἐκκλησιαστικῶν συγγραφέων, I, fasc. 1 (Constantinople, 1903), but they are virtually unobtainable, and are being reedited by Cyril Mango (see *supra,* p. 31 note 46). For Photius' letters, which are being reedited by L. G. Westerink, see my bibliography.

[25] Cf. N. G. Wilson, "Books and Readers in Byzantium," *Byzantine Books and Bookmen* (Washington, D.C., 1975), 4–8.

Though Photius was certainly far from typical, being with Leo the Mathematician the most learned man of his time, unusual men usually make the discoveries. If I am correct in conjecturing that Photius owned something like half the books described in the *Bibliotheca*, the mere fact that such a collection could be assembled is significant.[26] Though Photius tells us that some of his books were old, others must have been copied recently, and quite possibly at his order.[27] And he is not likely to have had the only copy of most of these books or to have been the only one to read most of the books that he read. Besides, what he read must have been in large part transmitted to his students and colleagues in teaching and conversation, and the *Bibliotheca* itself eventually became a means of transmission by being circulated to a greater extent than Photius had contemplated. Finally, informal though it was, the *Bibliotheca* was a philological work on a much larger scale than anyone had composed for centuries, and the fact that even one man could and would compose such a thing is impressive.

Thus the *Bibliotheca* was a product of a scholarly revival that was far advanced but was to advance still farther. Already by the mid-ninth century, iconophile scholars had been freed from persecution, the schools of the Magnaura and of Photius were beginning to produce students, and the numbers of the well-educated and the somewhat educated were increasing.[28] Photius had already written a short lexicon, and the little "Hesychius Epitome" was in circulation.[29] By the next century, Byzantium was ready for long and formal philological works and produced several of them, including the *Suda* and the encyclopedias commissioned by Constantine Porphyrogenitus.[30] These works formed a part of a new development in Byzantine scholarly literature that had begun with the overgrown private letter that we call the *Bibliotheca*. The *Bibliotheca* was something that Byzantium seldom produced: a real literary innovation.

[26] See p. 93 and note 52 *supra*.

[27] See p. 98 and note 8 *supra*.

[28] See p. 1 *supra*. In my article, "The Chronological Accuracy of the *Chronicle* of Symeon the Logothete for the Years 813–845," *DOP*, 33 (1979), 186–87, I argue that the school of the Magnaura was founded by Theophilus in 838 and either reestablished or expanded by Bardas in 843.

[29] See pp. 4, 31–32, and 36 *supra*.

[30] On these works, see Lemerle, *Humanisme*, 267–300.

TABLE I

Annotated Table of Contents to the *Bibliotheca*

For each work described in the *Bibliotheca,* this table gives the following information.

First line: the codex number and author's name. For codices that review more than one work, superscribed numbers (e.g., 13^1) denote the different works. The codex numbers of repeated reviews are italicized and cross-referenced. Names given in parentheses are not given by Photius and have been deduced; those in square brackets are given by Photius but are incorrect. For an index to the authors' names, see Table II.

Second line: the author's dates, with a source reference. These dates are given for the reader's convenience only and represent no original research on my part. The abbreviations used for dates and sources are as follows:

b. = born	fl. = flourished
C. = century	e. = early
d. = died	l. = late

m. = mid-

All dates are A.D. unless marked B.C. For an index to the authors by centuries, see Table IV.

Third line: the work's title. Titles in parentheses are not given by Photius and have been deduced; those in square brackets are given by Photius but are incorrect.

Fourth line: a subject classification, including the author's religion for religious works. The abbreviations used for authors' religions are as follows:

A = Arian Christian	Ma = Manichaean
G = Gnostic	Me = Monoenergist Christian
J = Jewish	N = Nestorian Christian
M = Monophysite Christian	O = Origenist Christian

X = Orthodox Christian

The abbreviations denoting the religious sects of writers who were associated with heresies after their death are put in square brackets. For an index to the codices by subject, see Table III.

Fifth line: the state of the work's preservation, and in the right-hand margin the "class" to which I have assigned Photius' description of the work. To determine whether works are preserved or not I have relied almost entirely on the reference works listed in my bibliography and on Henry's edition; some preserved works may have escaped my notice. My designation "fragments" means that fragments of the text survive outside Photius' works; "lost" means that no fragments of the text (except the title) survive outside Photius' works; and "unattested" means that the work is known only from Photius. References are given to Jacoby's *Fragmente der griechischen Historiker* (*FGrHist*), Geerard's *Clavis Patrum Graecorum* (*CPG*), and Halkin's *Bibliotheca Hagiographica Graeca* (*BHG*). The classes of descriptions, which are discussed in Chapter Six, are as follows:

I. Descriptions probably composed from memory: imprecise references

II. Descriptions probably composed by referring back to the original text (or possibly to notes on it):
   A. Precise references
   B. References by parts (for multipart works)
   C. Precise summaries
   D. Epitomes

III. Descriptions probably copied by Photius' secretary from reading notes taken before the *Bibliotheca* was compiled:
   A. Epitomes with introductions added by Photius for the *Bibliotheca*
   B. Epitomes without such introductions
   C. Excerpts, also without such introductions

For an index to the codices by these classes, see Table V.

In a few cases an additional note has been appended, marked by an *N*. For further information, the reader should consult the notes to Henry's edition and the reference works listed in the Bibliography.

1. Theodore (of Pharan?)
e. 7 C. (Beck, 430–31)?
That the Book of St. Dionysius is Genuine
exegesis (Me?)
unattested IIB

2. Hadrian
fl. *ca.* 440 (Bardenhewer, IV, 254–55)
Introduction to Scripture
exegesis (X)
preserved (*CPG*, 6527) I

3. Nonnosus
fl. *ca.* 530 (I. Kawar, in *BZ*, 53 [1960], 57–73)
History
history
lost (*FGrHist*, 673, frag. 165) IIC

4. Theodore (of Mopsuestia)
ca. 350–428 (*KP*, Theodorus III.1)
For Basil, Against Eunomius
apologetic [N]
fragments in Latin and Syriac (*CPG*, 3859) IIA

5. Sophronius
l. 4 C. (Bardenhewer, III, 283)
For Basil, Against Eunomius
apologetic (X)
unattested I

6. Gregory of Nyssa
ca. 330–*ca.* 394 (*KP*, Gregorios 2)
[*For Basil,*] *Against Eunomius*
apologetic (X)
preserved (see Quasten, III, 257–58) (*CPG*, 3135) I

7. Gregory of Nyssa
ca. 330–*ca.* 394 (*KP*, Gregorios 2)
(*Against Eunomius*)
apologetic (X)
preserved (see Quasten, III, 257–58) (*CPG*, 3135) I

8. Origen
ca. 185–before 253 (*KP*, Origenes 2)
De Principiis
dogmatic [O]
preserved in Latin translation IIC

9. Eusebius (of Caesarea) (=*13*[1])
260/65–339/40 (*KP*, Eusebios 7)
Praeparatio Evangelica
apologetic (A)
preserved (*CPG*, 3486) IIA

10. Eusebius (of Caesarea) (=*13*^{2})
260/65–339/40 (*KP*, Eusebios 7)
Demonstratio Evangelica
apologetic (A)
partly preserved (*CPG*, 3487) IIA

11. Eusebius (of Caesarea) (=*13*^{3})
260/65–339/40 (*KP*, Eusebios 7)
Praeparatio Ecclesiastica
apologetic (A)
partly preserved (see pp. 76–78 *supra*) I

12. Eusebius (of Caesarea) (=*13*^{4})
260/65–339/40 (*KP*, Eusebios 7)
Demonstratio Ecclesiastica
apologetic (A)
partly preserved (see pp. 76–78 *supra*) I

13^{1}, *13*^{2}, *13*^{3}, *13*^{4} = *9*, *10*, *11*, *12* (see pp. 76–78 *supra*)

14^{1}. Apollinarius of Hierapolis
fl. *ca.* 172 (*KP*, Apollinarios 4)
Against the Pagans
apologetic (X)
lost I

14^{2}. Apollinarius of Hierapolis
fl. *ca.* 172 (*KP*, Apollinarios 4)
On Piety
dogmatic (X)
unattested I

14^{3}. Apollinarius of Hierapolis
fl. *ca.* 172 (*KP*, Apollinarios 4)
On Truth
dogmatic (X)
lost I

15. Gelasius (of Cyzicus) (=*88*)
fl. *ca.* 475 (*KP*, Gelasios 2)
Ecclesiastical History
history (X)
preserved (*CPG*, 6034) IIA

16. —
431 (Beck, 45–46)
Acts of the Third Council
conciliar *acta* (X)
preserved I

17. —
451 (Beck, 46)
Acts of the Fourth Council
conciliar *acta* (X)
preserved IIC

18. —
553 (Beck, 46)
Acts of the Fifth Council
conciliar *acta* (X)
preserved in Latin, fragments in Greek IIC

19. —
680–81 (Beck, 46–47)
Acts of the Sixth Council
conciliar *acta* (X)
preserved I

20. —
787 (Beck, 47)
Acts of the Seventh Council
conciliar *acta* (X)
preserved I

21. John Philoponus
ca. 490–*ca.* 570
On the Resurrection
dogmatic (M)
fragments (*CPG*, 7272) I

22. Theodosius the Monk
l. 6 C. (Beck, 383)
Against John
apologetic (X?)
unattested I

23[1]. Conon (of Tarsus)
l. 6 C. (Beck, 394)
Against John
apologetic (M)
fragments? (*CPG*, 7283?) I

23[2]. Eugenius (of Seleucia)
l. 6 C. (Beck, 394)
Against John
apologetic (M)
fragments? (*CPG*, 7283?) I

23[3]. Themistius (of Alexandria) (or Theonas?)
l. 6 C. (Beck, 394)
Against John
apologetic (M)
fragments? (*CPG*, 7283?) I

24. —
565/77 (Beck, 394)
Acts Disputed Before Patriarch John
conciliar *acta* (M)
unattested IIC

25[1]. (Proclus of Constantinople?) [John Chrysostom]
bishop 434–46 (*KP*, Proklos 2)
On Death (22 sermons)
sermons (X)
unattested IIA
N. Since B. Marx, in his *Procliana* (*Münsterische Beiträge zur Theologie*, 23 [1940]) 44–49, assigns the surviving sermons of 25[2] and 25[3] to Proclus, this third part of the collection may also be his.

25[2]. (Proclus of Constantinople) [John Chrysostom]
bishop 434–46 (*KP*, Proklos 2)
On the Ascension (22 sermons)
sermons (X)
partly preserved (5 sermons) (*CPG*, 4531–35)
N. See under 25[1]. IIA

25[3]. (Proclus of Constantinople) [John Chrysostom]
bishop 434–46 (*KP*, Proklos 2)
On Pentecost (17 sermons)
sermons (X)
partly preserved (3 sermons) (*CPG*, 4536–38)
N. See under 25[1]. Marx thinks that the first sermon may actually be Chrysostom's. IIA

26[1]. Synesius of Cyrene
ca. 370–*ca.* 413 (*KP*, Synesios)
On Providence
dogmatic (X)
preserved (*CPG*, 5631) I

26[2]. Synesius of Cyrene
ca. 370–*ca.* 413 (*KP*, Synesios)
On Royalty
oratory
preserved (*CPG*, 5630) I

26[3]. Synesius of Cyrene
ca. 370–*ca.* 413 (*KP*, Synesios)
"on other things"
dogmatic? (X?)
preserved? I

26[4]. Synesius of Cyrene
ca. 370–*ca.* 413 (*KP*, Synesios)
Letters
letters (X)
preserved (*CPG*, 5640)
N. Read φησι with M at 5b line 35 (see *supra* p. 60 and note 37). IIA

27. Eusebius (of Caesarea)
260/65–339/40 (*KP*, Eusebios 7)
Ecclesiastical History
history (A)
preserved (*CPG*, 3495) IIA

28. Socrates
ca. 380–*ca.* 450 (*ODCC*)
Ecclesiastical History
history (X)
preserved (*CPG*, 6028) IIA

29. Evagrius Scholasticus
ca. 536–*ca.* 600 (*KP*, *Nachträge*, Euagrios 4)
Ecclesiastical History
history (X)
preserved (*CPG*, 7500) IIA

30. Sozomen
d. after 439 (*KP*, Sozomenos)
Ecclesiastical History
history (X)
preserved (*CPG*, 6030) IIA

31. Theodoret (of Cyrus)
393–*ca.* 466 (*KP*, Theodoretos 1)
Ecclesiastical History
history (X)
preserved (*CPG*, 6222) IIA

32. Athanasius
ca. 295–373 (*KP*, Athanasios)
Letters
letters (X)
preserved (*CPG*, 2123?) I

33. Justus of Tiberias
l. 1 C. (*RE*, Iustus 9)
Chronicle of the Jewish Kings in Family Trees
history (J)
lost (*FGrHist*, 734) IIA

34. (Julius) Africanus
ca. 160–*ca.* 240 (*ODCC*)
History
history (X)
fragments IIA

35. Philip of Side
e. 5 C. (*ODCC*)
Christian History (first 24 of 36 books)
history (X)
fragments (*CPG*, 6026) IIA

36. (Cosmas Indicopleustes)
fl. *ca.* 550 (*KP*, Kosmas)
Christian (*Topography*)
exegesis (X)
preserved (*CPG*, 7468) IIC

37. Anonymous
6 C. (see note)
On Politics
philosophy
partly preserved IIC
N. Cf. E. Barker, *Social and Political Thought in Byzantium* (Oxford, 1957), 63–66. I have learned from Professor A. S. Photiou that new portions of this work have now been discovered that identify it more securely with Photius' book.

38. Theodore of Mopsuestia
ca. 350–428 (*KP*, Theodoros III.1)
Interpretation of the Creation
exegesis [N]
fragments (*CPG*, 3827) IIA

39. Eusebius (of Caesarea)
260/65–339/40 (*KP*, Eusebios 7)
Against Hierocles
apologetic (A)
preserved (*CPG*, 3485) I

40. Philostorgius
ca. 368–*ca.* 439 (*ODCC*)
Ecclesiastical History
history (A)
fragments (*CPG*, 6032) IIC

41. John (Diacrinomenus) [of Aegeae]
d. after 526 (see pp. 69–70 *supra*)
Ecclesiastical History (first 5 of 10 books)
history (M)
fragments (*CPG*, 7509) IIA

42. Basil the Cilician
e. 6 C. (Beck, 376)
Ecclesiastical History (Book II of 3 books)
history (M?)
unattested IIC

43. John Philoponus (=*240*)
ca. 490–*ca.* 570 (*OCD*)
On the Hexameron
exegesis (M)
preserved (*CPG*, 7265) IIA

44. Philostratus (II) [of Tyre] (=*241*)
ca. 170–244/49 (*OCD*)
Life of Apollonius of Tyana
biography
preserved IIC

45. Andronicianus
fl. *ca.* 400 (*RE*, Andronikianos)
Against the Eunomians
apologetic (X)
unattested IIA

46[1]. Theodoret of Cyrus
393–*ca.* 466 (*KP*, Theodoretos 1)
Against Various Theses
apologetic [N]
preserved (see Quasten, III, 519–20) (*CPG*, 6215, 6219) IIB

46[2]. (Eutherius of Tyana) [Theodoret of Cyrus]
fl. *ca.* 431 (*RE*, Eutherios 3)
(*Confutationes*)
apologetic (N)
preserved (*CPG*, 6147) IIB

46[3]. Theodoret of Cyrus
393–*ca.* 466 (*KP*, Theodoretos 1)
Eranistes seu Polymorphus
apologetic [N]
preserved (*CPG*, 6217) IIB

47. Josephus
37/38–after 100 (*KP*, Iosephos 2)
(*Jewish War*)
history (J)
preserved IIC

48. (Hippolytus of Rome) [Josephus? Gaius of Rome?]
d. 235 (*KP*, Hippolytos 5)
On the Universe
dogmatic (X)
preserved IIC

49[1]. Cyril of Alexandria (=*169*[1])
d. 444 (*KP*, Kyrillos 1)
Against the Blasphemies of Nestorius
apologetic (X)
preserved (*CPG*, 5217) IIA

49[2]. Cyril of Alexandria
d. 444 (*KP*, Kyrillos 1)
(*Dialogues on the Trinity*)
apologetic (X)
preserved (*CPG*, 5216) I

49[3]. Cyril of Alexandria
d. 444 (*KP*, Kyrillos 1)
On (Adoration and) Worship in Spirit (and in Truth)
exegesis (X)
preserved (*CPG*, 5200) I

50[1]. Nicias the Monk
6 C. (Beck, 383)
Against the Seven Chapters of Philoponus
apologetic (X)
unattested I

50[2]. Nicias the Monk
6 C. (Beck, 383)
Against the Impious Severus
apologetic (X)
unattested I

50[3]. Nicias the Monk
6 C. (Beck, 383)
Against the Pagans
apologetic (X)
unattested I

51. Hesychius of Constantinople
m. 4 C. (*Dictionary of Christian Biography* [Boston, 1877–87], Hesychius 26)
On the Brazen Serpent
sermons? (X)
unattested IIA

52. —
compiled after 518 (Severus Patriarch of Antioch; cod. 52: 13b lines 26–28)
(*Collection of Acts Against the Messalians*)
conciliar *acta* (X)
unattested IIC

53. —
compiled after 442 (see note)
(*Collection of Acts Against Pelagius and Celestius*)
conciliar *acta* (X)
preserved in Latin, 2 of 7 acts preserved in Greek
N. See M. Aubineau, in *Revue de philologie,* 41 (1967), 232–41. IIC

54. —
compiled after 492 (Gelasius I Pope; cod. 54: 15a lines 24–28)
Copy of the Acts of the Bishops of the West Against the Doctrines of Nestorius
conciliar *acta* (X)
partly preserved (in texts of cod. 53) IIC

55[1]. John Philoponus
ca. 490–*ca.* 570 (*OCD*)
(*Against the Council of Chalcedon*)
apologetic (M)
fragments in Syriac (*CPG*, 7271) IIA

55[2]. John of Aegeae
m. 5 C. (see pp. 69–70 *supra*)
(*Against the Council of Chalcedon*)
apologetic (N)
unattested IIA

56. Theodoret of Cyrus
393–*ca.* 466 (*KP,* Theodoretos 1)
(*Compendium of Heretical Falsehood*)
apologetic [N]
preserved (*CPG*, 6223) IIA

57. Appian
after 81–before 161 (*OCD*)
Roman History
history
partly preserved IIC

58. Arrian
fl. *ca.* 130 (*KP*, Arrianos 2)
Parthica
history
fragments (*FGrHist*, 156, frags. 30–53) IIC

59. —
403 (Beck, 53)
(*Acts of the Synod of the Oak*)
conciliar *acta* (X but uncanonical)
lost IIC

60. Herodotus
484?–after 431 B.C. (*KP*, Herodotos 1)
Histories
history
preserved IIC

61. Aeschines (=*264*[1])
390/89–*ca.* 315 B.C. (*KP*, Aischines 2)
Orations (3 orations)
oratory
preserved IIA

62. Praxagoras of Athens
fl. *ca.* 337 (*RE*, Praxagoras 3)
History of Constantine
history
unattested (*FGrHist*, 219) IIC

63. Procopius (of Caesarea)
b. 490/507 (*KP*, Prokopios 3)
History (*of the Wars*)
history
preserved IIIA

64. Theophanes of Byzantium
l. 6 C. (Krumbacher, 243)
History
history
unattested (*FGrHist*, 673, frag. 166) IIIA

65. Theophylact (Simocatta)
e. 7 C. (Krumbacher, 247)
Histories
history
preserved IIIA

66. Nicephorus of Constantinople
ca. 758–829 (*ODCC*)
Breviarium
history
preserved IIA

67. Sergius Confessor
d. 832/42 (see p. 2 *supra*)
Ecclesiastical History
history (X)
unattested IIA

68. Cephalion
fl. 117/38 (*KP*, Kephalion 2)
(*Muses*)
history
fragments (*FGrHist*, 93) IIB

69[1]. Hesychius (of Miletus)
fl. 527/65 (*KP*, Hesychios 4)
Roman and General History
history
fragments IIC

69[2]. Hesychius (of Miletus)
fl. 527/65 (*KP*, Hesychios 4)
History of Justin and Justinian
history
unattested IIA

70. Diodorus Siculus (=*244*)
d. after 36 B.C. (*KP*, Diodoros 12)
(*Library of History*)
history
partly preserved IIC

71. Dio Cassius
fl. *ca.* 229 (*KP*, Cassius III.4)
(*Roman History*)
history
partly preserved IIC

72[1]. Ctesias of Cnidus
d. after 398 B.C. (*KP*, Ktesias)
Persica
history
fragments (*FGrHist*, 688, frags. 1–44) IIIA

72[2]. Ctesias of Cnidus
d. after 398 B.C. (*KP*, Ktesias)
Indica
history
fragments (*FGrHist*, 688, frags. 45–52) IIIA

73. Heliodorus
3 C. (*KP*, Heliodoros 5)
Aethiopica
novel
preserved IIC

74[1]. Themistius
ca. 317–*ca*. 388 (*KP*, Themistios)
Political Orations (36 orations)
oratory
partly preserved (34 of 36 orations) IIA

74[2]. Lesbonax (of Mytilene)
2 C. (*OCD*)
Political Orations (16 orations)
oratory
partly preserved (3 of 16 orations) IIA

75. John Philoponus
ca. 490–*ca*. 570 (*OCD*)
Against John the Scholastic
apologetic (M)
unattested IIA

76[1]. Josephus (=*238*)
37/38–after 100 (*KP*, Iosephos 2)
Jewish Antiquities
history (J)
preserved IIC

76[2]. Josephus
37/38–after 100 (*KP*, Iosephos 2)
(*Autobiography*)
biography (J)
preserved IIC

77[1]. Eunapius of Sardis
345/46–*ca*. 420 (*KP*, Eunapios)
Chronicle: New Edition
history
fragments IIC

77[2]. Eunapius of Sardis
345/46–*ca.* 420 (*KP*, Eunapios)
Chronicle: First Edition
history
fragments I

78. Malchus of Philadelphia
fl. *ca.* 500 (*KP*, Malchos 4)
Byzantiniaca (incomplete; see *RE*, Malchos 2)
history
fragments IIC

79. Candidus
d. after 491 (*KP*, Candidus 3)
History
history
lost (*FGrHist*, 748) IIC

80. Olympiodorus (of Thebes)
d. after 425 (*KP*, Olympiodoros 4)
History
history
lost IIIA

81. Theodore (of Mopsuestia)
ca. 350–428 (*KP*, Theodoros III.1)
On Magism in Persia
apologetic [N]
fragments? (*CPG*, 3861?) IIC

82[1]. Dexippus
ca. 210–after 274 (*KP*, Dexippos 2)
After Alexander
history
fragments (*FGrHist*, 100, frags. 8 and 31–36) IIC

82[2]. Dexippus
ca. 210–after 274 (*KP*, Dexippos 2)
Short History
history
fragments (*FGrHist*, 100, frags. 1–5 and 9–23) I

82[3]. Dexippus
ca. 210–after 274 (*KP*, Dexippos 2)
Scythica
history
fragments (*FGrHist*, 100, frags. 6–7 and 24–30) I

83. Dionysius of Halicarnassus
fl. 30/8 B.C. (*KP*, Dionysios 20)
(*Roman Antiquities*)
history
partly preserved IIA

84. Dionysius of Halicarnassus
fl. 30/8 B.C. (*KP*, Dionysios 20)
Synopsis
history
partly preserved (in original, not synopsis) IIA

85. Heraclianus of Chalcedon
fl. *ca.* 536 (Beck, 372)
Against the Manichaeans
apologetic (X)
fragments (*CPG*, 6801) IIC

86. John Chrysostom
ca. 349–407 (*KP*, *Nachträge*, Iohannes 15)
Letters
letters (X)
preserved (*CPG*, 4405) IIA

87. Achilles Tatius
fl. *ca.* 180 (*KP*, *Nachträge*, Achilleus Tatios 1)
Leucippe and Clitophon
novel
preserved IIA

88. Gelasius (of Cyzicus) [of Caesarea] (=*15*)
fl. *ca.* 475 (*KP*, Gelasios 2)
Ecclesiastical History
history (X)
preserved (*CPG*, 6034) IIC

89. Gelasius of Caesarea
d. 395 (*KP*, Gelasios 1)
Continuation of the Ecclesiastical History of Eusebius
history (X)
fragments in *Theodorus Lector* (ed. G. Hansen [Berlin 1971], 158–59)
(*CPG*, 3521) IIA

90. Libanius
314–*ca.* 393 (*KP*, Libanios)
(*Orations*)
oratory
preserved IIA

91[1]. Arrian
fl. *ca.* 130 (*KP*, Arrianos 2)
(Anabasis of) Alexander
history
preserved IIC

91[2]. Arrian
fl. *ca.* 130 (*KP*, Arrianos 2)
Indica
history
preserved IIA

92. Arrian
fl. *ca.* 130 (*KP*, Arrianos 2)
After Alexander
history
fragments (*FGrHist*, 156, frags. 1–11) IID

93. Arrian
fl. *ca.* 130 (*KP*, Arrianos 2)
Bithyniaca
history
fragments (*FGrHist*, 156, frags. 14–29) IIA

94. Jamblichus
ca. 100–after 165 (*KP*, Iamblichos 3)
(*Babyloniaca*)
novel
fragments IIIA

95. John of Scythopolis
bishop 536–50 (Beck, 376–77)
Against Those Separated from the Church
apologetic (X)
unattested IIA

96. George of Alexandria
patriarch *ca.* 620–*ca.* 630 (Beck, 460)
On Chrysostom
hagiography (X)
preserved (*BHG*, 873; *CPG*, 7979) IID

97. Phlegon of Tralles
d. after 140 (*KP*, Phlegon)
Compilation of Olympic Victors and Chronicles (read in part)
history
fragments (*FGrHist*, 257, frags. 1–34) IIC

98. Zosimus Comes
fl. *ca.* 500 (*KP*, Zosimos 2)
(*New History*)
history
preserved IIC

99. Herodian (of Syria)
ca. 180–after 238 (*KP*, Herodianos 2)
History
history
preserved IIC

100. Hadrian Augustus
76–138 (*KP*, Hadrianus 1)
Rhetorical Exercises
oratory
lost I

101[1]. Victorinus of Antioch
5 C. (very old under Zeno; cod. 101: 86a lines 7–10)
Consular Orations
oratory
unattested I

101[2]. Victorinus of Antioch
5 C. (see 101[1])
Imperial Orations
oratory
unattested I

102[1]. Gelasius of Caesarea
d. 395 (*KP*, Gelasios 1)
Against the Anomoeans
apologetic (X)
unattested IIA

102[2]. Diodorus of Tarsus
d. before 394 (*KP*, Diodoros 17)
On the Holy Spirit
dogmatic [N]
unattested IIA

103[1]. Philo Judaeus
15/10 B.C.–after 40 (*KP*, Philon 10)
Legum Allegoriae
exegesis (J)
preserved I

103[2]. Philo Judaeus
15/10 B.C.–after 40 (*KP*, Philon 10)
(*De Josepho*) (so K. Ziegler, in *RE*, Photius 13, cols. 702–3)
exegesis (J)
preserved I

104[1]. Philo Judaeus
15/10 B.C.–after 40 (*KP*, Philon 10)
(*De Judaeis*) (so K. Ziegler, in *RE*, Photius 13, col. 703)
devotional (J)
fragments I

104[2]. Philo Judaeus
15/10 B.C.–after 40 (*KP*, Philon 10)
(*De Vita Contemplativa*)
devotional (J)
preserved I

105[1]. Philo Judaeus
15/10 B.C.–after 40 (*KP*, Philon 10)
(*Legatio ad*) *Gaium*
apologetic (J)
preserved I

105[2]. Philo Judaeus
15/10 B.C.–after 40 (*KP*, Philon 10)
In Flaccum
apologetic (J)
preserved I

106. Theognostus of Alexandria
d. *ca.* 282 (*ODCC*)
Hypotyposes
dogmatic (O)
fragments IIC

107. Basil the Cilician
e. 6 C. (Beck, 376)
Against John of Scythopolis
apologetic (M?)
unattested IIC

108. Theodore of Alexandria
6 C. (Beck, 393)
Against Themistius
apologetic (M)
fragments? (*CPG*, 7295?) IIC

109. Clement of Alexandria
ca. 150–before 215 (*KP*, Clemens 6)
Hypotyposes
exegesis [O]
fragments (see Quasten, II, 16–17) IIA

110[1]. Clement of Alexandria
ca. 150–before 215 (*KP*, Clemens 6)
Paedagogus
apologetic [O]
preserved IIA

110[2]. Clement of Alexandria
ca. 150–before 215 (*KP*, Clemens 6)
(*Exhortation to the Pagans*)
apologetic [O]
preserved IIA

111[1]. Clement of Alexandria
ca. 150–before 215 (*KP*, Clemens 6)
Stromata
apologetic [O]
preserved IIA

111[2]. Clement of Alexandria
ca. 150–before 215 (*KP*, Clemens 6)
Quis Dives Salvetur?
exegesis [O]
preserved IIA

112–13[1]. [Clement of Rome]
ca. 380 (*KP*, Constitutiones apostolorum)
Apostolic Constitutions
regulations (A)
preserved IIC

112–13[2]. [Clement of Rome]
3 C. (*KP*, Clemens 7)
Recognitions
hagiography [A]
Latin translation IIC

112–13[3]. [Clement of Rome]
3 C. (*KP*, Clemens 7)
(*Homilies*) (see pp. 70–71 *supra*)
hagiography [A]
preserved (*BHG*, 321–41) I

114^{1}. [Leucius Charinus]
l. 2 C. (*ODCC*, Peter, Acts of St.)
Acts of St. Peter
hagiography (G)
partly preserved in Greek, Latin translation (*BHG*, 1482z–85) I

114^{2}. [Leucius Charinus]
l. 2 C.? (*ODCC*, John, Acts of St.)
Acts of St. John
hagiography (G)
partly preserved (*BHG*, 899–915p) I

114^{3}. [Leucius Charinus]
e. 3 C.? (*ODCC*, Andrew, Acts of St.)
Acts of St. Andrew
hagiography (G)
partly preserved (*BHG*, 93–94h) I

114^{4}. [Leucius Charinus]
e. 3 C.? (*ODCC*, Thomas, Acts of St.)
Acts of St. Thomas
hagiography (G)
preserved (*BHG*, 1800–31k) I

114^{5}. [Leucius Charinus]
l. 2 C. (*ODCC*, Paul, Acts of St.)
Acts of St. Paul
hagiography (X)
fragments in Greek, Coptic translation (*BHG*, 1451–52) I

115^{1}. Anonymous
4 C.? (perhaps near in date to 115^{2}, in same volume)
Against the Quartodecimans
chronology (X)
unattested IIC

115^{2}. Metrodorus
4 C.? (cf. V. Grumel, *La Chronologie* [Paris, 1958], 129)
Computation of Easter
chronology (X)
unattested IIA

116. Anonymous
4 C.? (perhaps soon after 115^{2}; cf. cod. 116: 91a lines 40–41)
On Easter
chronology (X)
unattested IIC

117. Anonymous
4 C.? (Eusebius latest author cited; cod. 117: 91b line 35)
For Origen
apologetic (O)
unattested IIC

118[1]. Pamphilus Martyr
d. 309 (*KP*, Pamphilos 4)
For Origen
apologetic (O)
Latin translation of first of 5 books; otherwise lost (*CPG*, 3476) IIC

118[2]. Eusebius (of Caesarea)
260/65–339/40 (*KP*, Eusebios 7)
For Origen
apologetic (A)
lost (*CPG*, 3476) IIC

119. Pierius (of Alexandria)
d. after 309 (Quasten, II, 111)
Sermons (12 sermons)
sermons (O)
fragments (see Quasten, II, 134–36) IIC

120. Irenaeus of Lyons
ca. 130–*ca*. 200 (*ODCC*)
Adversus Haereses
apologetic (X)
fragments in Greek, complete Latin translation IIC

121. Hippolytus (of Rome)
d. 235 (*KP*, Hippolytos 5)
Syntagma
apologetic (X)
fragments IIA

122. Epiphanius (of Salamis)
ca. 315–403 (*KP*, Epiphanios 1)
Panarium
apologetic (X)
preserved (*CPG*, 3745) IIA

123. Epiphanius (of Salamis)
ca. 315–403 (*KP*, Epiphanios 1)
Ancoratus
apologetic (X)
preserved (*CPG*, 3744) I

124. Epiphanius (of Salamis)
ca. 315–403 (*KP*, Epiphanios 1)
(title omitted)
apologetic? (X)
preserved? I

125[1]. Justin Martyr
ca. 100–*ca.* 165 (*ODCC*)
Apologia
apologetic (X)
preserved I

125[2]. Justin Martyr
ca. 100–*ca.* 165 (*ODCC*)
(*Dialogue with Tryphon*)
apologetic (X)
preserved I

125[3]. [Justin Martyr]
4/5 C. (*ODCC*, Justin Martyr)
(*Confutatio Dogmatum Quorundam Aristotelicorum*)
apologetic (X)
preserved I

125[4]. (Theodoret of Cyrus) [Justin Martyr]
393–*ca.* 466 (*KP*, Theodoretos 1)
(*Quaestiones et Responsiones ad Orthodoxos*)
dogmatic [N]
preserved (*CPG*, 6285) I
N. For the attribution, see Quasten, I, 206–7, and III, 548–49.

125[5]. (Theodoret of Cyrus?) [Justin Martyr] (see 125[4] N.)
393–*ca.* 466 (*KP*, Theodoretos 1)
(*Quaestiones Christianorum*)
dogmatic [N]
preserved I

125[6]. (Theodoret of Cyrus?) [Justin Martyr] (see 125[4] N.)
393–*ca.* 466 (*KP*, Theodoretos 1)
(*Quaestiones Graecorum*)
dogmatic [N]
preserved I

126[1]. Clement (of Rome)
l. 1 C. (*KP*, Clemens 7)
Epistle to the Corinthians
letter (X)
preserved IIA

126[2]. [Clement (of Rome)]
120/50 (*KP*, Clemens 7)
Second Epistle to the Corinthians
sermon (X)
preserved IIA

126[3]. Polycarp (of Smyrna)
ca. 69–*ca*. 155 (*ODCC*)
Epistle to the Philippians
letter (X)
partly preserved IIA

127. Eusebius (of Caesarea)
260/65–339/40 (*KP*, Eusebios 7)
Life of Constantine
biography (A)
preserved (*BHG*, 361x; *CPG*, 3496) IIC

128[1]. Lucian (of Samosata)
ca. 120–after 180 (*KP*, Lukianos 1)
For Phalaris
satire
preserved IIA

128[2]. Lucian (of Samosata)
ca. 120–after 180 (*KP*, Lukianos 1)
Dialogues of the Dead
satire
preserved IIA

128[3]. Lucian (of Samosata)
ca. 120–after 180 (*KP*, Lukianos 1)
Dialogues of Courtesans
satire
preserved IIA

128[4]. Lucian (of Samosata)
ca. 120–after 180 (*KP*, Lukianos 1)
(*Lucius or The Ass*) (see cod. 129: 96b lines 17–26)
novel
preserved I

128[5]. Lucian (of Samosata)
ca. 120–after 180 (*KP*, Lukianos 1)
(*True History*) (see cod. 166: 111b lines 35–37)
novel
preserved I

128[6]. Lucian (of Samosata)
ca. 120–after 180 (*KP*, Lukianos 1)
"other works"
satire?
preserved? I
N. Possibly 128[4] and 128[5] were the only "other works."

129. Lucius of Patrae (?)
e. 2 C. (see note)
Metamorphoses
novel
lost I
N. See pp. 68–69 note 10 *supra.*

130[1]. Damascius of Damascus
ca. 458–after 533 (*KP*, Damaskios)
On Marvelous Deeds
paradoxography
unattested IIA

130[2]. Damascius of Damascus
ca. 458–after 533 (*KP*, Damaskios)
Marvelous Tales of the Gods
paradoxography
unattested IIA

130[3]. Damascius of Damascus
ca. 458–after 533 (*KP*, Damaskios)
Marvelous Tales of Souls Appearing After Death
paradoxography
unattested IIA

130[4]. Damascius of Damascus
ca. 458–after 533 (*KP*, Damaskios)
Marvelous Animals
paradoxography
unattested IIA

131. Amyntianus
l. 2 C. (dedicated to Marcus Aurelius; cod. 131: 97a lines 10–11)
On Alexander
biography
lost IIA

132–35[1]. Palladius (of Methone)
e. 4 C. (*KP*, Palladios 1)
Rhetorical Exercises
oratory
lost I

132–35[2]. Aphthonius (of Antioch)
4/5 C. (*KP*, Aphthonios)
Rhetorical Exercises
oratory
unattested I

132–35[3]. Eusebius (of Emesa)
ca. 300–*ca*. 359 (*KP*, Eusebios 9)
Rhetorical Exercises
oratory
unattested (or preserved as *CPG*, 3525?) I

132–35[4]. Maximus (the Cynic?)
fl. *ca*. 380 (*KP*, Maximus I.12)?
Rhetorical Exercises
oratory
unattested I
N. Maximus the Cynic was from Alexandria (cf. cod. 132–35: 97a line 26), and is described by Gregory of Nazianzus as a λογογράφος and ῥήτωρ (PG, 37, col. 1341A).

136. Cyril (of Alexandria)
d. 444 (*KP*, Kyrillos 1)
Thesaurus
apologetic (X)
preserved (*CPG*, 5215) I

137. Eunomius (of Cyzicus)
d. *ca*. 394 (*KP*, Eunomios)
(*Apologeticus*)
apologetic (A)
preserved (*CPG*, 3455) I

138[1]. Eunomius (of Cyzicus)
d. *ca*. 394 (*KP*, Eunomios)
(*Apologia Pro Apologia*)
apologetic (A)
fragments (*CPG*, 3456) I

138[2]. Eunomius (of Cyzicus)
d. *ca*. 394 (*KP*, Eunomios)
Letters (about 40 letters)
letters (A)
lost IIA

139[1]. Athanasius
ca. 295–373 (*KP*, Athanasios)
Commentary on Ecclesiastes
exegesis (X)
unattested I

139[2]. Athanasius
ca. 295–373 (*KP*, Athanasios)
Commentary on the Song of Songs
exegesis (X)
fragments (*CPG*, 2141[6]) I

140[1]. Athanasius
ca. 295–373 (*KP*, Athanasios)
(*Orations Against the Arians*) (3 orations)
apologetic (X)
preserved (*CPG*, 2093) I

140[2]. [Athanasius]
l. 4 C.? (A. Puech, *Histoire de la littérature grecque chrétienne*, III [Paris, 1930], 84)
(*Fourth Oration Against the Arians*)
apologetic (X)
preserved (*CPG*, 2230) I

140[3]. Athanasius
ca. 295–373 (*KP*, Athanasios)
(*On the Incarnation and Against the Arians*)
apologetic (X)
preserved (*CPG*, 2806) I
N. On the identification, see Quasten, III, 29.

141. Basil (of Caesarea)
ca. 330–79 (*KP*, Basileios 4)
On the Hexameron
sermons (X)
preserved (*CPG*, 2835) I

142. Basil (of Caesarea)
ca. 330–79 (*KP*, Basileios 4)
Moralia
regulations (X)
preserved (*CPG*, 2877) I

143[1]. Basil (of Caesarea)
ca. 330–79 (*KP*, Basileios 4)
Canonical Letters
letters (X)
preserved (*CPG*, 2901) I

143[2]. Basil (of Caesarea)
ca. 330–79 (*KP*, Basileios 4)
Letters
letters (X)
preserved (*CPG*, 2900) I

144. (Basil of Caesarea) (=*191*)
ca. 330–79 (*KP*, Basileios 4)
Ascetica
regulations (X)
preserved (*CPG*, 2875–76) I

145. Helladius (of Alexandria)
fl. *ca*. 400 (*KP*, Helladios 2)
(*Usage of All Sorts of Style*)
lexicon
lost IIA
N. *145* may = *146, 147, 148* (see above, pp. 78–79 note 60). IIA

146. (Helladius of Alexandria?) (see *145*)
fl. *ca*. 400 (*KP*, Helladios 2)?
Lexicon of the Simple Style
lexicon
lost IIA

147. (Helladius of Alexandria?) (see *145*)
fl. *ca*. 400 (*KP*, Helladios 2)?
Lexicon of the High Style
lexicon
lost IIA

148. (Helladius of Alexandria?) (see *145*)
fl. *ca*. 400 (*KP*, Helladios 2)?
Lexicon of the Style of Political Oratory
lexicon
lost IIA
N. Read ἰδέας for the MSS' ἰδίως in title.

149[1]. (Valerius) Pollio
fl. 117/38 (*KP*, Valerius B.9)
Lexicon
lexicon
lost I

149[2]. Diogenianus (of Heraclea)
fl. 117/38 (*KP*, Diogenianos 2)
(*Lexicon*)
lexicon
lost I

150[1]. Julian
2 C. (*KP*, Julianos 12)
Lexicon of Words in the Ten Orators
lexicon
unattested I

150². Philostratus (I) [of Tyre]
2 C. (*OCD*)
(*Questions in the Orators*)
lexicon
lost I
N. See p. 70 note 22.

150³. (Valerius) Diodorus
m. 2 C. (*RE*, Diodoros 46)
(*Explanation of Questions in the Ten Orators*)
lexicon
lost I

151. Timaeus
1/2 C.? (cf. *KP*, Timaios 3)
On Terms in Plato
lexicon
preserved IIA

152¹. Aelius Dionysius
fl. 117/38 (*KP*, Dionysios 29)
Attic Words (*First Edition*)
lexicon
fragments IIA

152². Aelius Dionysius
fl. 117/38 (*KP*, Dionysios 29)
Attic Words (*Second Edition*)
lexicon
fragments IIA

153. Pausanias
fl. 117/38? (*KP*, Pausanias 9)
Lexicon
lexicon
fragments IIA

154–55¹. Boëthus
l. 2 C. (see under 154–55²)
Collection of Platonic Terms
lexicon
unattested IIA

154–55². Boëthus
l. 2 C. (dedicated [cod. 155: lines 19–20] to Athenagoras of Athens, fl. *ca.* 177; see *KP*, Athenagoras)
On Difficult Words in Plato
lexicon
unattested IIA

156. Dorotheus (of Ascalon?)
1 C. (*KP*, Dorotheos 1)?
On Foreign Words
lexicon
unattested IIA

157. Moeris
fl. *ca*. 200? (*KP*, Moiris 1)
Atticist
lexicon
preserved IIA

158. Phrynichus the Arab
2 C. (*KP*, Phrynichos 5)
Preparation for the Sophist
lexicon
fragments IIB

159[1]. Isocrates (=*260*)
436–338 B.C. (*KP*, Isokrates 2)
Orations (21 orations)
oratory
preserved IIB

159[2]. Isocrates
436–338 B.C. (*KP*, Isokrates 2)
Letters (9 letters)
letters
preserved IIB

160. Choricius of Gaza
6 C. (*KP*, Chorikios)
Orations
oratory
preserved (*CPG*, 7518) IIC

161. Sopatrus of Apamea
d. *ca*. 335 (*RE*, Sopatros 11)
Various Extracts
anthology
lost IIC

162. Eusebius (of Thessalonica)
l. 6 C. (Beck, 383–84)
Against Andrew
apologetic (X)
lost IIC

163. Vindanius Anatolius
4/5 C. (*RE*, Anatolios 14)
Collection of Farming Practices
agriculture
fragments IIA

164. Galen
129–99 (*KP*, Galenos)
On Schools
medicine
preserved IIC

165. Himerius (=*243*)
300/10–*ca*. 380 (*KP*, Himerios)
Orations [about 70 orations] (75 orations)
oratory
partly preserved IIB

166. Antonius Diogenes
fl. *ca*. 100 (*KP*, *Nachträge*, Diogenes 17)
The Wonders Beyond Thule
novel
unattested IIC

167. John Stobaeus
e. 5 C. (*KP*, Stobaios)
Extracts, Sayings, and Precepts
anthology
preserved IIB

168. Basil of Seleucia
bishop *ca*. 435–*ca*. 468 (*KP*, Basileios 5)
Sermons (15 sermons)
sermons (X)
preserved (*CPG*, 6656) IIB

169[1]. Cyril (of Alexandria) (=*49*[1])
d. 444 (*KP*, Kyrillos 1)
Against the Blasphemies of Nestorius
apologetic (X)
preserved (*CPG*, 5217) IIB

169[2]. Cyril (of Alexandria)
d. 444 (*KP*, Kyrillos 1)
(Second) Letter to Nestorius
letter (X)
preserved (*CPG*, 5304) IIA

169[3]. Nestorius
patriarch 428–31
(Second) Letter to Cyril
letter (N)
preserved (*CPG*, 5669) IIA

169[4]. Cyril (of Alexandria)
d. 444 (*KP*, Kyrillos 1)
(Third Letter to Nestorius)
letter (X)
preserved (*CPG*, 5317) IIA

169[5]. Cyril (of Alexandria)
d. 444 (*KP*, Kyrillos 1)
Letters
letters (X)
preserved (among *CPG*, 5301–5411) IIA

169[6]. Cyril (of Alexandria)
d. 444 (*KP*, Kyrillos 1)
Scholia on the Incarnation of the Only-Begotten
dogmatic (X)
partly preserved in Greek, complete Latin translation (*CPG*, 5225) IIB

170. Anonymous
l. 7 C.? (after Heraclius; cod. 170: 117b line 31)
Testimonies and Citations
anthology (X)
unattested IIC

171. Eustratius of Constantinople
fl. *ca.* 583 (Beck, 410–11)
(Refutation)
apologetic (X)
preserved (*CPG*, 7522) IIC

172–74[1]. (John) Chrysostom
ca. 349–407 (*KP*, *Nachträge*, Iohannes 15)
Homilies on Genesis (61 homilies)
sermons (X)
preserved (*CPG*, 4409) IIA

172–74[2]. (John Chrysostom)
ca. 349–407 (*KP*, *Nachträge*, Iohannes 15)
Homilies on Acts (55 homilies)
sermons (X)
preserved (*CPG*, 4426) IIA

172–74[3]. (John) Chrysostom
ca. 349–407 (*KP*, *Nachträge*, Iohannes 15)
Homilies on the Apostle
sermons (X)
preserved (*CPG*, 4427–40) I

172–74[4]. (John) Chrysostom
ca. 349–407 (*KP*, *Nachträge*, Iohannes 15)
Homilies on the Psalms
sermons (X)
preserved (*CPG*, 4413) I

175. Pamphila (of Epidaurus)
fl. 54/68 (*KP*, Pamphila)
Miscellaneous Historical Notes (8 of 33 books)
anthology
fragments IIC

176. Theopompus of Chios
b. *ca.* 378 B.C. (*OCD*)
(*Philippica*)
history
fragments (*FGrHist*, 115, frags. 24–246) IIC

177. Theodore (of Mopsuestia)
ca. 350–428 (*KP*, Theodoros III.1)
Against the Defenders of Original Sin
apologetic [N]
fragments in Latin translation (*CPG*, 3860) IIC

178[1]. Dioscorides Pedanius
fl. 41/68 (*KP*, Dioskurides 5)
Materia (*Medica*)
medicine
preserved IIC

178[2]. Dioscorides Pedanius
fl. 41/68 (*KP*, Dioskurides 5)
(*On Harmful Medicines*)
medicine
preserved IIC

178[3]. Dioscorides Pedanius
fl. 41/68 (*KP*, Dioskurides 5)
(*On Venomous Animals*)
medicine
preserved IIC

179[1]. Agapius
l. 3 C. (*RE*, Agapios 2)
Libelli
dogmatic (Ma)
unattested IIC

179[2]. Agapius
l. 3 C. (*RE*, Agapios 2)
Capita
dogmatic (Ma)
unattested IIC

180[1]. John Lydus
490–after 552 (*KP*, Lydos 2)
De Ostentis
science
preserved IIA

180[2]. John Lydus
490–after 552 (*KP*, Lydos 2)
De Mensibus
science
partly preserved IIA

180[3]. John Lydus
490–after 552 (*KP*, Lydos 2)
De Magistratibus
history
preserved IIC

181. Damascius of Damascus (=*242*)
ca. 458–after 533 (*KP*, Damaskios)
On the Life of Isidore the Philosopher
biography
lost IIC

182[1]. Eulogius of Alexandria (=*208*[1]=*280*[1])
patriarch 581–607 (Beck, 381)
On Dispensation
apologetic (X)
unattested (*CPG*, 6976) IIC

182[2]. Eulogius of Alexandria (=*208*[2] =*280*[2])
patriarch 581–607 (Beck, 381)
Against Novatus
apologetic (X)
unattested (*CPG*, 6976) IIC

183. Eudocia Augusta
ca. 400–*ca.* 460 (*RE*, Eudokia 1)
Paraphrase of the Octateuch
poetry (X)
lost (*CPG*, 6022) IIA

184[1]. (Eudocia Augusta)
ca. 400–*ca.* 460 (*RE*, Eudokia 1)
Paraphrase of Zacharias and Daniel
poetry (X)
lost (*CPG*, 6023) IIA

184[2]. (Eudocia Augusta)
ca. 400–*ca.* 460 (*RE*, Eudokia 1)
On Cyprian the Martyr
poetry (X)
fragments (*CPG*, 6024) IIC

185. Dionysius of Aegeae (=*211*)
1/3 C. (*RE*, Dionysios 124)
Dictyaca
medicine
unattested IIB

186[1]. Conon
fl. *ca.* 1 (*KP*, Konon 4)
Narrations
mythology
unattested (*FGrHist*, 26) IID

186[2]. [Apollodorus]
1 C. (*KP*, Apollodoros 5)
Epitome of Bibliotheca (cf. βιβλιδάριον, cod. 186: 142a line 38, σύνοψις, cod. 186: 142b line 6)
mythology
preserved? (as the Vatican epitome?) IIC

187. Nicomachus of Gerasa
ca. 120–96 (J. M. Dillon, in *Classical Review*, N.S., 19 [1969], 274–75)
Arithmetical Theology
arithmetic
lost IIC

188[1]. Alexander (of Myndus)
e. 1 C. (*RE*, Alexandros 100)
Collection of Wonders
paradoxography
unattested (*FGrHist*, 25, frag. 2) IIA

188[2]. Protagoras
fl. *ca.* 200 (*KP*, Protagoras 2)
Geography of the World
paradoxography
lost IIC

189[1]. Sotion
e. 1 C. (*KP*, Sotion 2a)
Strange Stories
paradoxography
fragments IIA

189[2]. Nicolaus of Damascus
ca. 64 B.C.–e. 1 C. (*KP*, Nikolaus 3)
Collection of Customs
paradoxography
fragments (*FGrHist*, 90, frags. 103–24) IIA

189[3]. Acestorides
1 C.? (perhaps near in date to 189[1] and 189[2], in the same volume)
Myths of the Town
paradoxography
lost (*FGrHist*, 28) IIA

190. Ptolemaeus (Chennus)
1 C. (*KP*, Ptolemaios B.3)
New History for Erudition
mythology
lost IIIA

191. Basil (of Caesarea) (=*144*)
ca. 330–79 (*KP*, Basileios 4)
Ascetica
regulations (X)
preserved (*CPG*, 2875–76) IIC

192A. Maximus Confessor
580–662 (*KP*, Maximus II.5)
Quaestiones ad Thalassium
exegesis (X)
preserved (*CPG*, 7688) IIB

192B. Maximus Confessor
580–662 (*KP*, Maximus II.5)
Letters (27 letters)
letters (X)
preserved (*CPG*, 7699) IIB

193^{1}. Maximus Confessor
580–662 (*KP*, Maximus II.5)
Liber Asceticus
devotional (X)
preserved (*CPG*, 7692) IIA

193^{2}. Maximus Confessor
580–662 (*KP*, Maximus II.5)
De Caritate
devotional (X)
preserved (*CPG*, 7693) IIA

194^{1}. Maximus Confessor
580–662 (*KP*, Maximus II.5)
Letter to George
letter (X)
preserved (*CPG*, 7699) IIA

194^{2}. Maximus Confessor
580–662 (*KP*, Maximus II.5)
Capita Gnostica
exegesis (X)
preserved (*CPG*, 7694) IIA

194^{3}. Maximus Confessor
580–662 (*KP*, Maximus II.5)
Letters (3 letters)
letters (X)
preserved (*CPG*, 7699) IIC

194^{4}. Maximus Confessor
580–662 (*KP*, Maximus II.5)
(*Ambigua ad Thomam*)
dogmatic (X)
preserved (*CPG*, 7705) IIC

194^{5}. Maximus Confessor
580–662 (*KP*, Maximus II.5)
Second Letter to Thomas
dogmatic (X)
preserved (*CPG*, 7700) IIA

195^{1}. Maximus Confessor
580–662 (*KP*, Maximus II.5)
(*To Marinus*)
dogmatic (X)
preserved (*CPG*, 7697) IIC

195[2]. Maximus Confessor
580–662 (*KP*, Maximus II.5)
Disputation with Pyrrhus
apologetic (X)
preserved (*CPG*, 7698) IIC

196[1]. Ephraem Syrus
ca. 300–73 (*KP*, Ephraim 1)
Sermons (49 sermons)
sermons (X)
preserved (among *CPG*, 3906–4067?) IIB

196[2]. Ephraem Syrus
ca. 300–73 (*KP*, Ephraim 1)
Sermon on Humility
sermon (X)
preserved (*CPG*, 3936) IIA

196[3]. Ephraem Syrus
ca. 300–73 (*KP*, Ephraim 1)
Sermon Against Laughter
sermon (X)
preserved (*CPG*, 3933) IIA

196[4]. Ephraem Syrus
ca. 300–73 (*KP*, Ephraim 1)
(*On Virtues and Vices*) (see D. Hemmerdinger-Iliadou, in *Dictionnaire de Spiritualité*, IV [Paris, 1958], 808)
sermon (X)
preserved (*CPG*, 3905) IIC

197[1]. (John) Cassian
ca. 360–after 430 (*KP*, Cassianus)
(*Institutes*)
regulations (X)
Latin original preserved, Greek lost IIC

197[2]. (John) Cassian
ca. 360–after 430 (*KP*, Cassianus)
(*Epitome of Conferences*)
hagiography (X)
Latin original preserved, Greek lost IIC

198. —
4/5 C. (*ODCC*, Apophthegmata Patrum)
(*Apophthegmata Patrum*)
anthology (X)
fragments, complete in Latin translation (*CPG*, 5560–74) IIB

199. John Moschus
ca. 550–619 (*ODCC*)
Pratum (Spirituale)
hagiography (X)
preserved (*CPG*, 7376) IIC

200[1]. Mark the Hermit
after 360–430 (*KP*, Marcus 7)
On the Spiritual Law
devotional (X)
preserved (*CPG*, 6090) IIC

200[2]. Mark the Hermit
after 360–430 (*KP*, Marcus 7)
Against the Melchisidecians
apologetic (X)
preserved (*CPG*, 6100) IIA

201[1]. Diadochus of Photice
fl. *ca.* 451 (*ODCC*)
Capita Gnostica
devotional (X)
preserved (*CPG*, 6106) IIB

201[2]. (Evagrius Ponticus) [Nilus (of Ancyra)]
ca. 345–*ca.* 400 (*KP*, Euagrius 3)
On Prayer
devotional (X)
preserved (*CPG*, 2452) IIA

201[3]. John of Carpathos
7 C. (Beck, 452)
Exhortation to the Monks Returned from India
devotional (X)
preserved (*CPG*, 7855) IIA

202[1]. Hippolytus (of Rome)
d. 235 (*KP*, Hippolytos 5)
Commentary on Daniel
exegesis (X)
partly preserved IIC

202[2]. Hippolytus (of Rome)
d. 235 (*KP*, Hippolytos 5)
On Antichrist
dogmatic (X)
preserved IIA

203. Theodoret of Cyrus
393–*ca.* 466 (*KP*, Theodoretos 1)
Commentary on Daniel
exegesis [N]
preserved (*CPG*, 6207) I

204[1]. Theodoret of Cyrus
393–*ca.* 466 (*KP*, Theodoretos 1)
Questions on the Octateuch
exegesis [N]
preserved (*CPG*, 6200) I

204[2]. Theodoret of Cyrus
393–*ca.* 466 (*KP*, Theodoretos 1)
(*Questions on Kings and Chronicles*)
exegesis [N]
preserved (*CPG*, 6201) I

205. Theodoret of Cyrus
393–*ca.* 466 (*KP*, Theodoretos 1)
Commentary on the Twelve Prophets
exegesis [N]
preserved (*CPG*, 6208) I

206[1]. Procopius (of Gaza)
ca. 465–*ca.* 528 (*KP*, Prokopios 2)
On the Octateuch
exegesis (X)
preserved (*CPG*, 7430) I

206[2]. Procopius (of Gaza)
ca. 465–*ca.* 528 (*KP*, Prokopios 2)
On Kings
exegesis (X)
preserved (*CPG*, 7430) I

206[3]. Procopius (of Gaza)
ca. 465–*ca.* 528 (*KP*, Prokopios 2)
On Chronicles
exegesis (X)
preserved (*CPG*, 7430) I

207. Procopius (of Gaza)
ca. 465–*ca.* 528 (*KP*, Prokopios 2)
On Isaiah
exegesis (X)
preserved (*CPG*, 7434) I

208[1]. Eulogius of Alexandria (*=182*[1] *=280*[1])
patriarch 581–607 (Beck, 381)
(*On Dispensation*)
apologetic (X)
unattested (*CPG*, 6976) IIC

208[2]. Eulogius of Alexandria (*=182*[2] *=280*[2])
patriarch 581–607 (Beck, 381)
(*Against Novatus*)
apologetic (X)
unattested (*CPG*, 6976) IIC

209. Dio of Prusa
ca. 40–after 110/11 (*KP*, Dion 3)
Orations (80 orations)
oratory
preserved IIB

210. [Caesarius of Nazianzus]
6 C. (*KP*, Caesarius 2)
Dialogues
dogmatic (X)
partly preserved (4 of 8 chapters) (*CPG*, 7482) IIB

211. Dionysius of Aegeae (*=185*)
1/3 C. (*RE, Dionysios 124)*
Dictyaca
medicine
unattested IIB

212. Aenesidemus (of Cnossus)
fl. *ca.* 40 B.C. (*KP*, Ainesidemos)
Pyrrhonian Books
philosophy
lost IIC

213. Agatharchides of Cnidus (*=250*)
ca. 200–after 131/32 B.C. (*KP*, Agatharchides)
On the Red Sea
history
fragments IIA

214. Hierocles (of Alexandria) (*=251*)
d. 431/32 (*KP*, Hierokles 6)
On Providence and Fate
philosophy
unattested IIC

215. John Philoponus
ca. 490–*ca.* 570 (*OCD*)
Against Jamblichus on Statues
apologetic (M)
unattested IIC

216. Oribasius (of Pergamum)
325–403 (*OCD*, Medicine)
Excerpts from Galen
medicine
lost IIC

217. Oribasius (of Pergamum)
325–403 (*OCD*, Medicine)
Collectiones Medicae
medicine
partly preserved IIC

218. Oribasius (of Pergamum)
325–403 (*OCD*, Medicine)
Synopsis ad Eustathium
medicine
preserved IIB

219[1]. Oribasius (of Pergamum)
325–403 (*OCD*, Medicine)
Ad Eunapium
medicine
preserved IIB

219[2]. Oribasius (of Pergamum)
325–403 (*OCD*, Medicine)
Euporista
medicine
partly preserved (as 219[1]; cf. cod. 219: 176b lines 11–23) IIA

219[3–8]. Oribasius (of Pergamum)
325–403 (*OCD*, Medicine)
(six other works) (see pp. 74–75 *supra*)
medicine
partly preserved I

220. Theon of Alexandria
4/e. 7 C. (*KP*, Theon 7)
Man
medicine
unattested IIC

221. Aëtius of Amida
fl. *ca.* 550 (*OCD*, Medicine)
Medical Work
medicine
preserved IIB

222. Jobius the Monk
6 C. (Beck, 383)
On the Incarnation
dogmatic (X)
fragments (*CPG*, 6984) IID

223. Diodorus of Tarsus
d. before 394 (*KP*, Diodoros 17)
Against (Astronomers, Astrologers, and) Fate
apologetic [N]
lost (*CPG*, 3821) IID

224. Memnon
1 C.? (*KP*, Memnon 5)
History (of Heraclea) (Books IX–XVI)
history
unattested (*FGrHist*, 434) IID

225. Eulogius of Alexandria
patriarch 581–607 (Beck, 381)
Against Theodosius and Severus
apologetic (X)
unattested (*CPG*, 6976) IID

226. Eulogius of Alexandria
patriarch 581–607 (Beck, 381)
Against Theodosius and Severus
apologetic (X)
unattested (*CPG*, 6976) IIC

227[1]. Eulogius of Alexandria
patriarch 581–607 (Beck, 381)
Against the Theodosians and Gaïnites
apologetic (X)
unattested (*CPG*, 6976) IIC

227[2]. Eulogius of Alexandria
patriarch 581–607 (Beck, 381)
Letter to Eutychius
letter (X)
unattested (*CPG*, 6976) IIA

228[1]. Ephraem (of Amida)
patriarch of Antioch 527–45 (Beck, 378)
Letters (11 letters)
letters (X)
unattested (*CPG*, 6908) IID

228[2]. —
537/38 (E. Honigmann, *Evêques et évêchés monophysites* [Louvain, 1951], 166)
Synod Against Syncleticus
conciliar *acta* (X)
lost (*CPG*, 6908) IIC

228[3]. Ephraem (of Amida)
patriarch of Antioch 527–45 (Beck, 378)
Letters (2 letters)
letters (X)
unattested (*CPG*, 6908) IIC

228[4]. Ephraem (of Amida)
patriarch of Antioch 527–45 (Beck, 378)
Festal Sermons (8 sermons)
sermons (X)
unattested (*CPG*, 6908) IIB

229[1]. Ephraem (of Amida)
patriarch of Antioch 527–45 (Beck, 378)
Treatises (4 treatises)
apologetic (X)
unattested (*CPG*, 6908) IID

229[2]. Ephraem (of Amida)
patriarch of Antioch 527–45 (Beck, 378)
(one other volume) (see p. 75 *supra*)
apologetic? (X)
unattested? I

230[1]. Eulogius of Alexandria
patriarch 581–607 (Beck, 381)
Treatises (3 treatises)
apologetic (X)
unattested (*CPG*, 6976) IID

230[2]. Eulogius of Alexandria
patriarch 581–607 (Beck, 381)
Letters (2 letters)
letters (X)
unattested (*CPG*, 6976) IID

230[3]. Eulogius of Alexandria
patriarch 581–607 (Beck, 381)
Sermons (3 sermons)
sermons (X)
unattested (*CPG*, 6976) IID

230[4]. —
589/90 (see pp. 75–76 *supra*)
Decree Proclaimed Against the Samaritans
conciliar *acta* (X)
unattested (*CPG*, 6976) IID

231[1]. Sophronius of Jerusalem
ca. 560–638 (*ODCC*)
Synodal Letter
letter (X)
preserved (*CPG*, 7635) IIC

231[2]. —
649? (Henry, V, 66 note)
(*Pro-Chalcedonian Anthology*)
conciliar *acta* (X)
lost IIC

232. Stephen Gobar
6 C.? (Beck, 394)
Florilegium
apologetic (M)
unattested (*CPG*, 7300) IIB

233. Germanus of Constantinople
ca. 634–*ca.* 733 (*ODCC*)
De Vera et Legitima Retributione
dogmatic (X)
unattested (*CPG*, 8022) IIC

234. Methodius (of Olympus)
d. *ca.* 311 (*ODCC*)
(*Aglaophon or*) *On the Resurrection*
dogmatic (X)
fragments, complete Slavonic translation IIIC

235. Methodius (of Olympus)
d. *ca.* 311 (*ODCC*)
(*Xeno or*) *On Creatures*
dogmatic (X)
lost IIIC

236. Methodius (of Olympus)
d. *ca.* 311 (*ODCC*)
On (God, Matter, and) Free Will
dogmatic (X)
partly preserved in Greek, complete Slavonic translation IIIC

237. Methodius (of Olympus)
d. *ca.* 311 (*ODCC*)
Symposium or On Chastity
dogmatic (X)
preserved IIIC

238. Josephus (=*76*[1])
37/38–after 100 (*KP*, Iosephos 2)
(*Jewish*) *Antiquities*
history (J)
preserved IIIB

239. Proclus
412–85 (*RE*, Proklos 4)?
Chrestomathia Grammatica
philology
fragments IIIB
N. See p. 50 note 53.

240. John Philoponus (=*43*)
ca. 490–*ca.* 570 (*OCD*)
On the Hexameron
exegesis (M)
preserved (*CPG*, 7265) IIIB

241. Philostratus (II) [of Tyre] (=*44*)
ca. 170–244/49 (*OCD*)
(*Life of*) *Apollonius* (*of Tyana*)
biography
preserved IIIC

242. Damascius (of Damascus) (=*181*)
ca. 458–after 533 (*KP*, Damaskios)
(*On the*) *Life of Isidore the Philosopher*
biography
lost IIIC

243. Himerius (=*165*)
300/10–*ca.* 380 (*KP*, Himerios)
Orations (I–XXXVI)
oratory
partly preserved IIIC

244. Diodorus Siculus (=*70*)
d. after 36 B.C. (*KP*, Diodoros 12)
Library (*of History*)
history
partly preserved IIIB

245. Plutarch
after 45–after 120 (*KP*, Plutarchos 2)
Parallel (*Lives*)
biography
preserved (The lost lives are not mentioned by Photius.) IIIC

246. (Aelius) Aristides
117–*ca*. 187 (*KP*, Aristeides 3)
Panathenaic
oratory
preserved IIIC

247–48. (Aelius) Aristides
117–*ca*. 187 (*KP*, Aristeides 3)
Against Plato, For Rhetoric (see p. 47 *supra*)
oratory
preserved IIIC

249. (Anonymous)
3/2 C. B.C. (H. Thesleff, *Ån Introduction to the Pythagorean Writings of the Hellenistic Period* [Åbo, 1961], 113)
Life of Pythagoras
biography
unattested IIIC

250. Agatharchides (of Cnidus) (=*213*)
ca. 200–after 131/32 B.C. (*KP*, Agatharchides)
On the Red Sea
history
fragments IIIC

251. Hierocles (of Alexandria) (=*214*)
d. 431/32 (*KP*, Hierokles 6)
On Providence (*and Fate*)
philosophy
unattested IIIC

252. (Anonymous)
741/52? (see p. 30 *supra*)
Life of St. Gregory Dialogus
hagiography (X)
unattested IIIB

253. (Anonymous)
7 C.? (see note)
Martyrdom of the Seven Holy Children
hagiography (X)
preserved? (*BHG*, 1599?) IIIB
N. See M. Huber, *Die Wanderlegende von den Siebenschläfern* (Leipzig, 1910), 37–59.

254. (Anonymous)
5 C. (H. Delehaye, in *Anatolian Studies Presented to W. H. Buckler* [Manchester, 1939], 79)
Martyrdom of Timothy the Apostle
hagiography (X)
preserved (or partly preserved?) (*BHG*, 1847) IIIB

255. (Anonymous)
6/7 C. (*ActaSS*, October IV [1780], 53–54)
Martyrdom of St. Demetrius
hagiography (X)
lost (*BHG*, 496b) IIIB
N. The *Life* in cod. Athon. Philoth. 9 is merely a transcription of cod. 255 as it appears in MS A.

256. (Anonymous)
m. 4 C. (M. Gedeōn, in Ἐκκλησιαστικὴ Ἀλήθεια, 4 [1884], 326 note 157)
Life of SS. Metrophanes and Alexander
hagiography (X)
preserved (*BHG*, 1279) IIIB

257. (Anonymous)
ca. 5 C. (cf. Henry, VIII, 215) (*Acta SS*, June II [1698], 13)
Life of St. Paul of Constantinople
hagiography (X)
preserved? (cf. Henry, VIII, 215) (*BHG*, 1472a?) IIIB

258. (Anonymous)
after 439/40 (B. Beck, *Die griechischen Lebensbeschreibungen des Athanasius* [diss. Jena, 1912], 80–81)
Life of St. Athanasius
hagiography (X)
unattested (=*BHG*, 184) IIIB

259. Antiphon
ca. 480–411 B.C. (*KP*, Antiphon 5)
Orations
oratory
preserved? (Photius may not have read those now lost.) IIIA

260. Isocrates (=*159*[1])
436–338 B.C. (*KP*, Isokrates 2)
Orations
oratory
preserved IIIA

261. Andocides
ca. 440–*ca*. 390 B.C. (*OCD*)
Orations (4 orations)
oratory
preserved IIIA

262. Lysias
ca. 459–*ca*. 380 B.C. (*OCD*)
Orations
oratory
preserved? (Photius may not have read those now lost.) IIIA

263. Isaeus
ca. 420–350 B.C. (*OCD* Isaeus 1)
Orations
oratory
preserved? (Photius may not have read those now lost.) IIIA

264[1]. Aeschines (=*61*)
390/89–*ca*. 315 B.C. (*KP*, Aischines 2)
Orations (3 orations)
oratory
preserved IIIA

264[2]. [Aeschines]
2 C.? (*KP*, Aischines 2)
Letters (9 letters)
letters
preserved IIIA

265. Demosthenes
384–322 B.C. (*KP*, Demosthenes 2)
Orations
oratory
preserved? (Photius may not have read those now lost.) IIIA

266. Hyperides
390/89–322 B.C. (*KP*, Hypereides)
Orations
oratory
preserved? (Photius may not have read those now lost.) IIIA

267. Dinarchus
ca. 360–after 292 B.C. (*KP*, Deinarchos)
Orations
oratory
preserved? (Photius may not have read those now lost.) IIIA

268. Lycurgus
ca. 390–324 B.C. (*KP*, Lykurgos 10)
Orations (not read)
oratory
(one oration preserved) IIIA

269. Hesychius of Jerusalem
d. after 451 (*ODCC*)
Encomium of St. Andrew
sermon (X)
preserved (*BHG*, 104; *CPG*, 6571) IIIC

270. (John) Chrysostom
ca. 349–407 (*KP*, *Nachträge*, Iohannes 15)
On St. Paul
sermon (X)
unattested? IIIC

271. Asterius of Amasea
d. after 341 (*ODCC*)
Sermons (10 sermons)
sermons (A)
partly preserved (6 of 10 sermons) (*CPG*, 3260–61) IIIC

272. Leontius of Arabissus
l. 7/e. 8 C. (Beck, 506)
On the Creation and On Lazarus
sermon (X)
unattested IIIC

273. Theodoret (of Cyrus)
393–*ca.* 466 (*KP*, Theodoretos 1)
On St. John Chrysostom (5 sermons, incomplete)
sermons [N]
unattested (*BHG*, 878t-x; *CPG*, 6225) IIIB

274[1]. John Chrysostom
ca. 349–407 (*KP*, *Nachträge*, Iohannes 15)
On the Forty Holy Martyrs
sermon (X)
unattested (or preserved and spurious? See Henry, VIII, 111 note 1.) (*BHG*, 1208n) IIIC

274². [John Chrysostom]
5 C.? (Photius himself considered these sermons spurious; cf. cod. 274: 510b lines 9–13, 510b lines 17–18, 511a lines 5–9.)
On the Beheading of St. John the Baptist (3 sermons)
sermons (X)
unattested IIIC

275¹. Hesychius of Jerusalem
d. after 451 (*ODCC*)
On St. James and David
sermon (X)
unattested (*CPG*, 6574) IIIC

275². [Modestus of Jerusalem]
l. 7/e. 8 C. (Beck, 454–55)
Sermons (3 sermons)
sermons (X)
partly preserved (1 of 3 sermons) (*CPG*, 7872, 7876, 7873) IIIC

276¹. Nilus (of Ancyra)
b. *ca.* 430 (*KP,* Neilos)
On Easter (2 sermons)
sermons (X)
unattested (*CPG*, 6078 [1–2]) IIIC

276². (Proclus of Constantinople) [Nilus (of Ancyra)]
bishop 434–46 (*KP,* Proklos 2)
On the Ascension (3 sermons)
sermons (X)
partly preserved (1 of 3 sermons) (*CPG*, 6078 [3–5]) IIIC
N. For the attribution, see J. G. Davies, in *Harvard Theological Review,* 49 (1956), 179–81.

277¹. (John) Chrysostom
ca. 349–407 (*KP, Nachträge,* Iohannes 15)
Sermons (17 apparently genuine sermons)
sermons (X)
partly preserved (5 of 17 sermons) (*CPG*, 4429, 4328, 4329, 4333, 4508) IIIC

277². (Severianus of Gabala) [(John) Chrysostom]
d. after 408 (*KP,* Severianos)
Sermons (3 sermons)
sermons (X)
preserved (*CPG*, 4188, 4204, 4200) IIIC
N. These are the 1st, 3rd, and 11th sermons cited by Photius.

277³. [(John) Chrysostom]
5 C.?
Sermons (4 spurious sermons)
sermons (X)
preserved (*CPG*, 4576, 4701, 4329, 4620) IIIC
N. These are the 5th, 6th, 13th, and 14th sermons cited by Photius.

278. Theophrastus
372/70–288/86 B.C. (*KP*, Theophrastos)
Treatises (9 treatises)
science
fragments (of 3 treatises) IIIB

279[1]. Helladius of Antinoöpolis
4 C. (*KP*, Helladios 1)
Chrestomathiae
philology
lost (*FGrHist*, 635) IIIB

279[2]. Hermias of Hermopolis
l. 4 C.? (*RE*, Hermeias 3)
Fatherland of Hermopolis and Other Poems
poetry
unattested (*FGrHist*, 638) IIIB

279[3]. (Aelius) Serenus
e. 2 C.? (*KP*, *Nachträge*, Aelius II.13a)
Plays
poetry
unattested IIIB

279[4]. Andronicus of Hermopolis
l. 4 C. (*RE*, Andronikos 21)
To Count Phoebammon
poetry
lost IIIB

279[5]. Horapollon
5 C.? (*KP*, Horapollon)
On Alexandria
poetry
lost IIIB

279[6]. Cyrus (of Panopolis)
d. after 457 (*KP*, Kyros 4)
To Duke Maurice
poetry
lost IIIB

280[1]. Eulogius of Alexandria (=*182*[1] =*208*[1])
patriarch 581–607 (Beck, 381)
(*On Dispensation*)
apologetic (X)
unattested (*CPG*, 6976) IIIC

280[2]. Eulogius of Alexandria (=*182*[2] =*208*[2])
patriarch 581–607 (Beck, 381)
(*Against Novatus*)
apologetic (X)
unattested (*CPG*, 6976) IIIC

TABLE II

Index to the Codices by Authors

See the introduction to Table I.

TABLE III

Index to the Codices by Subjects

See the introduction to Table I. Authors listed in Section A are Orthodox Christians unless indicated otherwise by one of the abbreviations on p. 117 *supra*.

A. Christian and Jewish

Chronology
- Metrodorus 115^{2}
- Anonymous 115^{1}, 116

Conciliar *Acta*
- 16, 17, 18, 19, 20, 52, 53, 54, 228^{2}, 230^{4}, 231^{2}
- 59 (uncanonical)
- 24 (M)

Devotional Works
- *Apophthegmata Patrum* 198
- Diadochus of Photice 201^{1}
- Evagrius Ponticus 201^{2}
- John of Carpathos 201^{3}
- Mark the Hermit 200^{1}
- Maximus Confessor 193^{1}, 193^{2}
- Philo Judaeus 104^{1}, 104^{2} (J)
  - See also Hagiography

Dogmatic Works
- Agapius 179^{1}, 179^{2} (Ma)
- Apollinarius of Hierapolis 14^{2}, 14^{3}
- [Caesarius of Nazianzus] 210
- Cyril of Alexandria 169^{6}
- Diodorus of Tarsus 102^{2} (N)
- Germanus of Constantinople 233
- Hippolytus of Rome 48, 202^{2}
- Jobius the Monk 222
- John Philoponus 21 (M)
- Maximus Confessor 194^{4}, 194^{5}, 195^{1}
- Methodius of Olympus 234, 235, 236, 237
- Origen 8 [O]
- Synesius of Cyrene 26^{1}, 26^{3}?
- Theodoret of Cyrus 125^{4}, 125^{5}?, 125^{6}? [N]
- Theognostus of Alexandria 106 (O)
  - See also Apologetics

Exegesis
- Athanasius 139^{1}, 139^{2}
- Clement of Alexandria 109, 111^{2}
- Cosmas Indicopleustes 36
- Cyril of Alexandria 49^{3}
- Hadrian 2
- Hippolytus of Rome 202^{1}
- John Philoponus *43*, *240*, (M)
- Maximus Confessor 192A, 194^{2}
- Philo Judaeus 103^{1}, 103^{2} (J)
- Procopius of Gaza 206^{1}, 206^{2}, 206^{3}, 207
- Theodore of Mopsuestia 38 (N)
- Theodore (of Pharan?) 1 (Me?)
- Theodoret of Cyrus 203, 204^{1}, 204^{2}, 205 [N]

Hagiography
- [Clement of Rome] 112-13^{2}, 112-13^{3} [A]
- George of Alexandria 96
- John Cassian 197^{2}
- John Moschus 199
- [Leucius Charinus] 114^{1}, 114^{2}, 114^{3}, 114^{4} (G)
- [Leucius Charinus] 114^{5}
- Anonymous 252, 253, 254, 255, 256, 257, 258

History
- Basil the Cilician 42 (M?)
- Eusebius of Caesarea 27 (A)
- Evagrius Scholasticus 29
- Gelasius of Caesarea 89
- Gelasius of Cyzicus *15*, *88*
- John Diacrinomenus 41 (M)
- Josephus 47, *76*^{1}, *238* (J)
- Julius Africanus 34
- Justus of Tiberias 33 (J)
- Philip of Side 35
- Philostorgius 40 (A)
- Sergius Confessor 67
- Socrates 28
- Sozomen 30
- Theodoret of Cyrus 31 [N]

Letters
- Athanasius 32
- Basil of Caesarea 143^{1}, 143^{2}
- Clement of Rome 126^{1}
- Cyril of Alexandria 169^{2}, 169^{5}
- Ephraem of Amida 228^{1}, 228^{3}
- Eulogius of Alexandria 227^{2}, 230^{2}
- Eunomius of Cyzicus 138^{2} (A)
- John Chrysostom 86

B. Secular and Pagan

TABLE IV

Index to the Codices by Centuries of Composition

See the introduction to Table I. Authors who were active in two centuries are italicized and listed under both, with their codex references given only under the earlier century.

Fifth Century B.C.
- *Andocides* 261
- Antiphon 259
- Ctesias of Cnidus 72[1], 72[2]
- Herodotus 60
- *Isocrates 159[1], 260*
- *Lysias* 262

Fourth Century B.C.
- Aeschines *61, 264[1]*
- *Andocides*
- Demosthenes 265
- Dinarchus 267
- Hyperides 266
- Isaeus 263
- *Isocrates*
- Lycurgus 268 (not read)
- *Lysias*
- *Theophrastus* 278
- Theopompus of Chios 176

Third Century B.C.
- *Theophrastus*

Third or Second Century B.C.
- Anonymous 249

Second Century B.C.
- Agatharchides of Cnidus *213, 250*

First Century B.C.
- Aenesidemus of Cnossus 212
- Diodorus Siculus *70, 244*
- Dionysius of Halicarnassus 83, 84
- *Nicolaus of Damascus* 189[2]

First Century A.D.
- Acestorides 189[3] (?)
- Alexander of Myndus 188[1]
- *Antonius Diogenes* 166
- [Apollodorus] 186[2]
- Clement of Rome 126[1]
- Conon 186[1]
- *Dio of Prusa* 209
- Dioscorides Pedanius 178[1], 178[2], 178[3]
- Dorotheus (of Ascalon?) 156 (?)
- Josephus 47, *76[1]*, *76[2]*, *238*
- Justus of Tiberias 33
- Memnon 224 (?)
- *Nicolaus of Damascus*
- Pamphila of Epidaurus 175
- Philo Judaeus 103[1], 103[2], 104[1], 104[2], 105[1], 105[2]
- *Plutarch* 245
- Ptolemaeus Chennus 190
- Sotion 189[1]

First or Second Century A.D.
- Timaeus 181 (?)

First, Second, or Third Century A.D.
- Dionysius of Aegeae *185, 211*

Second Century A.D.
- Achilles Tatius 87
- Aelius Aristides 246, 247–48
- Aelius Dionysius 152[1], 152[2]
- Aelius Serenus 279[3] (?)
- [Aeschines] 264[2] (?)
- Amyntianus 131
- *Antonius Diogenes*
- Apollinarius of Hierapolis 14[1], 14[2], 14[3]
- Appian 57
- Arrian 58, 91[1], 91[2], 92, 93
- Boëthus 154-55[1], 154-55[2]
- *Clement of Alexandria* 109, 110[1], 110[2], 111[1], 111[2]
- [Clement of Rome] 126[2]
- Cephalion 68
- *Dio of Prusa*
- Diogenianus of Heraclea 149[2]
- Galen 164
- Hadrian Augustus 100
- Irenaeus of Lyons 120
- Jamblichus 94
- Julian 150[1]
- *Julius Africanus* 34
- Justin Martyr 125[1], 125[2]
- Lesbonax of Mytilene 74[2]
- [Leucius Charinus] 114[1], 114[2] (?), 114[5]
- Lucian of Samosata 128[1], 128[2], 128[3], 128[4], 128[5], 128[6]
- Lucius of Patrae (?) 129
- *Moeris* 157
- Nicomachus of Gerasa 187
- Pausanias 153
- Philostratus I 150[2]
- Phlegon of Tralles 97
- Phrynichus the Arab 158
- *Plutarch*
- Polycarp of Smyrna 126[3]
- *Protagoras* 188[2]
- Valerius Diodorus 150[3]
- Valerius Pollio 149[1]

Third Century A.D.
- Agapius 179[1], 179[2]
- *Clement of Alexandria*
- [Clement of Rome] 112-13[2], 112-13[3]
- Dexippus 82[1], 82[2], 82[3]
- Dio Cassius 71
- *Eusebius of Caesarea 9, 10, 11, 12, 13[1], 13[2], 13[3], 13[4], 27,* 39, 118[2], 127
- Heliodorus 73
- Herodian of Syria 99
- Hippolytus of Rome 48, 121, 202[1], 202[2]
- *Julius Africanus*
- [Leucius Charinus] 114[3], 114[4] (?)
- *Methodius of Olympus* 234, 235, 236, 237
- *Moeris*
- Origen 8
- Pamphilus Martyr 118[1]
- Philostratus II *44, 241*
- Pierius of Alexandria 119
- *Protagoras*
- Theognostus of Alexandria 106

Fourth Century A.D.
- Andronicianus 45 (?)
- Andronicus of Hermopolis 279[4]
- *Aphthonius of Antioch* 132-35[2]
- Asterius of Amasea 271
- Athanasius 32, 139[1], 139[2], 140[1], 140[2], 140[3]
- Basil of Caesarea 141, 142, 143[1], 143[2], *144, 191*
- [Clement of Rome] 112-13[1]
- Diodorus of Tarsus 102[2], 223
- Ephraem Syrus 196[1], 196[2], 196[3], 196[4]
- Epiphanius of Salamis 122, 123, 124
- *Eunapius of Sardis* 77[1], 77[2]
- Eunomius of Cyzicus 137, 138[1], 138[2]
- *Eusebius of Caesarea*
- Eusebius of Emesa 132-35[3]
- Evagrius Ponticus 201[2]
- Gelasius of Caesarea 89, 102[1]
- Gregory of Nyssa 6, 7
- *Helladius of Alexandria 145, 146?, 147?, 148?*
- Helladius of Antinoöpolis 279[1]
- Hermias of Hermopolis 279[2]
- Hesychius of Constantinople 51 (?)
- Himerius *165, 243*

227^{1}, 227^{2}, 230^{1}, 230^{2}, 230^{3}, *280^{1}, 280^{2}*
Eusebius of Thessalonica 162
Eustratius of Constantinople 171
Evagrius Scholasticus 29
Heraclianus of Chalcedon 85
Hesychius of Miletus 69^{1}, 69^{2}
Jobius the Monk 222
John Diacrinomenus 41
John Lydus 180^{1}, 180^{2}, 180^{3}
John Moschus 199
John Philoponus 21, *43*, 55^{1}, 75, 215, *240*
John of Scythopolis 95
Malchus of Philadelphia
Nicias the Monk 50^{1}, 50^{2}, 50^{3}
Nonnosus 3
Procopius of Gaza
Sophronius of Jerusalem 231^{1}
Stephen Gobar 232 (?)
Themistius of Alexandria 23^{3}
Theodore of Alexandria 23^{3}
Theodosius the Monk 22
Theophanes of Byzantium 64
Zosimus Comes
Anonymous 37
Conciliar *acta* 18, 24, 52, 228^{2}, 230^{4}

Sixth or Seventh Century A.D.
Anonymous 255

Seventh Century A.D.
George of Alexandria 96
Germanus of Constantinople 233
John of Carpathos 201^{3}
John Moschus
Maximus Confessor 192A, 192B, 193^{1}, 193^{2}, 194^{1}, 194^{2}, 194^{3}, 194^{4}, 194^{5}, 195^{1}, 195^{2}
Sophronius of Jerusalem
Theodore (of Pharan?) 1 (?)
Theophylact Simocatta 65
Anonymous 170 (?), 253 (?)
Conciliar *acta* 19, 231^{2}

Seventh or Eighth Century A.D.
Leontius of Arabissus 272
[Modestus of Jerusalem] 275^{2}

Eighth Century A.D.
Germanus of Constantinople
Nicephorus of Constantinople 66
Anonymous 252 (?)
Conciliar *acta* 20

Ninth Century A.D.
Nicephorus of Constantinople
Sergius Confessor 67

TABLE V

Index to the Codices by Types

See the introduction to Table I and the discussion of the different "classes" in Chapter VI.

CLASS I. Descriptions Probably Composed from Memory: Imprecise References

Aphthonius of Antioch 132–35^{2}
Apollinarius of Hierapolis 14^{1}, 14^{2}, 14^{3}
Athanasius 32, 139^{1}, 139^{2}, 140^{1}, 140^{3}
[Athanasius] 140^{2}
Basil of Caesarea 141, 142, 143^{1}, 143^{2}, *144*
[Clement of Rome] 112-13^{3}
Conon of Tarsus 23^{1}
Cyril of Alexandria 49^{2}, 49^{3}, 136
Dexippus 82^{2}, 82^{3}
Diogenianus of Heraclea 149^{2}
Ephraem of Amida 229^{2}
Epiphanius of Salamis 123, 124
Eugenius of Seleucia 23^{2}
Eunapius of Sardis 77^{2}
Eunomius of Cyzicus 137, 138^{1}
Eusebius of Caesarea *11, 12,* 39
Eusebius of Emesa 132-35^{3}
Gregory of Nyssa 6, 7
Hadrian 2
Hadrian Augustus 100
John Chrysostom 172-74^{3}, 172-74^{4}
John Philoponus 21
Julian 150^{1}
Justin Martyr 125^{1}, 125^{2}, 125^{3}
[Leucius Charinus] 114^{1}, 114^{2}, 114^{3}, 114^{4}, 114^{5}
Lucian of Samosata 128^{4}, 128^{5}, 128^{6}
Lucius of Patrae 129
Maximus (the Cynic?) 132-35^{4}
Nicias the Monk 50^{1}, 50^{2}, 50^{3}
Oribasius of Pergamum 219$^{3-8}$
Palladius of Methone 132-35^{1}
Philo Judaeus 103^{1}, 103^{2}, 104^{1}, 104^{2}, 105^{1}, 105^{2}
Philostratus I 150^{2}
Procopius of Gaza 206^{1}, 206^{2}, 206^{3}, 207
Sophronius 5
Synesius of Cyrene 26^{1}, 26^{2}, 26^{3}
Themistius of Alexandria 23^{3}
Theodoret of Cyrus 125^{4}, 125^{5}?, 125^{6}?, 203, 204^{1}, 204^{2}, 205
Theodosius the Monk 22
Valerius Diodorus 150^{3}
Valerius Pollio 149^{1}
Victorinus of Antioch 101^{1}, 101^{2}
Conciliar *acta* 16, 19, 20

Class II. Descriptions Probably Composed by Referring Back to the Original Text (or Possibly to Notes on It)

A. Precise References

Acestorides 189^{3}
Achilles Tatius 87
Aelius Dionysius 152^{1}, 152^{2}
Aeschines *61*
Agatharchides of Cnidus *213*
Alexander of Myndus 188^{1}
Amyntianus 131
Andronicianus 45
Arrian 91^{2}, 93
Boëthus 154-55^{1}, 154-55^{2}
Clement of Alexandria 109, 110^{1}, 110^{2}, 111^{1}, 111^{2}
Clement of Rome 126^{1}
[Clement of Rome] 126^{2}
Cyril of Alexandria *49*^{1}, 169^{2}, 169^{4}, 169^{5}
Damascius of Damascus 130^{1}, 130^{2}, 130^{3}, 130^{4}
Diodorus of Tarsus 102^{2}
Dionysius of Halicarnassus 83, 84
Dorotheus (of Ascalon?) 156
Ephraem Syrus 196^{2}, 196^{3}
Epiphanius of Salamis 122
Eudocia Augusta 183, 184^{1}
Eulogius of Alexandria 227^{2}
Eunomius of Cyzicus 138^{2}
Eusebius of Caesarea *9, 10,* 27
Evagrius Ponticus 201^{2}
Evagrius Scholasticus 29
Gelasius of Caesarea 89, 102^{1}
Gelasius of Cyzicus *15*
Helladius of Alexandria *145, 146*?, *147*?, *148*?
Hesychius of Constantinople 51
Hesychius of Miletus 69^{2}
Hippolytus of Rome 121, 202^{2}
John of Aegeae 55^{2}
John of Carpathos 201^{3}
John Chrysostom 86, 172-74^{1}, 172-74^{2}
John Diacrinomenus 41
John Lydus 180^{1}, 180^{2}
John Philoponus *43*, 55^{1}, 75
John of Scythopolis 95
Julius Africanus 34
Justus of Tiberias 33
Lesbonax of Mytilene 74^{2}
Libanius 90
Lucian of Samosata 128^{1}, 128^{2}, 128^{3}
Mark the Hermit 200^{2}
Maximus Confessor 193^{1}, 193^{2}, 194^{1}, 194^{2}, 194^{5}
Metrodorus 115^{2}
Moeris 157
Nestorius 169^{3}
Nicephorus of Constantinople 66
Nicolaus of Damascus 189^{2}
Oribasius of Pergamum 219^{2}
Pausanias 153
Philip of Side 35
Polycarp of Smyrna 126^{3}
Proclus of Constantinople 25^{1}?, 25^{2}, 25^{3}
Sergius Confessor 67
Socrates 28
Sotion 189^{1}
Sozomen 30
Synesius of Cyrene 26^{4}
Themistius 74^{1}
Theodore of Mopsuestia 4, 38
Theodoret of Cyrus 31, 56
Timaeus 151
Vindanius Anatolius 163

B. References by Parts (Multipart Works)

Aëtius of Amida 221
Basil of Seleucia 168
[Caesarius of Nazianzus] 210
Cephalion 68
Cyril of Alexandria *169*^{1}, 169^{6}
Diadochus of Photice 201^{1}
Dio of Prusa 209
Dionysius of Aegeae *185, 211*
Ephraem of Amida 228^{4}
Ephraem Syrus 196^{1}

C. Precise Summaries

D. Epitomes

Class III. Descriptions Probably Copied by Photius' Secretary from Reading Notes Taken Before the *Bibliotheca* was Compiled

A. Epitomes with Introductions Added by Photius for the *Bibliotheca*

Aeschines *264*^{1}
[Aeschines] 264^{2}
Andocides 261
Antiphon 259
Ctesias of Cnidus 72^{1}, 72^{2}
Demosthenes 265
Dinarchus 267
Hyperides 266
Isaeus 263
Isocrates *260*
Jamblichus 94
Lycurgus 268
Lysias 262
Olympiodorus of Thebes 80
Procopius of Caesarea 63
Ptolemaeus Chennus 190
Theophanes of Byzantium 64
Theophylact Simocatta 65

B. Epitomes without Introductions Added by Photius for the *Bibliotheca*

Aelius Serenus 279^{3}
Andronicus of Hermopolis 279^{4}
Cyrus of Panopolis 279^{6}
Diodorus Siculus *244*
Helladius of Antinoöpolis 279^{1}
Hermias of Hermopolis 279^{2}
Horapollon 279^{5}
John Philoponus *240*
Josephus *238*
Proclus 239
Theodoret of Cyrus 273
Theophrastus 278
Anonymous 252, 253, 254, 255, 256, 257, 258

C. Excerpts without Introductions Added by Photius for the *Bibliotheca*

Aelius Aristides 246, 247–48
Agatharchides of Cnidus *250*
Asterius of Amasea 271
Damascius of Damascus *242*
Eulogius of Alexandria *280*^{1}, *280*^{2}
Hesychius of Jerusalem 269, 275^{1}
Hierocles of Alexandria *251*
Himerius *243*
John Chrysostom 270, 274^{1}, 277^{1}
[John Chrysostom] 274^{2}, 277^{3}
Leontius of Arabissus 272
Methodius of Olympus 234, 235, 236, 237
[Modestus of Jerusalem] 275^{2}
Nilus of Ancyra 276^{1}
Philostratus II *241*
Plutarch 245
Proclus of Constantinople 276^{2}
Severianus of Gabala 277^{2}
Anonymous 249

TABLE VI

References to Books in Photius' Letters and *Amphilochia*

The following lists include only books that Photius refers to as if he had read them, including books that he quotes or plagiarizes. I have omitted references that I cannot identify. Authors and titles in parentheses are not given by Photius but can be inferred. Photius included letter no. 28 in the *Amphilochia* as no. 93; these two numbers are italicized in each list. If a book is reviewed in the *Bibliotheca,* its codex number is given after its entry; in the two cases in which the *Amphilochia* is textually identical with the *Bibliotheca,* an equal sign precedes the codex number. If a book is not reviewed in the *Bibliotheca* but might have been excluded as a school text (see pp. 6–7 *supra*), it is marked with an asterisk. References to Scripture, of which there are many, are excluded from the lists. The letters are cited from *Letters* (Valettas' edition), the *Amphilochia* from PG 101 unless otherwise specified.

A. Letters

Aesop, no. 94, p. 419
Antimachus, no. *28,* p. 317
Aristophanes, no. *28,* p. 317 and no. 127, pp. 447–48*
Aristotle, letters, no. 233, p. 545
Aristotle, other works, no. 6, p. 224 and no. 208, p. 545*
Basil of Caesarea, letters, no. 233, p. 545 (cod. 143)
[Brutus], letters, no. 233, p. 545
Callimachus, no. *28,* p. 317
[Clement of Rome], *Apostolic Constitutions,* no. 4, p. 176 (cod. 112–13)
(Conon, *Narrations*), no. 118, p. 441 (cod. 186)
[Demosthenes], letters, no. 233, p. 545
Demosthenes, orations, no. *28,* p. 317 and no. 135, p. 452 (cod. 265)
(Diogenes Laertius), no. 6, p. 224 and no. 101, p. 425
Eusebius of Caesarea, no. 73, p. 399 (codd. 9–13, 27, 39, 118, or 127?)
Gregory (of Nazianzus?), letters, no. 233, p. 545
(Homer), no. *28,* p. 317 and no. 100, pp. 424–25*
Isidore (of Pelusium), letters, no. 233, p. 545

(Julian?), letters, no. 233, p. 545
Julian (*Against the Galilaeans*), no. 66, p. 370
Leo and Galaton, no. 135, p. 452
Libanius, letters, no. 233, p. 545
Nicephorus the Philosopher, panegyric, no. 114, p. 435
Nicephorus the Philosopher, treatise, no. 244, p. 550
[Phalaris], letters, no. 233, p. 545
Plato, dialogues, no. *28*, p. 317, no. 64, p. 368, no. 66, p. 375, and no. 233, p. 545*
Plato, letters, no. 233, p. 545
Sophocles (lost play), no. 64, p. 368
(Stephen Gobar), no. 5, pp. 196–97 (cod. 232)
(Theodoret of Cyrus, *Ecclesiastical History*), no. 73, p. 399 (cod. 31)
Thucydides, no. *28*, p. 317*
Acts of the Council of Gangra, no. 4, p. 177
Acts of the Council of Side, no. 3, p. 155 (cod. 52)
Acts of the Quinisext Council, no. 4, pp. 176–77

B. *Amphilochia*

Antimachus, no. *93*, col. 600D
Apollinarius (of Laodicea), (*Commentary on Matthew*), no. 1, col. 92A–B
Aratus, no. 151, col. 813B–C
Aristophanes, no. *93*, col. 600D*
(Aristotle), *Categories*, nos. 137–47, cols. 760A–812A*
Asterius (the Sophist), no. 312, cols. 1161B–C
Asterius of Amasea, *On the Martyrdom of St. Euphemia*, no. 312, col. 1161B–C
Asterius of Amasea, other sermons, no. 312, col. 1161B (cod. 271?)
Athanasius, no. 119, col. 700A (codd. 32, 139, or 140?)
Basil of Caesarea, *Against Eunomius*, no. 119, col. 700A
Basil of Caesarea, "everywhere," no. 240, col. 1040B (codd. 141–44 and 191?)
Callimachus, no. *93*, col. 600D and no. 151, col. 813D
Cyril of Alexandria, no. 243, cols. 1044B–45C (codd. 49, 136, or 169?)
Demosthenes, no. *93*, col. 600D (cod. 265)
[Dionysius (the Areopagite)], no. 119, cols. 697D–700A
(Eulogius of Alexandria, *On Dispensation*), no. 132, col. 728A–B (codd. 182=208=280)
Euripides, *Lamia*, no. 150, col. 812C
Eusebius of Caesarea, no. 219, col. 997D (codd. 9–13, 27, 39, 118, or 127?)
(Germanus of Constantinople, *De Vitae Termino*), no. 149, in PG 98, cols. 90–103
Gregory of Nazianzus, *Theological Orations*, no. 70, cols. 440C–441A
Gregory of Nazianzus (*Homilia II in Pascha*), no. 36, col. 257A–D
Gregory of Nazianzus (*Oratio II de Filio*), no. 78, cols. 489B–501B
Gregory of Nazianzus (*Oratio in S. Lumina*), no. 233, col. 1028B–C
Homer, no. 93, col. 600D*

(Jobius the Monk, *On the Incarnation*), no. 188, cols. 909A–913B and no. 191, cols. 924C–929B (cod. 222)

John Chrysostom, *On the Incomprehensible*, no. 119, col. 700B–C

John Chrysostom, sermons, no. 159, col. 836B–no. 170, col. 865C (=cod. 277: 516a line 33–523a line 34, 523b line 13–524b line 16)

John Chrysostom, sermons, no. 161, col. 848A and no. 217, col. 984C–D (codd. 172–74, 270, or 277?)

[John Chrysostom], *On Fasting*, no. 130, col. 725A

John Climacus, no. 273, cols. 1100C–1104A

(John of Damascus?), no. 36, col. 252B

Julian (*Against the Galilaeans*), no. 101, cols. 616D–633B and no. 109, cols. 649D–652A

Maximus Confessor (*To Marinus*), no. 80, cols. 508A–541C (cod. 195)

[Menander], *Gnomic Sayings*, no. 151, col. 813C*

[Modestus of Jerusalem], sermons, no. 158, cols. 833C–836B (=cod. 275: 511b line 21–512a line 8)

Origen (*Commentary on Genesis*?), no. 70, cols. 440C–441A

Origen (*Commentary on John*), no. 1, cols. 89D–92A (probably also no. 217, col. 984B–C; cf. Quasten, I, 262)

Plato, no. 77, cols. 477D–489B, no. 83, col. 553B, and no. 93, col. 600D*

(Polychronius of Apamea, *Preface to Job*), no. 152, col. 816A–C

Sophocles, no. 83, col. 553B*

(Theodoret of Cyrus, *Quaestiones in Octateuchem*), nos. 249–81, cols. 1053C–1113B (cod. 204)

Thucydides, no. 93, 600D*

TABLE VII

Parallels to the *Bibliotheca* in the *Suda,* "Sophronius," and Theodorus Lector

These are the biographical passages for which Photius seems to have used the "Hesychius Epitome" (see Chapter Four). Soph. stands for "Sophronius."

Cod. 13 (Eusebius): 4b lines 8–12; *Suda,* II, 472 lines 29–31; Soph., chap. 89, 48 lines 22–24.

Cod. 14 (Apollinarius of Hierapolis): 4b lines 15–21; *Suda* omits; Soph., chap. 36, 24 line 28–25 line 5.

Cod. 34 (Julius Africanus): 7a lines 7–8 and 15–14; *Suda* ("Africanus"), I, 433 line 30–434 line 3; Soph., chap. 73, 40 line 31–41 line 9.

Cod. 48 (Gaius of Rome): 12a lines 10–17; *Suda* omits; Soph., chap. 68, 38 lines 14–20.

Cod. 58 (Arrian): 17b lines 11–20 and 22–23; *Suda,* I, 350 lines 8–12.

Cod. 60 (Herodotus): 19b lines 38–42; *Suda* (Thucydides), II, 721 lines 16–21, (ὀργᾶν), III, 552 lines 2–4.

Cod. 73 (Heliodorus): 51b lines 40–41; *Suda* omits; Theodorus Lector, 82 lines 28–30.

Cod. 74 (Themistius): 52a lines 15–21; *Suda,* II, 690 line 26–691 line 3.

Cod. 90 (Libanius): 67b lines 20–21: *Suda,* III, 267 lines 14–19.

Cod. 105 (Philo): 86b lines 4–26: *Suda,* IV, 737 line 11–738 line 8: Soph., chap. 21, 14 line 6–16 line 3.

Cod. 111 (Clement of Alexandria): 89b line 38–90a line 3; *Suda* omits; Soph. chap. 48, 29 line 13–30 line 13.

Cod. 112–13 (Clement of Rome): 90b lines 5–17; *Suda* omits; Soph. chap. 25, 18 lines 2–17.

Cod. 118 (Pamphilus and Eusebius): 92b lines 19–22; *Suda* (Origen), III, 620 lines 3–6; Soph., chap. 63 (Origen), 37 lines 1–3; cod. 118: 93a lines 26–29; *Suda* omits; Soph., chap. 83 (Pamphilus), 45 line 30–46 line 5.

Cod. 119 (Pierius): 93a lines 31–35, 93b lines 19–30; *Suda* omits: Soph., chap. 84, 46 lines 13–24.

Cod. 120 (Irenaeus): 94a lines 11–22; *Suda* omits; Soph., chap. 45, 27 line 14–28 line 15.

Cod. 121 (Hippolytus of Rome): 94a lines 34–43; *Suda,* II, 662 lines 4–5; Soph., chaps. 70 (Hippolytus) and 71 (Ambrose), 39 line 8–40 line 5 (see pp. 55–56 *supra*).

Cod. 125 (Justin Martyr): 94b line 38–95a line 16; *Suda,* II, 645 line 24–646 line 5; Soph., chap. 33, 22 line 29–23 line 20.

Cod. 160 (Choricius of Gaza and Procopius of Gaza): 102b line 37–103a line 13; *Suda* omits, but see p. 58 *supra*.
Cod. 189 (Nicolaus of Damascus): 146a lines 8–12; *Suda*, III, 467 line 31–468 line 2.
Cod. 196 (Ephraem Syrus): 160b lines 33–35; *Suda* omits; Soph., chap. 123, 57 lines 16–22.
Cod. 201 (Nilus of Ancyra): 163b lines 14–18; *Suda* omits, but see pp. 57–58 *supra*.
Cod. 209 (Dio of Prusa): 165a line 32–165b line 8; *Suda*, II, 117 lines 4–10.
Cod. 210 (Caesarius of Nazianzus): 168b lines 19–20; *Suda*, III, 86 lines 1–2.

Bibliography

The following bibliography includes only materials that are relevant to the study of the *Bibliotheca* as such. It usually does not include texts of, and articles on, the 386 books reviewed in the *Bibliotheca*, unless these materials refer specifically to the *Bibliotheca*.

A. Primary Sources

Hermogenis opera, ed. H. Rabe, Rhetores Graeci, VI (Leipzig, 1913).

Mansi, G., *Sacrorum conciliorum nova et amplissima collectio*, repr. J. B. Martin, L. Petit, et al. (Paris-Leipzig, 1901–).

Nicetas Paphlago, *Vita S. Ignatii archiepiscopi Constantinopolitani*, PG, 105, cols. 487–574.

Philostorgius, *Kirchengeschichte*, ed. J. Bidez and F. Winkelmann, 2nd ed., GCS, 21 (Berlin, 1972).

Photius, *Amphilochia*, PG, 101; ed. S. Oikonomos (Athens, 1858).

——, *Bibliotheca*, ed. I. Bekker, 2 vols. (Berlin, 1824–25); ed. R. Henry, 8 vols. (Paris, 1959–77); for the *pinax* see E. Martini, under Secondary Works.

——, *Contra Manichaeos*, PG, 102, cols. 15–264; preface, ed. C. Astruc et al., "Les sources grecques pour l'histoire des Pauliciens d'Asie Mineure," *TM*, 4 (1970), 180–83.

——, *Photii Patriarchae lexicon*, ed. S. A. Naber (Leiden, 1864–65); *Der Anfang des Lexikons des Photios*, ed. R. Reitzenstein (Leipzig-Berlin, 1907).

——, *Photiou Epistolai*, ed. I. Valettas (London, 1864); *Sanctissimi Patriarchae Photii archiepiscopi Constantinopoleos epistolae XIV*, ed. A. Papadopoulos-Kerameus (St. Petersburg, 1896); ed. PG, 102, cols. 585–990.

——, *Photiou Homiliai*, ed. B. Laourdas, in *Hellenika*, suppl. 12 (Thessalonica, 1959); see also Mango, under Secondary Works.

Proclo Crestomazia, ed. D. Ferrante (Naples, 1957).

Pseudo-Symeon, see [Symeon Magister].

"Sophronius," *Hieronymi de viris inlustribus*, ed. O. von Gebhardt, *TU*, 14. 1B (1896).

Suidae Lexicon, ed. A. Adler, 5 vols. (Leipzig, 1928–38).

[Symeon Magister], ed. I. Bekker, in Theophanes Continuatus, *Chronographia*, Bonn ed. (1838), 601–760.

Theodorus Lector, *Kirchengeschichte*, ed. G. C. Hansen, GCS, 54 (Berlin, 1971).

Theophanes Continuatus, *Chronographia*, ed. I. Bekker, Bonn ed. (1838).

B. Secondary Works

Ahrweiler, H., "Sur la carrière de Photius avant son patriarcat," *BZ*, 58 (1965), 348–63.

Aubineau, M., "Photius, Bibliothèque: Codex 53: Sur les Pélagiens," *Revue de philologie, de littérature, et d'histoire anciennes*, 41 (1967), 232–41.

Atsalos, B., *La Terminologie du livre-manuscrit à l'époque byzantine*, in *Hellenika*, suppl. 21 (Thessalonica, 1971); concluded in *Hellenika*, 24 (1971), 5–32, and *Hellenika*, 25 (1972), 78–102.

Ballheimer, R., *De Photi vitis decem oratorum* (diss. Bonn, 1877).

Bardenhewer, O., *Geschichte der altkirchlichen Literatur*, 5 vols. (Freiburg-St. Louis, Mo., 1913–32).

Beck, H.-G., *Kirche und theologische Literatur im byzantinischen Reich* (Munich, 1959).

Becker, P., *De Photio et Aretha lexicorum scriptoribus* (diss. Bonn, 1909).

Birt, T., *Das antike Buchwesen in seinem Verhältnis zur Literatur* (Berlin, 1882).

Bouquet, A. C., "The References to Josephus in the *Bibliotheca* of Photius," *Journal of Theological Studies*, 36 (1935), 289–93.

Bury, J. B., *A History of the Eastern Roman Empire from the Fall of Irene to the Accession of Basil I* (London, 1912).

Chatzis, A., "Der Philosoph und Grammatiker Ptolemaios Chennos: Leben, Schriftstellerei und Fragmente. I, Einleitung und Text," *Studien zur Geschichte und Kultur des Altertums*, VII.2 (Paderborn, 1914).

Christ, W. von, *Geschichte der griechischen Literatur*, 6th ed. (Munich, 1920–24).

Coppola, C., "Contributo alla restituzione del testo della lettera a Tarasio, proemiale della 'Biblioteca' di Fozio," *Rivista di Studi Bizantini e Neoellenici*, 12–13 (1975–76), 129–53.

Dain, A., "À propos de l'étude des poètes anciens à Byzance," *Studi in onore di Ugo Enrico Paoli* (Florence, 1956), 195–201.

——, "La transmission des textes littéraires classiques de Photius à Constantin Porphyrogénète," *DOP*, 8 (1954), 33–47.

Devreesse, R., *Introduction à l'étude des manuscrits grecs* (Paris, 1954).

A Dictionary of Christian Biography, 4 vols. (Boston, 1877–87).

Diller, A., "Photius' *Bibliotheca* in Byzantine Literature," *DOP*, 16 (1962), 389–96.

Dvornik, F., "The Embassies of Constantine-Cyril and Photius to the Arabs," *To Honor Roman Jakobson: Essays on the Occasion of his Seventieth Birthday*, I (The Hague, 1967), 569–76.

——, *Les Légendes de Constantin et de Méthode vues de Byzance* (Prague, 1933).

——, "The Patriarch Photius in the Light of Recent Research," *Berichte zum XI. Internationalen Byzantinisten-Kongress*, III.2 (Munich, 1958), 1–56.

——, "Patriarch Photius, Scholar and Statesman," *Classical Folia*, 13.2 (1959), 3–18 and 14.1 (1960), 3–22.

——, *The Photian Schism, History and Legend* (Cambridge, 1948).

——, "Photius' Career in Teaching and Diplomacy," *Byzantinoslavica*, 34 (1973), 211–18.

Elter, A., *De Joannis Stobaei codice Photiano*, I (diss. Bonn, 1880).

Freese, J. H., *The* Library *of Photius*, I (New York, 1920) (an unfinished annotated translation of the *Bibliotheca*).

Gärtner, H., "Charikleia in Byzanz," *Antike und Abendland*, 15 (1969), 47–69.

Geerard, M., *Clavis Patrum Graecorum:* II and III (Turnhout, 1974–79).
Gouillard, J., "Deux figures mal connues du second iconoclasme," *Byzantion,* 31 (1961), 371–401.
Grumel, V., *La Chronologie,* Traité d'études byzantines, I (Paris, 1958).
——. *Le Patriarcat byzantin:* Ser. I, *Les Regestes des actes du patriarcat de Constantinople.* I, *Les Actes des patriarches,* fascs. 2 and 3 (Constantinople, 1936–47).
Hägg, T., *Photios als Vermittler antiker Literatur: Untersuchungen zur Technik des Referierens und Exzerpierens in der Bibliotheke* (Uppsala, 1975).
——, "Photius at Work: Evidence from the Text of the *Bibliotheca,*" *GRBS,* 14 (1973), 213–22.
——, review of Henry, I–VII, in *Göttingische Gelehrte Anzeigen,* 228 (1976), 32–60.
Halkin, F., "La Date de composition de la *Bibliothèque* remise en question," *AnalBoll,* 81 (1963), 414–17.
Hartmann, G., *Photios' Literarästhetik* (Borna-Leipzig, 1929).
Heimannsfeld, H., *De Helladii Chrestomathia quaestiones selectae* (diss. Bonn, 1911).
Hemmerdinger, B., "Le 'Codex' 252 de la *Bibliothèque* de Photius," *BZ,* 58 (1965), 1–2.
——, "Les 'Notices et extraits' des bibliothèques grecques de Bagdad par Photius," *REG,* 69 (1956), 101–3.
Hergenröther, J., *Photius, Patriarch von Konstantinopel: Sein Leben, seine Schriften und das griechische Schisma,* 3 vols. (Regensburg, 1867–69).
Impellizzeri, S., "L'Umanesimo bizantino del IX secolo e la genesi della *Biblioteca* di Fozio," *Studi storici in onore di Gabriele Pepe* (Bari, 1969), 211–66.
Irigoin, J., "Centres de copie et bibliothèques," *Byzantine Books and Bookmen* (Washington, D.C., 1975), 17–27.
——, "Survie et renouveau de la littérature antique à Constantinople (IXe siècle)," *CahCM,* 5 (1962), 287–302.
Jenkins, R., "A Note on Nicetas David Paphlago and the *Vita Ignatii,*" *DOP,* 19 (1965), 241–47.
Der Kleine Pauly, 5 vols. (Stuttgart, 1964–75).
Klinkenberg, J., *De Photi Bibliothecae codicibus historicis* (diss. Bonn, 1913).
Krumbacher, K., *Geschichte der byzantinischen Litteratur,* 2nd ed. (Munich, 1897).
Kugeas, S., Ὁ Καισαρείας Ἀρέθας καὶ τὸ ἔργον αὐτοῦ (Athens, 1913).
Kustas, G. L., "History and Theology in Photius," *Greek Orthodox Theological Review,* 10 (1964), 37–74.
——, "The Literary Criticism of Photius: A Christian Definition of Style," *Hellenika,* 17 (1962), 132–69.
——, *Studies in Byzantine Rhetoric* (Thessalonica, 1973).
Lemerle, P., "L'Histoire des Pauliciens d'Asie Mineure d'après les sources grecques," *TM,* 5 (1973), 1–144.
——, *Le Premier humanisme byzantin: Notes et remarques sur enseignement et culture à Byzance des origines au Xe siècle* (Paris, 1971).
Mango, C., "The Availability of Books in the Byzantine Empire, A.D. 750–850," *Byzantine Books and Bookmen* (Washington, D.C., 1975), 29–45.
——, *The Homilies of Photius, Patriarch of Constantinople: English Translation, Introduction, and Commentary* (Cambridge, Mass., 1958).

——, "The Liquidation of Iconoclasm and the Patriarch Photios," *Iconoclasm*, ed. A. A. M. Bryer and J. Herrin (Birmingham, 1977), 133–140.
Martini, E., "Studien zur Textgeschichte der *Bibliotheke* des Patriarchen Photios von Konstantinopel: I, Der Alte *Pinax*," Ὁ ἐν Κωνσταντινουπόλει Ἑλληνικὸς Φιλολογικὸς Σύλλογος, Πεντηκονταετηρὶς 1861–1911, suppl. to 34 (1921), 297–318.
——, *Textgeschichte der Bibliotheke des Patriarchen Photios von Konstantinopel:* I, *Die Handschriften, Ausgaben und Übertragungen* (Leipzig, 1911).
Mayer, A., review of A. Vonach, "Die Berichte des Photios über die fünf älteren attischen Redner," *Commentationes Aenipontanae*, 5 (1910), 14–76, in *BZ*, 20 (1911), 220–23.
Nogara, A., "Note sulla composizione e la struttura della *Biblioteca* di Fozio, Patriarca di Costantinopoli I," *Aevum*, 49 (1975), 213–42.
Oikonomidès, N., *Les Listes de préséance byzantines des IXe et Xe siècles* (Paris, 1972).
Orth, E., *Photiana* (Leipzig, 1928).
——, *Die Stilkritik des Photios* (Leipzig, 1929).
The Oxford Classical Dictionary, 2nd ed. (Oxford, 1970).
The Oxford Dictionary of the Christian Church, 2nd ed. (Oxford, 1974).
Palm, J., *Über Sprache und Stil des Diodoros von Sizilien: Ein Beitrag zur Beleuchtung der hellenistischen Prosa* (Lund, 1955).
Pattenden, P., "The Text of the *Pratum Spirituale*," *Journal of Theological Studies*, 26 (1975), 38–54.
Paulys Real-Encyclopädie der classischen Altertumswissenschaft, new rev. ed. by G. Wissowa and W. Kroll (Stuttgart, 1893–1979).
Puech, A., *Histoire de la littérature grecque chrétienne*, 3 vols. (Paris, 1928–30).
Quasten, J., *Patrology*, 3 vols. (Westminster, Md.-Utrecht, 1950–60).
Ševčenko, I., *Etudes sur la polémique entre Théodore Métochite et Nicéphore Choumnos* (Brussels, 1962).
——, "Hagiography of the Iconoclast Period," *Iconoclasm*, ed. A. A. M. Bryer and J. Herrin (Birmingham, 1977), 113–31.
——, review of Lemerle, *Humanisme*, in *American Historical Review*, 79 (1974), 1531–35.
Severyns, A., *Recherches sur la Chrestomathie de Proclos*, 4 vols. (Liège-Paris, 1938–63).
——, "Les Vies parallèles de Plutarque dans la *Bibliothèque* de Photius," *Mélanges offerts à A. M. Desrousseaux* (Paris, 1937), 435–50.
Skeat, T. C., "The Use of Dictation in Ancient Book-Production," *Proceedings of the British Academy*, 42 (1956), 179–208.
Speck, P., *Die kaiserliche Universität von Konstantinopel*, Byzantinisches Archiv, 14 (Munich, 1974).
Tomberg, K.-H., *Die* Kaine Historia *des Ptolemaios Chennos* (Bonn, 1968).
Treadgold, W. T., "Photius on the Transmission of Texts (*Bibliotheca*, Codex 187)," *GRBS*, 19 (1978), 171–75.
——, "The Preface of the *Bibliotheca* of Photius: Text, Translation, and Commentary," *DOP*, 31 (1977), 343–49.
——, "The Recently Completed Edition of the *Bibliotheca* of Photius," *Byzantinoslavica*, 41 (1980) (forthcoming).
——, review of Hägg, *Photios*, in *Speculum*, 52 (1977), 978–80.
——, "The Revival of Byzantine Learning and the Revival of the Byzantine State," *American Historical Review*, 84 (1979), 1245–66.

Tsantsanoglou, K., Τὸ Λεξικὸ τοῦ Φωτίου, Χρονολόγηση-Χειρόγραφη Παράδοση, *Hellenika,* suppl. 17 (Thessalonica, 1967).
Van Thiel, H., *Der Eselsroman,* 2 vols., Zetemata, 54 (Munich, 1971–72).
Vasiliev, A. A., *Byzance et les Arabes,* I (Brussels, 1935).
Vonach, A., "Die Berichte des Photios über die fünf älteren attischen Redner," *Commentationes Aenipontanae,* 5 (1910), 14–76.
Vryonis, Sp., Jr., "The Will of a Provincial Magnate, Eustathius Boilas (1059)," *DOP,* 11 (1957), 263–77.
Wentzel, G., "Die griechische Übersetzung der *Viri inlustres* des Hieronymus," *TU,* 13.3 (1895).
Wilson, N. G., "Books and Readers in Byzantium," *Byzantine Books and Bookmen,* (Washington, D.C., 1975), 1–15.
——, "The Composition of Photius' *Bibliotheca,*" *GRBS,* 9 (1968), 451–55.
——, "The Libraries of the Byzantine World," *GRBS,* 8 (1967), 53–80.
Ziegler, K., "Photios 13," *RE,* 20 (1941), cols. 667–737.

Addenda

Baldwin, B., "Malchus of Philadelphia," *DOP,* 31 (1977), 89–107.
——, "Photius and Poetry," *Byzantine and Modern Greek Studies,* 4 (1978), 9–14.
Blumenthal, H., "Photius on Themistius (Cod. 74): Did Themistius Write Commentaries on Aristotle?", *Hermes,* 107 (1979), 168–82.
Halkin, F., *Bibliotheca Hagiographica Graeca,* 3rd ed., 3 vols. (Brussels, 1957) and *Auctarium* (Brussels, 1969).
Hunger, H., *Die hochsprachliche profane Literatur der Byzantiner,* 2 vols. (Munich, 1978).
Jacoby, F., ed., *Die Fragmente der griechischen Historiker,* 3 vols. in 16 parts (Berlin-Leiden, 1923–58).
Nogara, A., "Sergio il Confessore e il cod. 67 della *Biblioteca* di Fozio, Patriarca di Costantinopoli," *Aevum,* 52 (1978), 261–66.
Van Hook, L., "The Literary Criticism in the *Bibliotheca* of Photius," *Classical Philology,* 4 (1909), 178–89.

INDICES

See also Tables I–VII, which are not covered by these indices.

A. GENERAL

[ ] indicates supposed author

B. GREEK

C. CODICES